# THE MAKING OF TRON

## HOW TRON CHANGED VISUAL EFFECTS AND DISNEY FOREVER

By

William Kallay

Foreword by Harrison Ellenshaw

*The Making of Tron: How Tron Changed Visual Effects and Disney Forever*
By William Kallay

"Kodaliths Explained by Harrison Ellenshaw" used by permission from publisher Don Shay. Original article, entitled "Tronic Imagery," appeared in *Cinefex*, April 1982, written by Peter Sørenson. Additional text by Harrison Ellenshaw (2011).

Cover by Richard Winn Taylor II

Back cover photograph by Alexandria Kallay

Back cover description written by William Kallay and Judy Shuler

ISBN:
0615494501

ISBN 13:
978-0-615-49450-0

Dedicated to my family, friends, and to the visionaries of *Tron*.

# TABLE OF CONTENTS

# ACKNOWLEDGEMENTS

A book is a collaborative effort. An author hopes he can take numerous conversations with people involved on a groundbreaking film like *Tron*, and try to turn their words into a cohesive story. Without the gracious assistance of *everyone* I spoke with in regard to *Tron*, this book would have not been possible. Thank you all! I found that *Tron* still means so much to those who worked on it.

I would be remiss if I did not point out a few of the folks who helped me out from the beginning.

Harrison Ellenshaw has been supportive of not only this project from the beginning, but is also a valuable friend. He patiently answered my questions, endless *Tron* emails, offered encouragement in my moments of doubt, and offered valuable and constructive criticism after reading endless drafts of this book. Sometimes he was as ruthless as a college professor. But as a result of his honesty, he helped me become a better writer. He taught me to "plus" what I already thought was good. I value Harrison's professionalism, knowledge and very funny stories he told me about making *Tron*. Harrison, you are a class act and I cannot thank you enough.

Richard Taylor not only gave me incredible insight into *Tron*, but he also introduced me to Steven Lisberger. Both Richard and Steven have been very helpful, honest, and gracious in answering my questions. Richard and Steven, you are brillant visionaries and great guys.

Jerry Rees was one of the first artists I interviewed for this book. Despite Jerry's amazing accomplishments over the years since *Tron*, he is one of the most down-to-earth persons I know. I learned a lot about animation, filmmaking, studio politics, and the simple joys of having a dog.

Raulette Woods has been a lifesaver in regards to this book. She went out of her way on her own time to facilitate many of the interviews you have read here. She was a huge supporter in getting this book written from the very beginning. I cannot thank you enough, Raulette.

David Arnspiger is perhaps the biggest *Tron* fan in the world. Because of his dedication to the film and maintaining a collection of rare *Tron* artifacts, I was able to step back in time and enter the world of *Tron*. Thank you, David.

When I was down on this project, Michael Bonifer introduced me to the idea of using CreateSpace to publish this book. Michael is a "never say never" guy. Thank you, Michael.

Judy Schuler was my fabulous copy editor on this book. No matter how many times the drafts were scrutinzed by myself and Harrison, there was still room for improvement. Judy was excellent in making the book better. Thank you, Judy.

I have always loved writing, but I have always dreaded writing bibliographies. Thankfully, Becky Gogel stepped up to provide me guidance. She told me that writing a bibliography "was a piece of cake." She was right. Thank you, Becky.

A big thank you goes to my Kickstarter.com friends who came in at the last minute to help fund this book, and to John Van Vliet for introducing me to the site.

Thank you to my mom and dad for giving me the wisdom of writing, encouragement to stand tall, and the ability to have a sense of humor when things seemed their bleakest. I love you mom and dad.

I especially want to thank Loretta and Alexandria for being patient with me. This book took a lot of time to research and write, and without your support, it could not have been made. I love you.

Thank you to:

Tonya Agurto, Ioan Allen, Ross Anderson, David Arnspiger, Adam Becker, Jim Blinn, Peter Blinn, Michael Bonifer, Bruce Boxleitner, Jeff Bridges, William and Patty Bumpus, Glenn Campbell, John Canemaker, Wendy Carlos, Chris Casady, Ed Catmull, CreateSpace, Gina Draker, Art Durinski, Douglas Eby, Ralph Eggleston, Harrison Ellenshaw, Brian Ellis, Tammy Evers, Annemarie Franklin, Michael Fremer, Jean "Moebius" Giraud, Becky Gogel, Howard Green, Stuart Green, Wendy Gross, Laura Guillen, Peter Gullerud, John Hughes (Rhythm and Hues), Richard Hardesty, Thomas Hauerslev, Rob Hummel, Don Iwerks, Leslie Iwerks, Jim Jimirro, Alexandria Kallay, Loni Kallay, Loretta Kallay, Mike Kallay, Christopher Keith, Kickstarter.com, Jeffrey Kleiser, Gene Kozicki, Bill Kroyer, Carly Kuhn, Donald Kushner, Tony Lamberti, Chris Lane, John Lasseter, Wendy Lefkon, Peggy Lisberger, Steven Lisberger, Bruce Logan A.S.C., Bonnie MacBird, Derek Maki, Leonard Maltin, Syd Mead, Diane Disney Miller, Ron Miller, Michael Minkler, Kenny Mirman, Tim McGovern, Amelia McPartlon, Cindy Morgan, Ray Morton, Walter Murch, John Norton, Rosanna Norton, Barrie O'Brien, Ellen Pasternack, Pixar Publicity Team, Becky Pedretti, Patty Proctor, Jerry Rees, Stephanie Robinson, Darrell Rooney, Kristine Roper, Georgia Scheele, John Scheele, Judy Schuler, Nancy Seltzer, Frank Serafine, Jean Sievers, Roger Servick, Don Shay, Gregg Shay, Dan Shor, Jesse Silver, Alvy Ray Smith, David R. Smith, Victoria Smith, Charles Soloman, Anne Stark, Richard Winn Taylor II, Randy Thom, Lynda Thompson, Shawna Tice, John Van Vliet, Cardon Walker, David Warner, Robert C. Weisgerber, Daniel Weisinger, John Whitney, Jr., Tom Wilhite, Arne Wong, Greg Wood, Raulette Woods

# WHAT IS TRON?

## Foreword by Harrison Ellenshaw

Recently a cousin from Florida and her two grown children were visiting my studio here in L.A. I was showing them my collection of *TRON* memorabilia. She is an interior designer and art teacher so I imagined she would be very interested in seeing some of the amazing illustrations and artwork done for the original film.

As I always do, when reliving my experience of working on such an iconic film, my enthusiasm began to build as I pulled out more and more ephemera. Everyone seemed genuinely interested as I explained the complexities of backlight compositing, computer imagery and visual effects budgets.

I was on a roll, telling my small but very polite audience about filming top secret government lasers at Lawrence Livermore Labs, the glamour of working with Hollywood movie stars like Jeff Bridges and the pure fascination of *TRON's* rotoscoping and multiple formats, when my cousin looked turned to her son and whispered, "What's *TRON*?"

So this book is for her. It is also for the fans who love *TRON*, but especially it is for those of us who had the privilege of being part of a very unique and creative filmmaking experience which was like nothing that came before... or since.

- Harrison Ellenshaw,
associate producer and co-visual effects supervisor, *TRON*

# INTRODUCTION

In the summer of 1982, nearly every kid in America played video games. Blasting robots, gobbling electronic dots, and zapping alien invaders from the sky was preferable to going outside to play. It did not matter if the game was played in a noisy arcade, or on the floor in front of a television set. Video games sent kids to exciting worlds and challenged their imagination.

That summer, every major studio released films that eventually became classics. *Poltergeist*, *Star Trek: The Wrath of Khan*, *Blade Runner*, *The Road Warrior*, *E.T. The Extra-terrestrial*, and *The Thing* dazzled audiences with strong stories, unforgettable characters, and eye-popping visual effects. Film geeks regard the summer of 1982 as the best ever.

In that mix of films was a highly risky and ambitious film called *Tron*. The story about a video game programmer zapped into a computer was intriguing. It was the first feature film in history to use extensive computer animation. The studio releasing it, Walt Disney Productions, was counting on the film to blow audiences away. After years of mediocre movies and tepid box office returns, it desperately needed a hit. The studio figured it could not go wrong with a major film about video games.

This is the story behind the making of one of the most groundbreaking films ever made, *Tron*. Using unproven computer technology and old-fashioned visual effects magic, a rag-tag group of ex-hippies, computer effects artists, and Disney's "Crown Prince" brought the world of *Tron* to the big screen. It is the story of immense artistic risk, creative ingenuity, creative clashes, technological achievement, and personal sacrifice. The making of *Tron* was one of the most challenging films ever made. It is also the story about how *Tron* transformed Walt Disney's studio.

When *Tron* was brought to Walt Disney Productions by writer/director Steven Lisberger and producer Donald Kushner, the studio was in a desperate struggle to reinvent itself. After Walt Disney's death in 1966, the company stayed financially stable for a few years. But by the mid-1970s, changes in popular culture and society turned the once proud studio into the laughing stock of the film industry. To stay relevant, Disney's management decided to shake up their stale family film formula. They promoted a young executive who, without any qualms, took a huge risk on making *Tron*.

*Tron* would spark a number of innovations and changes in the film industry. If not for *Tron*, there would be no Pixar as it exists today. There would be no Disney studio as we now know it.

CGI visual effects would have most likely taken a long time to come to fruition. There would be no *Tron: Legacy* (2010). *Tron* was as influential to the film industry as *2001: A Space Odyssey* (1968) and *Star Wars* (1977).

Ever since I saw *Tron* in the summer of 1982, I have always been intrigued by how it was done. How was it made? Who made it? Why it was so influential? With so many story lines and people involved with *Tron*, I had to ask myself some questions. What was this book going to be about? Was it going to be about the film's legendary lineup of visual effects wizards? Would it strictly be about the use of computer graphics in filmmaking? Would it be about how Walt Disney Productions was under tremendous pressure to change? In truth, the book is about all of that, and a lot more.

The book you are now reading represents nearly five years of dedication to bring the making of *Tron* to readers. The result is comprised of hours of interviews, travel, hundreds of emails, numerous phone calls, detective work, frustration, rejection, soul searching, and ultimate joy. I received unprecedented cooperation from the very people who made the film. Everyone I interviewed has been open and honest about their experiences of working on *Tron*. Everyone I interviewed has consented to be recorded on audio and/or video tape. These are their quotes and their memories. All quotes, except where noted, are on the record. As with any story with historical context, there are going to be differing perspectives on events, quotes, locations and so forth. I have tried to the best of my ability to maintain accuracy.

This is an independent study on how *Tron* was made. This book was not authorized by the Walt Disney Company or any of its divisions. However, I believe this is the most thorough and accurate account on the making of *Tron* available. And if you are a fan of Disney, you will get an inside look at the studio that few people have read about.

I truly hope you enjoy reading about *Tron*. Find your inner Kevin Flynn, grab a handful of quarters, and head to the arcade. *The Making of Tron: How Tron Changed Visual Effects and Disney Forever* awaits you.

- William Kallay
September 3, 2011
Anaheim, California

# Chapter 1

# *FUTUREBOWL*

Blip. Blip. A tiny square block, lit by radiant white light, bounces across a black-and-white television screen. It has the momentum of a racquetball, hitting the wall with so much force, it pings across the television screen at high velocity. On the other side of the screen awaits a virtual white ping pong paddle. The paddle eagerly moves up and down, ready to hit the square block. A virtual ping pong net bisects the television screen.

The block crashes into the paddle and immediately bounces back into the wall, ricocheting into another white paddle waiting to hit it back. Blip. Blip. Back and forth the game goes until the square block is hit out-of-bounds. A point is awarded to the winner of this match. The square block returns to the screen, and the virtual ping pong match starts again.

Steven Lisberger was playing the video game *Pong* at his in-laws' house. Like many Americans during the mid-1970s, his in-laws had caught video game fever and bought a *Pong* game console for their family room. By this point in time, though, *Pong* was a relic gathering dust on the shag carpet. But its influence on modern culture was astounding. Americans embraced this new form of game play.

It was not difficult to walk into a restaurant or bar and find a game like *Pong* or Space *Invaders* lighting up a player's face. If there was an arcade within the eyesight of a kid, he would no doubt beg his parents for quarters. Playing video games was addictive.

Lisberger had an epiphany. Looking at the television screen filled with electronic energy, he thought about what was on the other side of that television screen. What if living beings were inside those video games? What if there was an electronic world that lived and breathed, just as humans do? What if there were electronic warriors battling each other for their freedom? The concept of a human going into the computer world was intriguing to Lisberger. He kept the idea in the back of his mind.

## STEVEN LISBERGER

Born in New York City in 1951, Lisberger was nominated for a Student Academy Award for his animated short, *Cosmic Cartoon* (1973), with fellow School of Boston Museum of Fine Arts student,

Eric Ladd. Lisberger eventually opened up his own animation studio in the heart of Boston with a small staff of animators and artists.

Boston was far away from the Hollywood myth-making machine. This city of antique American Revolutionary War monuments and modern skyscrapers seemed to be the last place where an animator could make a living. Yet Lisberger managed to do just that by producing a number of local and national animated commercials. Dark haired with dark eyes and a piercing stare, Lisberger was extremely talented, smart, and determined. A natural salesman, he could pitch a project to the best agencies in the business.

Lisberger was one of a small group of up-and-coming animators. Among his peers were animators Tim Burton, John Lasseter, Glen Keane, Bill Kroyer, Jerry Rees, John Musker and Ron Clements. Even though Lisberger was on the opposite coast running his tiny studio, he reflected a new generation of artists who experimented with new animation techniques.

Children who grew up during the 1970s would be familiar with one of his ads for Bubblelicious Bubblegum. It features a young boy trying a piece of gum. He blows a huge bubble and the bubble lifts him into the air high above of his house and into outer space. The animation was as trippy and colorful as any of the eye-popping commercials of the day.

"With a few exceptions, I don't have a lot of fond memories of commercial work," says Lisberger.

One of the ads made at the studio included a neon warrior by animator John Norton. The image of bright light shining through its scarcely drawn body on a pitch black background was striking. The warrior moves with fluidity, flinging two neon discs at the viewer where they converge. The animation caught your eye. Lisberger licensed the ad to radio stations around the country who used it for their television commercials.

Lisberger's studio included a group of talented people, most of which were in their twenties. True to being a creative filmmaker, he had many more ideas running through his creative mind. His dream was that he wanted to make an animated feature film.

## PAINT TO PIXELS

On the outskirts of the entertainment industry, a new revolution was taking place in labs and in garages around America. Just as the automobile forever changed transportation, software designers changed how the world communicated, functioned, and lived. No longer were computers seen as plot devices in movies (i.e. HAL in Stanley Kubrick's *2001: A Space Odyssey—1968*). Nor were they only used in large corporations and government facilities. Computers had begun to enter the mainstream public in small doses. Under the guise of video games, people were beginning to use computers.

The 1970s saw amazing technology advances thanks to the likes of Steve Jobs, Steve Wozniack, Bill Gates and Paul Allen. And even more significantly, a research and development division of one of the world's most influential companies would change the world forever.

A little known division of Xerox (a Wall Street darling that "invented" the modern-day copier) became a hotbed for computer innovation. Xerox had invested in the Palo Alto Research Center

(PARC) in California. This was an experimental laboratory that would usher in some of the biggest breakthroughs, including the laser printer and graphical user interface (GUI), though Xerox would not capitalize on these inventions.

As a student at the University of Utah, Ed Catmull had created a digital version of his own hand in 1972 as a part of his PhD dissertation. While it may seem easy to do in this day of motion capture and body scans, Catmull's work was quite revolutionary. The short demo, called *Hand*, showed promise in the field of computer graphics. Utilizing polygons and raster graphics, Catmull's demo would be used in the 1976 film, *Futureworld*.

He joined Alvy Ray Smith at the campus of New York Institute of Technology. They had been doing extraordinary work in computer graphics and animation. The pair had an idea of making an animated feature with computers, but the technology was not ready yet.

Alvy Ray Smith was the opposite of Catmull. Catmull was small in stature with a clean-cut look. Smith was burly with long hair and beard. He seemed like he would be more at home at a ZZ Top concert than in a computer lab, but behind the rocker looks was a brilliant mind. After seeing a demonstration of SuperPaint by PARC resident Dick Shoup, Smith was hooked on the possibilities of what could be done with computer graphics. He was eventually hired at PARC, but left to work at NYIT with Catmull.

"The owner of NYIT, Alexander Schure, was our first patron," says Smith. Suddenly he and Catmull had a laboratory all their own to experiment and push the digital envelope.

Meanwhile in the mid-1970s, Steven Lisberger saw a demonstration given by Dr. Phil Mittelman at M.I.T. Mittelman founded Mathematical Applications Group, Inc. (MAGI) in 1966. The company had computer simulation software called Synthavision. It was used to study nuclear radiation exposure. Mittelman was not the first person who had dabbled in computer animation, but the development of Synthavision was a remarkable breakthrough. One simulation done through Synthavision was of a Boeing helicopter in the early 1970s. Instead of a flat one-dimensional image, the helicopter was fully three-dimensional, in color, and moved around the screen with fluid motion.

"When I saw the basic shapes, circles and cylinders that Phil was using, it clearly made me think of model drawing class," says Lisberger. "Everyone knows that animated figures are first roughed out in basic shapes, so I thought its only a matter of time before this stuff is used artistically, first to create objects and then some form of crude animated figures."

He saw potential in those polygons and pixels.

"I had met the people at MAGI at Long Island Tech. I was really impressed with these people because they were going where, to use the cliché, no one had gone before. And I thought that's what I wanted to do as an artist—to go where people haven't gone before."

## ANIMALYMPICS AND FUTUREBOWL

Lisberger Studios was barely making ends meet by doing commercial work.

"I was aware of the fact that animation studios have to create characters that they own to make money," says Lisberger. "You know, the Mickey Mouse thing."

Disney had Mickey Mouse, Donald Duck, Goofy and all of its animated princesses. Warner Bros. had Bugs Bunny, Daffy Duck, Porky Pig and Elmer Fudd. MGM had Tom & Jerry. Hanna-Barbera had Fred Flintstone and Scooby-Doo. Lisberger Studios had the video warrior and Olympic animal athletes.

The studio began to work on two major projects. One was two television specials about the upcoming 1980 winter and summer Olympic Games. The studio would use animated animals as athletes. The specials would be cut together and also released as a feature film overseas.

The other project was an animated feature film called *Futurebowl*. Lisberger had written an outline about gladiatorial video warriors competing on a game grid inside a computer. Putting the video warrior inside that game could provide endless possibilities for an animated movie.

The three-page outline for *Futurebowl* was written in 1978 at the same time *Animalympics* was being created. According to the U.S, Copyright Office website, Lisberger Studios is listed under "Authorship of Application." Lisberger is spelled incorrectly, and there is no mention of Steven's name. It is probably safe to say that it was Lisberger who wrote that outline, as it was his concept. Walt Disney Productions would transfer to copyright to itself on August 24, 1981.

For such a small independent studio, Lisberger had high ambition and some foresight. Arcade games started making inroads in the American public's desire for recreational entertainment by the late 1970s. Already, *Space Invaders* had been a huge hit, paving the way for Atari's *Asteroids* to make a killing at the arcade. The game pitted a vector graphic spaceship against floating asteroids and flying saucers. Millions of kids and teens regularly crowded around the game console for their chance to blast meandering digital rocks. Video games were now entrenched in the psyche of American youth.

America had also been riding high on the last Olympic Games held in 1976. Before he became a reality TV show star on *Keeping up with the Kardashians*, Bruce Jenner was a world-class athlete during the Montreal Olympic Games. He broke records and won gold. Dorothy Hamill charmed television viewers with her ice skating performance during the Innsbruck, Austria Olympic Winter Games. With the upcoming 1980 Moscow Olympics, there was another opportunity for Americans to show off their athletic prowess. The Olympics brought out a sense of patriotism in Americans.

"*Animalympics* was going to ride the trend of the Olympics," says Lisberger, "And *Futurebowl* should ride the video game trend which was happening. It wasn't that much of a mystery to put those pieces together."

There was a lot of potential for the Lisberger Studios to not only capitalize on two major trends, but to also expand and possibly become a major player in animation. The only real major animation studio during the 1970s was Disney, and its animated output had dwindled since Walt Disney's death in 1966. Most of the other studios were either closed down, or only sporadically made cartoons.

Television animation was still fairly strong. Hannah-Barbera, Ruby-Spears and Filmation produced most of the cartoons during the 1970s for Saturday morning television. Perhaps if the Lisberger Studios could get a show going on television, there was a possibility that the video game warrior and *Futurebowl* could have a shot at the big screen.

## VENICE BEACH, LISBERGER STUDIOS AND BILL KROYER

Venice Beach, California is both quaint and bizarre. Built by Abbot Kinney in the 1900s, the little beach city was designed to emulate Venice, Italy with its canals. In the early days, the city was an elegant playground for Los Angeles residents. Roller coasters, piers, amphitheaters, swimming pavilions and gondola riding lent to the charm of this town. By the 1960s, Venice became an artist colony where poets and upcoming rock bands like The Doors thrived.

Lisberger moved his studio out to Venice by 1978, taking with him Donald Kushner, Roger Allers, Dave Stephan, Darrell Rooney, Peter Mueller, Ken Boge, Paul Nevitt, Michael Fremer and John Norton. The charming little town was now famous for oddball street entertainers, Arnold Schwarzenegger and Muscle Beach. The fledgling studio would feel right at home where artists painted murals and roller skating babes cruised the bike path. Kushner, a former lawyer and stage show producer, found a building a few blocks away from the blue Pacific and housed the studio there at 1510 Andalusia Avenue. The studio was filled with young and talented artists who would eventually make their own mark on the film industry.

With the studio embarking on two major projects, it needed talent. Lisberger and Kushner started making phone calls.

Thirty miles away at Walt Disney Productions in the San Fernando Valley, a young self-taught animator named Bill Kroyer was learning classic Disney animation techniques along side animators John Lasseter, Brad Bird, Jerry Rees, and Tim Burton. They were a part of the studio's animation training program. Kroyer caught the animation bug early as a kid growing up in Chicago.

"Chuck Jones came to Chicago to speak at a film festival and I had made him watch one of my films, recalls Kroyer. "He was really generous and then said to me, 'You should go to California and learn to be an animator.' So I thought if Chuck Jones says this, I gotta go to California. So I packed up and went to California."

Work at the fabled studio was good, but it was not stimulating. *The Fox and the Hound* was on the production slate, but its lackluster storyline was a far cry from Disney's heyday. One project that was very promising was *The Black Cauldron*, a dark epic featuring a young warrior, flying dragons and an evil skull-faced villain named the Horned King. The young animators were enthused about the possibilities of mixing up the Disney formula. But production issues and budget problems slowed the film's journey to theaters, and enthusiasm waned.

"I was at Disney and being trained by the old guys and really learning classic animation, says Kroyer. "I was there working on a couple films and that's when Steve Lisberger came to town. He was going to set up this company and do *Animalympics*. So he actually came to Disney and pitched to all of us young guys. 'I got a new studio. It's going to be really exciting. You guys should leave Disney and come and work for me.' I'm the only one that did. At the time, Disney was ready to do *The Black Cauldron* and it didn't look very exciting to me."

Kroyer became Lisberger's animation director on *Animalympics*.

## ARNE WONG AND DONALD KUSHNER

The Venice studio first became active doing commercial work. Though this was not Steven's favorite task, it paid the bills and his staff, plus kept his feature film projects rolling along. Lisberger continued to hire. One of his excellent finds was Arne Wong. He was an animator whose love for surfing became a part of his short films. He would later apprentice at Disney.

"I had originally planned a life career as a surfer in Hawaii," says Wong, "but one fateful day at Pupakea, one break over from Pipeline, I paddled into a 10-12 ft. monster wave. When I washed up the beach later barely alive, I realized that I wasn't going to be the surfer I dreamed of being. I returned home and finished college, making short animated surf films."

Others who joined the new small studio to work on *Animalympics* included Roger Allers, who would co-direct *The Lion King* (1994), and direct *Open Season* (2006), and Brad Bird, who would direct *Iron Giant* (1999), *The Incredibles* (2004), *Ratatouille* (2007) and *Mission: Impossible – Ghost Protocol* (2011).

*Animalympics* was an ambitious project for a large animation studio, let alone a boutique studio near the beach. But Lisberger and his staff were ambitious enough to tackle it and *Futurebowl*.

The concept for *Animalympics* revolved around colorful animal characters participating in Olympic Games on a fictional island. The animation team used bold colors and dimensional shaping on the characters to give them more form and function. The result gave the production a high-quality appearance, even though the budget for the film was low. The animation itself was fluid and nothing like what was seen on television or in some of the films of the era. Considering that the Lisberger staff was small, it still used its talent to produce excellent work. They also used a technique called backlit animation that had been pioneered by a television commercial artist named Richard Taylor.

Kushner, with his negotiating skills, sold the project to NBC, which was airing the Olympic Games. What better way than to get children to watch *Animalympics*, then their parents and grandparents would watch the regular games? It could be a ratings bonanza for NBC, and Lisberger Studios would be on the map.

"Donald's a sort of quiet power," says Lisberger. "He's not too up front with you. He doesn't push. He was very instrumental in landing the *Animalympics* deal. And whenever I had doubts about can we really move forward from this point, Donald always said, 'Let's do it, and I'll try my best.' He tried his best to build the road running ahead of me, six inches at a time. Once in a while, I almost stepped down into the abyss. At the last second, Donald got a step ladder jerry rigged so we wouldn't completely fall down."

## MICHAEL FREMER AND CHRIS LANE

When Lisberger was still in Boston working on the early stages of the film, they contacted Michael Fremer to lend some voices and ideas for character names. He was a "shock jock" in Boston, predating Howard Stern's act by a few years. He had been popular around the city and the artists at Lisberger loved listening to him.

"They heard all my stuff and they contacted me," says Fremer. "I met the artists and saw the storyboards. They said come up with names for the characters. I came up with some very funny names, if I do say so myself. There was a Russian weightlifter, an elephant, and I named him Ivan Dizavensky. Then there was a female Russian and I named her Lyudmila Steponutova."

Fremer moved out with the studio staff to California a short time later. Because of the small size of the studio, his new job on the film was not only to supply character voices, but also to work on the soundtrack, sound mix and seek out other actors.

One of the first actors he hired was Harry Shearer, who at the time was part of a comedy troupe called the Credibility Gap. Shearer was immensely talented and could do a variety of voices, but at the time, he was unknown. He later found fame doing voices for *The Simpsons*. His characters included C. Montgomery Burns, Waylon Smithers, and Ned Flanders. He also did a killer impression of Vin Scully, the famous announcer for the Los Angeles Dodgers. At one recording session, Shearer brought in his own talent to the Lisberger Studios by the name of Billy Crystal.

Crystal was best known at the time as the character of Jodie Dallas on the ABC network show, *Soap*. He had not found fame yet beyond the show, but he would crack up the artists with his dead-on impressions of Mohammad Ali and Howard Cosell. He would later play leads in *When Harry Met Sally* (1989) and *City Slickers* (1991), as well as being a popular host of the Oscars telecast.

Fremer's other coup in the voice department was getting Gilda Radner to play most of the female character voices. By this time, she was hugely popular on *Saturday Night Live*. Because of her schedule on the show, her lines had to be recorded in New York City. Lisberger and Fremer flew out to meet her and record.

"She was at the height of her fame at that point," recalls Fremer. "The afternoon after the rehearsal for this *Saturday Night Live*, she said to us, 'Okay guys, you each grab an arm. You ready?' We didn't know what we were supposed to be ready for. We said okay. We walked out of the elevator and it was like a vacuum where everything gets sucked in. My head would turn and it would be like, 'Hey, Roseanne Roseannadanna! *Nevermind*!' Every cliché, everything she ever did on the show, yelling back at her. It was a blast."

While waiting for their ride from New York's JFK Airport into Manhattan to record with Radner, Lisberger stared at a *Pong* video game console in the lobby. Its black-and-white television screen blasted video pong images at thousand of JFK passengers each day. After studying it for a minute, he turned to Fremer.

"What if we're creating this reality? We are like God and we're creating this new world inside the television."

What was Lisberger talking about? Then it dawned on him. He was talking about the *Futurebowl* concept taking place back at the Venice studio.

As *Animalympics* was finishing and getting ready to go to NBC, Lisberger began honing in on his original idea for the electronic gladiator and *Futurebowl*.

"Instead of it just being a *Pong* game, it was an electronic video game/football game the warriors were in," says Lisberger. "In that draft, I already had technical computer aspects, but I didn't know very much. I didn't know how computers really were laid out and how they worked. I knew that I wanted a Master Program and he was the emperor that sends people to die on the games. I wanted HAL to be that guy."

He pounded away at the script and focused on a new plot. It borrowed from the 1960 film, *Spartacus* and placed the electronic gladiator into a video game. Just imagine Kirk Douglas battling inside a video game!

"What did Kirk Douglas do in *Spartacus*? asks Lisberger. "He escaped from the gladiatorial arena. I thought: If you're an electronic warrior, and you're fighting in a video game, where are you going to escape to? You're going to escape to another part of the computer."

The film would also be visionary and cutting edge.

"I was really influenced a lot by *Yellow Submarine*," recalls Lisberger. "I was influenced by movies that took you to a whole new world. Originally it was going to be all animated with backlit glowing characters and some cel paint, only Flynn would be a live action character."

The character of Flynn, at this point, was not fully developed.

For *Futurebowl*, Lisberger began looking around town for staffing to augment his visionary concept. He was very adept in choosing who would work for him. Like a good baseball scout, he could pick talent and use their skills to build a winning team.

One of the influential artists he brought aboard was Chris Lane. Lane specialized in incredible production design, giving the director, and in some cases, studios, ideas of how a film would look. He would prove himself to be ideal for Lisberger's electronic warrior movie.

"I went to see his rather cute film studio in Venice," recalls Lane. "We went upstairs and he began to tell me about his ideas. He stumbled around a bit. I kept waiting for something that was going to jump out, but nothing did. That is until he said, 'I have another idea I'm calling *Futurebowl*, which is about this guy that is into computer games and somehow gets bolted into the insides of the computer and has to try to find a way to get out of this huge tech world.' At that point I said, 'That's your film! You've got something with this!'"

Lane was hired as the film's production designer.

"Steve couldn't pay my full film salary, so Donald wrote in the contract that I would receive the balance of my payments and an extra fee for being the designer on *Futurebowl*," says Lane. "That money would come to me on the sale of the project to a studio or backer of the film. I signed the contract and we went forward with it."

The other main designs of the film were done by John Norton, who had designed the electronic warrior that was featured in those Boston radio ads. His and Chris Lane's early designs set in motion the look and feel of the film. Kroyer also developed the concept art and storyboards. Roger Allers did the first designs of the MCP.

*Futurebowl* was eventually rechristened as *Tron*.

"My father-in-law was an electrical engineer who worked at the DuPont Experimental Station," relates Lisberger. "He started his own company and called it Peltron. This name was derived from *The Pelidna,* the name of his sailboat. I liked the word *tron* to signify electronic."

## BONNIE MACBIRD AND DARRELL ROONEY

With some proceeds NBC paid upfront for *Animalympics*, Lisberger hired Lane and additional staff members. One of them was a successful story development executive at Universal Pictures named Bonnie MacBird.

She had worked for Ned Tanen, a powerful executive who was the legendary head of features. He was perhaps most famous for nearly sidetracking George Lucas' career after seeing an early screening of *American Graffiti*. He hated the film so much he wanted to send it directly to television. According to legend, Francis Ford Coppola told Tanen he would buy the movie right there and release it himself. Tanen relented and the film went on to become a monster hit with Oscar nominations, including one for Best Picture of 1973. He later produced the John Hughes teen classic, *The Breakfast Club* (1985).

MacBird had a very comfortable job at Universal, according to Lane. She was well paid and worked for arguably one of the biggest personalities in the film business. Lisberger had at one point come to Universal to pitch an idea called *Lightning* to Jennings Lang. He was a producer on the lot, having been an executive producer on some of Universal's *Airport* sequels. He produced the 1977 film, *Rollercoaster*. Lang teamed MacBird with Lisberger to try and develop the story.

"We hit it off and enjoyed working together," says MacBird. "We had complimentary talents, his for strong visual effects and mine for a real sense of story and character. I left Universal and joined Lisberger Studios with an initial plan to write two feature films which he and I would co-produce and Steven would direct. One of them was *Tron*."

MacBird would be one of the early members of the *Tron* team, working alongside Lisberger, Fremer and Lane.

"My producing consisted of line producing the test shoots for a process we were investigating with a cutting edge blue screen technique with Paul Vlahos, searching for the right actor for Flynn for the test shoots (and later the film)," recalls MacBird.

Vlahos eventually won an Academy Award of Merit in 1995 for his Ultimatte blue screen process.

One of Lisberger's original artists who came out from Boston, Darrell Rooney, was not only asked to start doing storyboards, but he was the first live action model for *Tron*. As the production concepts grew larger, and the scripts were revised, it was decided to turn *Tron* into a combination live-action/animated film. Rooney was videotaped in a small corner of the Venice Studio against a black background. He represented different video game characters that inhabited what would be called the "Electronic World." Some were cowboys. Some were gladiators throwing invisible "Deadly Discs." Rooney wore his own street clothes, except for the cowboy hat he wore to play a cowboy.

"I wasn't an actor or anything," recalls Rooney. "So I did these things. I was really embarrassed. I guess they added effects to them. I don't even think I saw the finished product, but I'm sure it was part of the whole package they took around to the studios to pitch the project."

Looking at snapshots of the Venice studio, it is clear that it was a fun moment in time for most employees who worked there. Most of the artists were still in their twenties, many beginning their careers and families. *Animalympics* had the signs of being a hit for not only NBC, but for Lisberger Studios and its staff. The *Tron* concept was beginning to grow and could be something spectacular, too. It was clear that most people working at Lisberger held their boss in high regard.

Lane was excited about working for Lisberger, too. Lisberger brought in computer parts like circuit boards, and the two would put their heads together to create the world of this electronic fantasyland. Using black paper and Prismacolors, he began sketching out how the insides of a computer would look.

"It was very free floating in the early stages and I felt free to imagine the world as I saw it, and other times the way Steve was envisioning it," says Lane. "We had good back-and-forth exchanges. But as time went on, Steve became more his spontaneous self and would walk in and want to go in a completely different direction at times, or try something out on the spot."

Along with John Norton, Andy Probert, and Peter Mueller, Lane created some astounding early concepts for the computer world. The "Electronic World" was inhabited by electronic gladiators who glowed neon light and had hyper-muscular bodies that would make Arnold Schwarzenegger envious.

Various creatures that might be found in video games of the era were present. A character named Scout, storyboarded by Rooney, floated around the "Electronic World" without legs. There was an electric bull and horse that could have lived in a western video game.

The world itself was alive with neon and backlighting. The electronic gladiator that was featured in Lisberger's radio ad was now more refined and tougher looking. In this artwork were early renditions of what would become the Light Cycle, a futuristic motorcycle. The arenas where the electronic gladiators battled were gigantic. Many of the artist renderings are copyrighted 1979 by Lisberger Studios.

According to Lane, he took a stab at the script and showed it to Lisberger. Since the studio was very small with about sixty-five people employees, it was probably not unusual for other artists to write their own screenplay draft. Many screenplays can and will go through numerous re-writes and different authors.

"I showed him my rough treatment for the screenplay and he liked it a lot, but said that he had just signed on Bonnie and had to let her do her thing to get her going," recalls Lane.

"When Bonnie came in we hit it off and I would also show her what I had been designing," Lane continues. "Together with Steve, we started to plan out the early stages of the story along with the visuals that would go along with it. Many times I would present ideas of my own as possibilities and other times Steve or Bonnie would come up with a new direction to work on."

But it was Lisberger who planted the seed in everyone's minds about this computer warrior character.

"The thing about Steve is he's always been an amazing idea person," says Rooney. "*Animalympics* was his idea. Some things that preceded me were his idea. *Tron* was his idea. I don't remember if Steven was talking about *Tron* in Boston or not. It may not have been until we moved to California, which was in September 1978, working down in Venice. At some point the seeds of *Tron* were born. It was a brilliant idea."

10

# Chapter 2

# *SUSPENDED ANIMATION*

Walt Disney Productions was a dreammaking factory. Located in Burbank, a sleepy bedroom community in Southern California, the fabled studio was the place where magic was made. Here the iconic characters of Mickey Mouse, Donald Duck, Goofy, Pinocchio, Dumbo, and Mary Poppins were brought to life. It was here that Kirk Douglas battled a giant squid, and the Mouseketeers taught children how to sing and dance.

The studio was built with profits from Walt Disney's *Snow White and the Seven Dwarfs* (1937). Built to resemble a college campus, the studio had a comfortable atmosphere that was condusive to creativity. Nicely paved streets like Mickey Avenue and Dopey Drive meandered past the Animation and Camera Buildings. Large beautiful shady trees and grassy areas provided comfortable spots in which to relax. The studio commissary served hot meals for lunch. Nearly everyone dressed nicely for work. It is no wonder that Walt himself probably enjoyed walking through the studio property thinking of the new worlds he was going to conquer.

When Walt passed away in 1966, the world had changed radically after his death. It was more cynical, angry and scary. The Vietnam War changed the perception that war was like a John Wayne movie. Politicians were under scrutiny and were not trusted anymore. Music shifted from Sinatra to Hendrix. Sports became further integrated. Cinema became very diverse. Fashion and personal appearance went from conservative to wild. Rebellion was the rule of the times.

Walt Disney Productions still managed to be a bright spot in family entertainment and was happy to provide it. It was a safe haven for those who did not adhere to the changes of the 1960s and 1970s. Families still looked to Disney for wholesome entertainment. But to a cynical visitor, Walt Disney Productions was a place trapped in time. It was as though fairies had cast a spell over the studio to protect it from a changing world. The fabled studio fell into a deep slumber and would not awaken.

## WALT DISNEY: BUILDING MAGIC

The Walt Disney studio property at 500 Buena Vista Drive is sometimes mistaken as the birthplace of Mickey Mouse. In truth, the iconic cartoon character was conceived in Walt Disney's creative mind, and was born at the original Disney Brothers Studio, located on Hyperion Drive in Silver Lake, a small community in Los Angeles. Walt founded the studio with his older brother Roy Oliver Disney in 1923. Walt was the creative and ingenious dreamer, while Roy was the quiet and responsible businessman. It was there that Walt and his lead animator (and business partner), Ub Iwerks, began the foundation for the iconic character of Mickey Mouse.

Walt was born in Chicago on December 5, 1901. Growing up on a farm, he showed an early talent in drawing. By the time he was in his early twenties, he went into the animation business in Kansas City. Not content with being just an animator, he embarked on a journey that would forever change his career. With a 35mm motion picture film camera, he, along with Iwerks and Roy, created a series of live-action short films that put actress Virginia Davis into a world of animated characters. The *Alice Comedies* put Walt Disney and his fledgling studio on the map in the early 1920s.

The *Alice Comedies* were popular with movie audiences, but they ran their course. That was when Walt created Oswald the Lucky Rabbit. The financial success of the *Oswald* shorts opened the door for the Disney Brothers to move out to California to open their studio on Hyperion Avenue. Ub Iwerks later joined them.

Oswald the Lucky Rabbit was a cute cartoon creation by Walt. Iwerks animated the character and the Disney Brothers Studio had a hit. Unfortunately, Oswald was taken away by Walt's film distributor, Charles Mintz. Walt was left without a cartoon character to keep his new studio in business.

Walt desperately needed a new cartoon character to keep his studio alive. The legend goes that Walt came up with Mickey while on a train ride from New York to California. Walt sketched out an appealing cartoon mouse and told his wife, Lillian, "I'm going to call him Mortimer Mouse."

Lillian allegedly balked. "That's a horrible name, Walt. Why don't you call him Mickey?"

The first Mickey Mouse cartoon was a parody of the public's fascination with pilot, Charles A. Lindbergh. The film, *Plane Crazy*, received some interest from studios around Hollywood, but no one picked it up for distribution. Walt figured to get Mickey Mouse out into the public's eye, new movie technology was the cheese.

By the late 1920s, a number of inventors, both independent and under the employment of large studios like Warner Bros. and Fox Film Corporation, created new ways of syncing sound with motion pictures. *Don Juan* (1926), a 1927 Fox newsreel about Lindbergh's historic transatlantic flight, *The Jazz Singer* (1927), and *The Lights of New York* (1928) were hits with the public.

Using primitive sound recording equipment from an unscrupulous businessman named P.A. Powers, Walt and a small group of his studio employees recorded the sound, music and sound effects for an animated short by Iwerks, *Steamboat Willie*.

Debuting at the Colony Theater in New York City on November 18, 1928, *Steamboat Willie* was a sensation with audiences. The film was not the first sound cartoon, though numerous publications (and no doubt Disney's publicity department) said otherwise. Max Fleischer's series of *Song Cartune* shorts beat Disney's creation by four years.

But Disney had two elements in his favor. Mickey, as simplistic as he looked in those early cartoons, had a particular charm that set him apart from other cartoon characters. Adults and children seemed to gravitate toward this simple character. His simplicity and eventual friendly demeanor helped him become the most iconic cartoon character of all-time.

Walt also realized sound was going to be the future of cinema. The Powers Cinephone sound system, allegedly built from other patents, could be installed in almost any movie theater in the country. With movie theater exhibitors and studios realizing the profit potential of sound movies, the film industry changed in very little time. Silent films were out and sound films were in. From the moment that Mickey whistled "Turkey in the Straw," Disney instantly turned his studio into an animation powerhouse.

The success of the Mickey Mouse cartoons lead the Disney Brothers Studio into an incredible period of growth. *The Silly Symphonies* were a way for Disney's animators to experiment with different characters, stories, and techniques. The first short was *The Skeleton Dance* (1929), a delightfully animated short by Iwerks. The animation staff continued to improve their skills on nearly every Mickey Mouse and *Silly Symphony* short. Walt, even at a young age, was a stickler for high quality. Animation, which was considered by audiences to be nothing more than toss-away entertainment, was refined into an art form by Disney and his staff.

## TECHNICOLOR AND *SNOW WHITE* CHANGE THE DISNEY STUDIO

Technicolor had been around since the 1900s, but it took a number of years until it made its way into Hollywood's subconscious. By 1932, Walt scrapped a *Silly Symphony* already being filmed in black-and-white, *Flowers and Trees*, in favor of shooting it in Technicolor. Roy, who prided himself on keeping the studio financially above water, cringed at his brother's latest idea. He reluctantly allowed Walt to pursue making the film in Technicolor. The short was a smash hit and from that moment on the Disney studio made every one of its cartoons in color. Out of this series came the immensely popular short, *The Three Little Pigs* (1933).

Not finished with innovation, Walt encouraged the development of the multiplane camera for use on another *Silly Symphony*, *The Old Mill* (1937). Now that the studio had conquered sound and Technicolor, it was going to combine them with the illusion of three-dimensions.

Disney's engineers built the multiplane camera, which was a tall device where animators stacked layers of animation cels and backgrounds in succession. With a 35mm motion picture camera anchored on top, peering down through the multiple layers of cels, the camera, in effect, saw a three-dimensional image. The effect from the multiplane camera was stunning, adding depth to even Disney's simplest cartoon shorts. With all of this technical innovation at the hands of his staff, Walt felt it was time to take his studio's future endeavors to a higher level.

Walt filled his studio with some of the most inventive people in the movie business. His featured animators were relatively young men he later referred to as the "Nine Old Men." Les Clark, Marc Davis, Ollie Johnston, Milt Kahl, Ward Kimball, Eric Larson, John Lounsbery, Woolie Reitherman, and Frank Thomas were considered to be the top animators at Disney. He surprised them with a revolutionary idea he wanted to tackle—an animated feature film.

Walt had loved the story of *Snow White and the Seven Dwarfs* since he was a newsboy back in Kansas City. He had seen a silent film version of it and the story always remained in his mind. He decided, much to the chagrin of Roy and Bank of America (the bank that helped fund many of Disney's projects), that the studio would embark on an animated feature version of *Snow White and the Seven Dwarfs*.

*Snow White and the Seven Dwarfs* was an extremely risky venture for any studio, let alone Walt's. Although Walt Disney Productions was considered to be one of the smaller studios outside the exclusive club of major studios: MGM, Warner Bros., Universal, Paramount, 20th Century Fox and Columbia, it had an amazingly diverse staff of animators and artists who could be called upon for almost any task. Yet the concept of producing a feature-length cartoon was unheard of in Hollywood. Walt did not care what the film industry thought of his "folly." He cared about telling a great story.

The release of *Snow White and the Seven Dwarfs* in 1937 brought Walt and the studio prosperity. It was the highest grossing film in history at that point. The film won over cynics who believed that a cartoon feature would fail. Parents found the film charming, entertaining and in the end, emotionally moving. Children loved the dwarfs and laughed aloud at Dopey. The Wicked Queen scared the daylights out of children, yet they still loved the film enough to want to see it again.

Walt's gamble paid off handsomely. The studio, which might have been bankrupt had *Snow White* failed, was flush with cash. Most importantly, Disney's gamble took what was perceived as kiddie entertainment, animation, and placed it amongst the higher echelon of cinema. Walt talked Roy into building a new state-of-the-art studio in Burbank from the profits.

Over the next few decades, the studio produced a remarkable string of animated classics including *Pinocchio* and *Fantasia* (1940), *Dumbo* (1941), *Bambi* (1942), *Cinderella* (1950), *Alice In Wonderland* (1951), *Peter Pan* (1953), *Lady and the Tramp* (1955), *Sleeping Beauty* (1959), *101 Dalmatians* (1961) and *The Jungle Book* (1967).

## WALT MOVES FORWARD

During World War II, Walt Disney Productions remained busy by making films for the war effort. After the war, the studio made compilation feature films such as *Make Mine Music* (1946), cartoon shorts, and occasional features like *Song of the South* (1946). But the studio was still trying to recover from the financial losses it incurred during World War II.

The studio needed a hit film and by 1950, it had one in *Cinderella*. It was a huge box office hit and it was seen as a return to Disney's classic animation style. It was around this time that Walt pushed forward an idea he had in his mind for years: an amusement park where families could enjoy the day together. But he needed funding to build it. Defying Hollywood's reluctance to enter the world of television, Walt jumped in. He created a show called *Disneyland* and it was an immediate hit. He used the show as a vehicle to essentially advertise his studio's projects, but also to use it to help fund his new amusement park called Disneyland. It was a brilliant move. Walt, as the show's host, became a national icon.

Disneyland is now a part of American culture. But in 1955, when the park opened in Anaheim, California, it was a wild concept. Amusement parks that operated prior to Disneyland's opening were usually tawdry, dirty places. Walt turned the concept of the amusement park upside down by creating the theme park. Guests, as he called customers, entered a world away from reality. Guests escaped into the darkest jungles of the world on the *Jungle Cruise*, or visited the world of fairy tales (as told by Disney) in Fantasyland. With this single concept of a theme park, Walt and his "Imagineeers" reinvented the way outdoor entertainment would be experienced forever.

By the time Walt opened Disneyland, the company was rapidly expanding. The *Disneyland* television series was a Sunday night staple in millions of households. One of the shows featured on it, *Davy Crockett*, was a huge success. Kids loved the adventures starring Fess Parker and Buddy Ebsen. Walt Disney Productions sold millions of coonskin caps to kids as a result. Children raced home after school to watch *The Mickey Mouse Club*, and to this day, nearly anyone can sing its theme song. By 1959, Walt initiated a huge expansion of Tomorrowland and introduced the world to the themed steel roller coaster ride, the Matterhorn.

By the 1960s, Walt's Imagineering unit created fantastic worlds and concepts for Disneyland. They also created robotic Audio-Animatronic figures, bringing characters to three-dimensional reality in his theme park. Animals on the *Jungle Cruise* and birds in *The Enchanted Tiki Room* charmed guests with their realism. For the 1964 New York World's Fair, Imagineers created a life-like presentation of America's 16th president in *Great Moments with Mr. Lincoln* for the Illinois State pavilion. The Audio-Animatronic figure of Abraham Lincoln, voiced by actor Royal Dano, was eerily realistic. Audiences flocked to the pavilion to get a glimpse of Walt Disney's latest creation.

Walt Disney represented an American ideal. His films could present a happy and carefree world in which laughs were key (*The Absent Minded Professor*—1960), or where wishes came true (*Cinderella*). Walt made sure his employees, known as cast members, were clean cut at Disneyland. The theme park was always maintained with clean walkways and freshly painted facades. Viewers of his movies and visitors to his theme park expected top notch entertainment. The Disney name represented high quality and an escape from the outside world. People gravitated to the fantasy worlds Disney created.

"Walt Disney had succeeded because he had touched and made relatable the storytelling, which was very American," says Harrison Ellenshaw, who would eventually work on *Tron*.

In 1964, the studio released *Mary Poppins*. This remarkable film starred Julie Andrews, Dick Van Dyke, David Thomlinson and Glynis Johns in a big screen adaption of P. L. Traver's book. Directed by Robert Stevenson, every asset of Disney's creativity was used. First and foremost, the film told an engaging story. Second, it continued Walt's penchant for finding extraordinary musical talent. Brothers Richard M. and Robert B. Sherman wrote some of the most memorable songs in film history, such as "Chim Chim Cheree," "A Spoonful of Sugar," and "Feed the Birds." Third, the studio's Animation Department performed outstanding work. And fourth, the studio's visual effects department was at the top of its game in bringing the world of *Mary Poppins* to life. The film was practically perfect in every way.

As nostalgic as Walt was for the good old days, he liked change. Once a project was finished, he encouraged his staff to come up with new ideas or "plus" existing ones. He discouraged sequels to his successful films, but he was not above expanding on an original concept like Disneyland. The creation of Disney World in Central Florida was his desire to expand upon the concepts he had for Disneyland. With the amount of acreage his staff secretly bought, he could build nearly anything he wanted.

But sadly, Walt had been seriously ill for awhile. Smoking had damaged his lungs and cancer had developed. Despite an obvious change in appearance, he managed to keep his illness secret, even to his most devoted employees.

On December 15, 1966, Walt Disney passed away. In his last hours, he was looking toward the future. His last major project before his death was EPCOT (Experimental Prototype Community of Tomorrow).

His death from lung cancer was a shock. His family lost a caring man who was a father, brother and father-in-law. To the world, they lost an iconic person who made magical movies and a magical place called Disneyland. His studio staff lost their leader.

Walt Disney was a charismatic leader, devoted family man, wonderful storyteller, a true innovator, and father figure to the public and his devoted employees. He could be a difficult boss, moody, financially risky, and a perfectionist. His death marked the end of an era, and to some, the end of his magic kingdom.

He left the company in capable hands and it continued to expand after his death. Roy O. Disney made it his priority to build and open his brother's final dream project, Disney World (rechristened Walt Disney World by Roy), in Orlando, Florida in 1971. *The Love Bug* was the number one hit movie in 1969 and kept Disney's coffers flowing, proving that both children and hippies could enjoy a family flick. Merchandising of Disney characters and stories kept the studio humming along. Continuous rereleases of some of its animated feature films also kept a new generation entertained. Just as the world was transitioning, Walt Disney Productions was changing, too. It just did not know it yet.

## UNDER NEW MANAGEMENT

Roy O. Disney passed away shortly after the opening of Walt Disney World in 1971, leaving the company under the leadership of Donn B. Tatum (chairman of the board and CEO), E. Cardon Walker (president and COO), Roy E. Disney (a vice president) and Ron Miller (another vice president).

Walker was a studio veteran who had worked his way up into the board room. Walker was loyal to Walt and wanted to continue with what he perceived were Walt's wishes. Under his leadership, the studio was the icon of family entertainment. In 1973, record profits from the animated version of *Robin Hood* and theme parks kept the company moving along.

"We haven't gone in any new directions," Walker told *Time* magazine in 1973. "The name has become a guarantee. If it says Walt Disney Productions, a family can be assured that they're not going to be shocked in any way—bored maybe sometimes, but never shocked."

*Robin Hood* was a hit, but it was an uninspired piece of work from a studio that once prided itself on high-quality animation and storytelling. Animated by a small number of the studio's veteran animation staff, the film was not in the same league of Disney's past achievements. Since the release of *Sleeping Beauty* in 1959, animation at the studio became less involved with finesse and more involved with simplicity and cost cutting. Just three years earlier, *The Aristocats* demonstrated the lack of passion in the animated art form.

There was also a huge problem on the horizon. The "Nine Old Men" were retiring or close to retirement. Walt's famed animation unit was in limbo. How was the studio going to replace those aging animators?

There was a drive to train new animators from CalArts, a school in which Walt had invested money. The idea was for veteran Disney animators to train students in the studio's traditional techniques. Once the students graduated and came to work at Disney, they would be ready to continue the Disney animation tradition.

The studio continued to produce live action movies, but they were largely forgettable. *Island at the Top of the World* (1974), *One of Our Dinosaurs is Missing* and *Gus* (both 1976) were Disney movies, but they lacked Disney magic. Audiences still saw these movies, but they were also rushing to see movies like *The Godfather* (1972), *The Exorcist* (1973) and *Jaws* (1975). Those films were far more mature than anything that Disney was producing. They were made by young directors who were not raised in the traditional studio system. These films had modern cinematography and looked contemporary. They were edgy and exciting. They were fresh. Disney's films of the 1970s felt archaic and tiresome.

The only Disney film made during this time that broke studio convention was *Freaky Friday* (1976). Assuredly directed by Gary Nelson, it dealt with the modern problems of being an adolescent girl, played by Jodie Foster. The film was an anomaly in the studio's normal fare. Most of its films starred old Hollywood actors who did not register on the radar of Disney's prime demographic: teenagers and children. No self respecting teenager was going to beg their parents to see a movie starring Helen Hayes.

In 1976, Walker became CEO of Walt Disney Productions. By 1977, Roy E. Disney, Walt's nephew and Roy's son, left the Disney board. Fed up with the lack of change he thought the company needed, Roy eventually embarked on a takeover attempt.

Still, the company grew. It added *The New Mickey Mouse Club* to its television roster, and continued building major new attractions at its California and Florida theme parks. Plans were made to finally build EPCOT in Florida and build a Disneyland in Japan. But within the ranks, there were rumblings for change. Some were desperately trying to reinvent the studio.

# Chapter 3

# *COLLAPSE*

In the 1970s, computers were a new concept to most people. Certainly they were used in major corporations and some tinkering types created primitive computers at home. Mostly they were out of the hands of most ordinary people. Lisberger was intrigued by computers and computer games enough to base a story around their environment. But he was the first to admit even he was not completely computer savvy. He needed to do some research.

He, along with MacBird, Fremer, and other artists, traveled to Northern California to get into the minds of computer geniuses. One of the places they visited was Apple. At the time, it was a small company in an industrial park in Cupertino.

"Lisberger was an Apple guy," says Fremer. "He made some phone calls and we took a day trip up to Cupertino. We go upstairs and there are these circuit boards and these guys tinkering with stuff. One guy says, 'You know, in ten years everyone's going to have a computer in their house.' I walked out of there and said, 'These people are out of their fucking minds! What are you going to do with a computer in your house?' I have to look back and laugh."

Further into the research process, Lisberger and his team visited Xerox Corporation's PARC (Palo Alto Research Center) facilities. This was perhaps the most influential computer research center on earth. Their brain trust included Alvy Ray Smith (for one year) and Alan Kay. Kay was one of the wizards of not only PARC, but the entire computer industry. His invention of a program called Smalltalk utilized a graphical user interface (GUI), which used icons to allow users to quickly find their documents and programs on their desktop computer. He is also credited for conceiving the laptop computer. He earned a Ph.D. and M.S. in Electrical Engineering from the University of Utah.

PARC's inventors concocted wild concepts, including the laser printer, the Superpaint frame buffer (an early computer animation program), the Ethernet, and the Xerox Alto (a personal workstation). Steve Jobs, Steven Wozniack, and Bill Gates took a tour of PARC. Allegedly they took some of those ideas and made both Microsoft and Apple into the behemoths we know of today.

PARC was a playground for the *Tron* team to learn and enjoy the optimistic future of computers. Lisberger was caught up in Kay's bright outlook.

"I heard him talk at length about how we were all going to attain our digital freedom through the PC," says Lisberger. "I take my art as sort of a spiritual expression. I'm a '60s person, so a revolution is always part of the formula. It sounded like *Spartacus* in a way. At the time, I was very fascinated by Jungian psychology. One of the core tenants of Jungian psychology is that within each of us, if you step back and you look at yourself, there's a potentially great person. The best you can be lies within you. And computers have all this potential, as Alan laid out. Would they bring out the best in us as users?"

Lisberger realized that, in what would become a catch line for *Tron's* radio promotion, a part of everyone lives in a computer. We are the "users" and there are "programs," or alternate versions of us, living and breathing inside these machines. Those programs take our cues, our emotions, our desires, and create their own alternate world. They carry with them our names, our checkbook account numbers, and essentially our lives.

MacBird was also intrigued by Kay's vision of the future.

"I traveled up to Palo Alto with Steven and another person where we met with Alan," she recalls. "He regaled us for four hours about computers and history and art and music and theater and education and children. He loved the project. We were bowled over. We hired him as the Technical Consultant for the film. He began flying down often to L.A. to work with us."

Kay and MacBird eventually married.

Fed with inspiration, the small team came back to the Venice studio and continued to brainstorm. MacBird had acting connections within the film industry and stand-up comic circuit. She brought in an actor named Larry Anderson who taught improvisation classes to the Lisberger staff. He would do new blue screen tests for the animators working on *Tron*. Kay even became part of the action.

"He'd come down Friday afternoon just to come to Lisberger Studios and sit around and b.s. with us about what the movie can be," says Kroyer. "That was pretty amazing."

Lisberger further got the staff into the mood for the film by playing electronic music.

"Groups like Claus Scholts, Tangerine Dream and Brian Eno were making their way into the record stores," says Lane. "Some of the guys were picking up their albums. The music filled the studio all the time until there were some complaints. We waited for whoever to leave the studio and then we turned it back up."

## CANCELLED

Jimmy Carter meant well. A former peanut farmer from Georgia, he was elected governor of that state. He ran for President of the United States and beat out Gerald Ford. Americans wanted a change from the ugliness brought about by the Richard Nixon years. They got it in Carter, but it was not what they bargained for.

Seen as a passive American president, Carter presided over four years of weak leadership. The economy was in the pits, while American morale was low after the end of the Vietnam War. Americans were taken hostage in Tehran, Iran at the American Embassy, starting the Iran Hostage Crisis. Carter sent in a small military squadron of helicopters to rescue them, but three crashed in a desert sandstorm and the mission was aborted. The Cold War between the United States and

Russia had come to a head due to the nuclear arms race and Russia's invasion of Afghanistan. In a rare show of force as president, Carter boycotted the 1980 Moscow Olympic Games.

Athletes, who had trained hard to compete, were angry. Americans, looking for more vindication after beating Russia in the huge 1980 "Miracle on Ice" hockey game were shocked. The staff of Lisberger Studios was stunned. NBC would not have the Summer Olympic Games to air, and Lisberger Studios would not have a place to show *Animalympics*. All of their hard work, all of their time, spent on a project that would not see the light of day.

In 1980, outlets for a children's program like *Animalympics* were limited. Cable was just starting to make inroads in households across America. There were only three major networks, CBS, NBC and ABC. Without NBC to broadcast Olympic Games, *Animalympics* had limited appeal at that point. The winter version of the film did air, but it was not enough to keep Lisberger's studio afloat. Videocassette rentals were still in their infancy, so that revenue was virtually nonexistent.

"The whole Olympics fiasco happened and basically the studio was going to close," says Rooney. "I think Steve's plan was to be independent with *Tron* from the proceeds of *Animalympics* and all that went out the window."

With *Animalympics* finished, but not airing, he had to get *Tron* somewhere to keep his studio running. He could no longer be independent. It was time to focus and get a major studio to fund to the project. By this point in time, screen tests had been done with Darrell Rooney and Larry Anderson. The storyboards and sketches for *Tron* filled most of the offices at Lisberger Studios. Lisberger had a bold and ambitious vision to bring the film to life. What was still being written was a suitable screenplay, and that is where the relationship between Lisberger and MacBird began to fray.

If one were to graph the development of *Tron*, based on interviews of the principle participants in the film, there seems to be reasonable agreement that Lisberger and MacBird worked well together up until a point in time. There does not seem to be much debate that she was instrumental in some of the early development of the film. In Lisberger's skills in finding talent, he knew that MacBird's studio experience would be valuable to the production.

In short time, MacBird was involved with producing some of the early Lisberger Studio tests for *Tron*. She was instrumental in introducing Lisberger to Alan Kay, as well as getting Larry Anderson to perform for the animators. She had major connections at Universal. She was supposed to be one of the producers along with Donald Kushner. Lisberger and MacBird's different ideas about which creative direction the script should take would fracture their friendship for good. And with any fractured friendship, each person has their supporters and detractors.

In all major movies, a screenplay goes through numerous revisions. Sometimes these revisions can be done by the original writer, other times by a number of writers. In some cases, the original writer is paid, then is not credited as the screenwriter. In many cases, that credit is arbitrated by the Writer's Guild of America. As a token, the original writer can be given an associate or executive producer credit. To writers, a screenplay is their "baby." They have nurtured it, created its characters and spent hundreds of hours developing it. When another writer tinkers with the script, or if there is a disagreement over who is the author, friction develops.

In the case of *Tron*, based on interviews of the early stages of its development, a few of Lisberger Studio employees took a stab at the script. Lisberger toiled away on the script for two years based on his original *Futurebowl* outline. Lane allegedly did at least one draft. Kushner worked with both Lisberger and MacBird in developing the script. Michael Fremer sat down at a typewriter and tried to improve what he thought was a weak screenplay.

"I'm reading this script and it's just written like a greeting card," says Fremer. "No emotional life. I wasn't a script writer, I admit. But I'd been to movies. I actually sat down and wrote my own script. They couldn't have been too thrilled about that. Steve actually took a meeting with me at my house. I was very critical of what was going on. I said this is so wooden. His attitude was, 'Well, it's inside of a computer.'"

Lisberger's original concept and script for *Tron* involved video game warriors with a *Spartacus* theme of gladiatorial battles. The film would be abstract like Walt Disney's *Fantasia*. It would be funded by his studio for about $10 million, but the studio was in financial straits after the Olympics debacle.

"We realized there was no way we can finance this movie. We just can't do it," says Lisberger. "Then we shopped it. At that point, we shopped it with a script that I had been working on for probably two years at that point with the storyboards. I had a lot of my own money into that thing. Hundreds of thousands of dollars. It was a very difficult time."

According to MacBird's accounts of the script's progress, both she and Lisberger worked together on the script, but it was she who wrote it.

"I am the original writer of *Tron*," she says. "Steven disputes this. However it was upheld by a Writer's Guild arbitration. He had a lot of input into the eight or so drafts that I did, however they were in the way of reading what I wrote and making comments and suggestions. Development execs and producers everywhere do this. The writer is the one who sits there, facing the blank page, solving the problems, writing the dialogue, creating the 'moments'—and they get the writing credit. I've been both and I know the difference."

Lisberger's position was that MacBird and he found themselves going in totally different creative directions regarding the plot, characters, dialogue, and tone of the script.

"She was hired as an experienced film executive and co-producer," says Lisberger. "I thought we needed that because we were the little new studio from out of town. I think she could have made a real contribution in that area, but she veered off sharply into her own take on things. It got political in a studio that had no politics up to that point. When she gambled that she could impress the creative team, and me, with her approach, in spite of the fact that we didn't expect that from her, she revealed that her taste and mine regarding *Tron* were polar opposites. She took her shot and it didn't work. It was wall-to-wall silly, sitcomy. I had been struggling to make this deep and give it meaning on many levels."

One of MacBird's concepts for the film involved a young pizza delivery guy, named Flynn, who messes with computers in an AI (artificial intelligence) lab and falls inside the computer's world. The film would have a more comedic tone, yet contain much of the film's action elements that are seen today. Robin Williams, then hot from the television show, *Mork & Mindy*, was MacBird's choice in the lead role of Flynn. Lisberger wanted an unknown actor.

In a draft written by MacBird, dated March 14, 1980, the film opens with a Light Cycle duel which eventually appears in the final film. Warriors in the "Electronic World" are shot through tubes to enter the "simulation areas for the games." The character of Tron is a key character in this world and is considerably more heroic in the script than he appears in the final film. The character of the Bit has quite a bit of dialogue and desires to become a "program." Sark is present in the script, but does not have much of a personality. The Master Control Program (also known as the MCP) and Dumont have fairly big roles in the script. Two advisors to the MCP, Frick and Frack, are used as comic relief. Gibbs runs the "AIC Corporation," a giant computer company.

The lead characters of Alan and Lora are very prominent in the "Real World" sections of the script. They work together as computer experts. She carries around a "Dynabook" notebook-type computer and is extremely smart. Alan is brilliantly smart, and he acts like Flynn does in the final film as a computer hacker.

Flynn eventually shows up as Lora's boyfriend later into the script. He is portrayed as an immature smart ass who so happens to be an excellent computer hacker. It takes almost an hour for Flynn to shoot into the "Electronic World" and it is Tron who eventually saves the day.

For a script written by a novice screenplay writer, it is structured with fast-paced storytelling. The opening sequences in the "Electronic World" are exciting and written well with good visuals. The characters of Alan and Lora are well-developed and likable. Unfortunately, Flynn is portrayed as if he is an obnoxious thirteen year-old boy. He nearly derails the story. The script meanders in different directions without a clear focus in what it is trying to say.

In a screenplay draft written by Lisberger, dated September 1980, he writes a more complex film with less of a comedic tone. Both his and MacBird's scripts open with the exciting Light Cycle battle. But Lisberger's script goes in a different direction. Flynn is given more structure and acts mostly mature. He is likable and a bit feisty. He and Lora are lovers, and there is no love triangle as it is seen in the final film. The Bit is more developed as a character and gains sympathy from the reader in his quest to help his "programs." In both scripts, Tron performs an incredible feat by jumping a canyon in the "Electronic World" with his Light Cycle.

Lisberger's script is infused with heart and an exhilarating chase sequence between Tron's Solar Sailer galleon and a destroyer across the "Electronic World" landscape. Interspersed in Lisberger's script are storyboards and drawings of the characters and world of *Tron*. Some of the most dynamic drawings are of Sark, who has a snake-like head, and the Bit, who is a spherical floating ball.

Lisberger's script is not perfect and does meander, as well. But it has a stronger structure and plot. It has several side characters who come into the screenplay and disappear without an impact on the plot. Neither Alan, Lora nor Flynn are dynamic characters the audience would gravitate toward. The Bit is actually the most sympathetic character in both versions of the script.

"Basically I came up with the story," claims MacBird. "Steven had the name *Tron* and a backlit, macho character which he had originally designed for a radio station ad in Boston. He wanted this character to be a 'video game warrior' and to have an adventure-animated flick built around this idea. In the business of movies, this is a notion, not a story idea."

The Writer's Guild of America read and arbitrated all the material including *Futurebowl* and came to a different conclusion than MacBird.

According to MacBird, she came up with "the entire skeletal storyline; the characters of Flynn, the Bit, the MCP, Alan (based on Alan Kay), and Laura, as well as Tron (not his visual concept, but his characteristics)."

"I almost wish what she believes was true," says Lisberger, "then I wouldn't have had to work my ass off on the script for all those years."

With rewrites, the script evolved into the basic story of hot shot computer programmer, Kevin Flynn, and his battle against the evil ENCOM Corporation. He would get beamed into the computer world to battle for his life. While there, he meets a video game warrior named Tron who is the alter ego to Flynn's friend, Alan. Together with a female video warrior named Yori, they fight on the Game Grid and ultimately battle Sark and the MCP.

In a long conversation with Lisberger, it became clear that his vision for the film as an electronic gladiatorial epic served as the backbone of the film. He also cited the subject of duality which plays a significant part in the film.

"I'm a person who believes in duality," he says. "If you look at every movie when a story says there is one world, and then there is another world. One of the reasons why *The Matrix* (1999) works so well is it doesn't say that in the beginning. It just says there's one world. We seem to have this enormous drive to create a doppelganger for this world, and that is *Tron*."

Lisberger also mentions the idea of a Master Program in the earliest concept of what would become *Tron* in the treatment of *Futurebowl*.

"I had seen *2001* and I loved HAL and I knew that I wanted a Master Program. He'd be the emperor that sends people to die on the games."

Yet MacBird claims she came up with the character of the MCP.

"To me, this was Steve's film, not Bonnie's film," says Rooney. "The quintessential piece of dialogue Bonnie brought to the film, and it epitomizes her and this shows my opinion, was the evil nemesis in the film, the MCP. There were characters called Frick and Frack. And they were very subservient, and they would say, 'Yes, your MC-penis.'"

# Chapter 4

# *RADICAL CHANGE*

*Star Wars* caught everyone by complete surprise.

Released on May 25, 1977, the space fantasy ignited the imagination of audiences around the country. Filled to the brim with dazzling visual effects, triumphant music, a rousing story, snappy dialogue, and memorable characters, George Lucas' film struck a nerve.

People who saw it could not wait to tell their friends. They told their friends the movie had a walking dog character named Chewbacca, a princess with wild hair, laser-gun battles, a scary villain named Darth Vader, and amazing special effects. Word of mouth spread quickly. Children could not wait to see the film for the first time or the tenth time. This was a must-see event for audiences of all ages.

Although the film borrowed liberally from old movie serials Lucas used to watch as a child, he managed to tap into the core of what made those serials exciting: the childlike need for adventure. He figured out a way, through numerous script rewrites, to take audiences to worlds they had never been to. At the same time, he created a core of characters who were fun, endearing, and relatable.

The film's visual effects were nothing like audiences had seen before. The only other film in recent memory to have stunning effects like *Star Wars* was Stanley Kubrick's *2001: A Space Odyssey*. As great as those effects were, they were stilted in being artistic and graceful. The effects in Lucas' space fantasy were fluid and fun. Starships raced across the screen, banked, and flew right at the camera. They fired laser beams and blew up. This was the stuff of every kid's dreams.

Lucas was surprised with the success of the film he created. Indirectly quoted, he was fond of saying he expected it would make around $16 million. This was approximately the amount Disney movies made. It was a comfortable take at the box office. But *Star Wars* shattered not only the average take on a Disney film, but the grosses on *The Godfather*, *The Exorcist*, and *Jaws* by a long shot. Studios around Hollywood scrambled to find their next box office hit. Suddenly everyone in the film industry, from the big studios to schlocky filmmakers, wanted to make the next *Star Wars*.

Lucas did not make the film to change the industry. But its groundbreaking use of visual effects, effect on box office grosses, and the use of Dolby Stereo brought the film industry into the modern age. Now nearly every big "event" film had to have the latest state-of-the-art visual effects, had to perform better than *Star Wars*, and had to have a loud Dolby Stereo soundtrack.

In June of 1977, Walt Disney Productions released two of its own highly anticipated films, *The Rescuers* and *Herbie Goes To Monte Carlo*. The animated *Rescuers* was considered by many to be the studio's return to former glory. This was the swan song for Disney animators Frank Thomas, Ollie Johnston, Milt Kahl, Wolfgang Reitherman, John Lounsbery, and Ken Anderson. Don Bluth also showed off his animation skills. It was a charming tale about mice who are called into rescue a little girl from the evil Madame Medusa. The film performed well at the box office. *Herbie Goes To Monte Carlo* also did respectable business.

Yet there was an underlying current streaming through Disney and the film business that the studio was living on borrowed time. The success of *Star Wars* was a clear shot across Disney's bow. It was felt by many that *Star Wars* should have been made by Disney. The studio's core audience of families and children was growing more mature. They wanted more spice in their film diet. Kids who were nine years old were more sophisticated at that age than their parents were. They could handle watching a movie that was loaded with violence and strong language. The "PG" rating, which was being slapped on many films during the 1970s, was generally accepted as a safe rating for children. Their eyes would not pop out at the sight of violence and their ears would not bleed from hearing bad words. A "G" rating was considered a death knell at the box office.

At this time, Disney released only "G" rated films. In looking at the studio's output during this era, every one of its films, with the possible exception of *Freaky Friday*, was carefully diluted to appeal to a broad family base. The films did not have much, if any violence, and words like "damn" or "hell" were not uttered.

The studio's older catalog of films was actually tinged with situations that would generally garner a "PG" rating today. In *Snow White and the Seven Dwarfs*, the Wicked Queen's transformation into an ugly hag gave children nightmares. In *Pinocchio*, Lampwick's transformation into a donkey is frightening. The fact that some characters in the film smoked would make the ratings board look twice today. In *Fantasia*, there were suggestions of "artistic" nudity. Yet these films continually received "G" ratings during their releases in the 1970s. The closest the studio got to a "PG" rating was in 1975. They were about to rerelease Walt Disney's version of *Treasure Island* (1950) in theaters. But it was violent enough to garner a "PG" rating. Disney vigorously fought the board and lost. The studio relented and cut the film's violence to get a "G" rating.

For several years, Walt Disney Productions was the leader in family entertainment. Very few studios could compete in this area. By the time *Star Wars* entered the public's imagination, Disney films were considered blasé. The Disney board forgot Walt's ability to entertain almost any audience member, regardless of age.

There was a sense of denial that the world outside of Disney had changed. Children under the age of eighteen were now listening to KISS, Led Zeppelin, The Eagles, Fleetwood Mac and David Bowie. By the time those children grew into teenagers, they went to concerts, bought band T-shirts, and smoked pot. They went to movies that featured hard core profanity, violence and maybe even nudity. They cursed. They made out. They were teenagers who probably influenced their younger siblings to get into the world debauchery.

These were the same teenagers who were forking over millions of dollars to see *Star Wars*, again and again. The other major studios recognized that the under-eighteen market was hugely profitable. Disney did not see the value and potential. The films it approved for production were steeped in what the board thought Walt might like, not what the public wanted to see. Most of the members of the Disney board were in their 50s. They were clueless about what kids wanted. As a result, its market share suffered badly. By 1978, according to author Leonard Maltin's book, *The Disney Films*, its market share in the United States and Canada fell from six percent in 1977 to four percent in 1979.

Disney could not play with the bigger studios. Though its theme parks continued to draw huge crowds and earned stunning revenues, the company was extremely weak on the film side. Without a substantial hit, the studio was in danger. Roy E. Disney took issue with the current management and its inability to produce hits. His main concern was that his uncle's film studio unit was nearly stagnant and in danger of being shut down. That would be a serious blow to his uncle and father's legacy. The studio needed new blood and searched frantically for it.

## TOM WILHITE

Tom Wilhite was someone who would have appealed to Walt's sensibilities. Walt, though he did not give praise to his employees, admired people with a creative mind and hard work ethic. Born in Keswick, Iowa in 1952, Wilhite got his foot in the door by the age of nineteen as comedian Groucho Marx's agent. He was soon working for one of the biggest public relation firms in Hollywood, Rogers & Cowan. After successfully placing Fleetwood RV products in Walt Disney World's camping grounds, he joined Disney in 1977 to head their television publicity department. By the age of twenty-four, he was the head of both television and feature film publicity for Walt Disney Productions.

"I'd learned a lot in the time I worked for Rogers & Cowan," recalls Wilhite. "In any case, like many young people of my generation who grew up watching Walt Disney himself on TV, I was enamored of the whole idea and vision of Disney. It was exciting to go to work there. My immediate reaction was very favorable. I liked the people."

Wilhite was a rarity at the Disney—he was young. He quickly embedded himself into the culture of Disney. He familiarized himself with the history and lore of the studio, while maintaining his drive to freshen up the place with new ideas. One of his first assignments was to publicize a new and ambitious film the studio was producing, *The Black Hole*. The film was going to feature cutting edge visual effects on par with *Star Wars* and it was to feature art direction and visual effects supervised by Disney's legendary matte painter, Peter Ellenshaw.

## DISNEY'S VISUAL EFFECTS DEPARTMENT

Over the years, numerous books about Disney have focused on the studio's animation department, and rightly so. There was no peer for the studio's commitment to high-quality animation. What is not known is that the studio had one of the best visual effects departments in the film business. Disney was one of the few studios that kept its visual effects department operating for years after other studios closed theirs down. Most of the films made at the Disney studio, with few exceptions, had visual effects. Composite shots, mechanical effects, matte paintings or a combination of all of those contributed to the success of many of the studio's films.

By the late 1960s, most of the major studios began consolidating, tearing down soundstages and selling their valuable back lots for real estate. Films were no longer just shot in Hollywood. With quieter, lighter weight cameras, and faster film stocks, shooting a movie took film crews to distant locales worldwide. Disney stayed independent, still shooting its features on the studio back lot, while still maintaining its animation and visual effects departments.

When it came to the art of filmmaking, visual effects were treated by the public and media as secondary citizens. Directors seemed to get credit for their vision. Actors got credit for making films come alive. But the technicians, the people who often times could save a movie from disaster, were treated with indifference.

When it came to fantasy and science fiction films, they were relegated to "B" movie status. Certainly, films such as *Forbidden Planet* (1956) challenged the notion that science fiction was only made for children and devoted fans. (It is worth noting that the film featured some Disney animation for the monster "Id.") Science fiction and fantasy films usually made money and gained a following by devoted fans, but the visual effects did not get much respect. That is until Stanley Kubrick turned that perception around with *2001: A Space Odyssey*.

With a huge budget and talented crew that included Tom Howard, Wally Veevers, Douglas Trumbull, Con Pederson and James Dickson, Kubrick set out to blow any misconceptions about science fiction and visual effects out of the water. Though the film confused some audience members and impressed others with its mysterious story, it was a solid hit for MGM. It was the swan song for the storied studio, and would be Kubrick's last epic film before he delved into more small scale films like *A Clockwork Orange* (1972). The story kept audiences talking for years, but it was the visual effects that set the bar at an almost unreasonable height.

Most studios were trying to make rebel films to capitalize on *Easy Rider* (1969). *Bonnie and Clyde* (1967), *Rosemary's Baby* (1968), and *Midnight Cowboy* (1969) shifted the way Hollywood made movies. Movies were to become more contemporary, edgy, and controversial. Audiences flocked to theaters as a result. Disney still specialized in making family fantasy.

Disney's answer to these adult movies was *Bedknobs and Broomsticks* (1971), a rather lifeless tale starring the wonderful Angela Landsbury. It had the makings of a Disney hit. There were songs by the Sherman Brothers who scored *Mary Poppins* and wrote many of Disney's theme park songs including *It's a Small World*. It took place in Britain and even actor David Tomlinson was cast. He played Mr. Banks in *Mary Poppins*. Unfortunately, the film missed the mark with forgettable songs and a slow-moving story. The intention was good, but not good enough. The film did moderate business since there were not a lot family films in the marketplace. It earned Oscar nominations for Art Direction, Costume Design, Music Scoring and won for Special Visual Effects.

In all the years that Disney's visual effects unit existed prior to *2001: A Space Odyssey* and *Star Wars*, the crew hardly received attention except for an occasional Academy Award nomination or win. Here was a group who brought the Nautilus to life in *20,000 Leagues Under the Sea* (1954), and made Fred McMurray fly an old jalopy powered by Flubber in *The Absent Minded Professor*. The Disney visual effects artists, despite their numerous Oscar nominations and wins and their impressive resume, quietly did their work at the studio.

The public and the media perception of visual effects films changed with Kubrick's *2001: A Space Odyssey*. But it was George Lucas and his company, Industrial Light + Magic, that turned visual effects and the people who made them into rock stars. Suddenly, visual effects guys such as John Dykstra, Dennis Muren, and Richard Edlund were famous.

It was the young turks of the *Star Wars* generation who would get the press and become heroes to a generation of film geeks. That is until *The Black Hole* invaded the Disney studio lot, and one of the studio's last remaining icons would finally get his moment in the spotlight. His work on the film would bridge a gap between the old way of doing visual effects, and the new way of doing them. It signaled the beginning of major changes at the studio.

## THE DISNEY STUDIO

The Walt Disney studio was a pioneer in visual effects long before *2001: A Space Odyssey* and *Star Wars* hit movie screens. Walt's own involvement with visual effects began early in his career with the *Alice Comedies*. He employed live action and animation techniques to place an actor inside a cartoon world. Rival animator, Max Fleischer (*Popeye*) used a similar concept in the *Out of the Inkwell* series by placing an animated character into live-action scenes with actors. Disney simply reversed the idea and Iwerks pulled this visual effect off with near perfection.

Disney continued on with the actor-in-animation concept for years, carefully refining it into an art form. There were live action sequences done in many of the studios feature films including *Saludos Amigos* (1943), *The Three Caballeros* (1945), and *Make Mine Music*. His animators also used the technique in *Song of the South* where James Baskett interacted with animated animals. On *Walt Disney's Wonderful World of Color* television series, Donald Duck (Clarence Nash) made occasional appearances with Walt.

Walt had the foresight to expand his studio beyond animated features. After he bought property in Burbank, he wanted to make sure soundstages were built for live-action feature film production. The first one was built in 1940. World War II sidelined any live-action feature film plans as the U.S government took over the studio and its soundstages for war purposes.

A few years after the war, Disney ramped up production on not only live-action features, but on building Disneyland. The stages were used for building some of the theme park's future attractions, which would be shipped down to Anaheim. The paddle wheeler, *Mark Twain*, was entirely built from scratch in Burbank then trucked down to Anaheim.

Part of Disney's studio magic lies within the vast spaces of its soundstages. This is where Kirk Douglas fought the giant squid in *20,000 Leagues Under the Sea*. It is where Annette Funicello and the Mouseketeers of *The Mickey Mouse Club* sang and danced. It is the location of Walt's famed office set where he introduced many episodes on his television program. It is also where *Mary Poppins* floated down from the clouds to Cherry Tree Lane. For several decades, the studio's shops were abuzz with activity in building everything from the Nautilus, to the elaborate sets used in *The Black Hole*. Even writer/actor Jack Webb borrowed the soundstages to shoot some episodes of *Dragnet* (1951-1959).

When Walt became fully committed to both animation and live-action films, he decided to make a huge splash. *20,000 Leagues Under the Sea* was Walt's signal to the rest of the film industry he that was serious about making live-action movies. And what a glorious debut it was.

Starring Kirk Douglas, James Mason, Paul Lukas, and Peter Lorre, *20,000 Leagues Under the Sea* was a triumph in filmmaking. It was one of those rare adventure films that featured excellent acting, a superb storyline that was faithful to the original Jules Verne book, mature and assured direction by Richard Fleischer, and some of the most brilliant visual effects committed to film.

It was on this film that Peter Ellenshaw showcased his talent of matte painting and visual effects prowess. His work became a signature for nearly every Disney live-action production for decades.

## PETER ELLENSHAW

It is important to shine a spotlight on Ellenshaw's work for Disney. An Englishman with a witty sense of humor, he was a consummate artist who worked mainly in matte painting, yet had a great talent for other visual effects. He was considered to be one of Walt's closest friends, as well as one his most trusted artists, having worked on numerous visual effects in the studio's live-action productions. By 1979, Ellenshaw had been long retired, citing that the business was not the same after Walt died. *The Black Hole* was such a massive production that his expertise and guidance were needed. He came out of retirement to be the production designer and visual effect supervisor on the film.

Ellenshaw's step father, Percy Day, was one of the first artists to work in matte painting. This art form was a way of making scenes in a film seem larger than they really were, or to add elements to a scene that did not exist on location or on a set. The simplest method in matte painting involved blocking out a section of a large piece of glass where live-action would take place.

For example, a matte painter like Day or Ellenshaw painted an ornate ceiling to extend a Victorian ballroom, or paint ships to create a bustling harbor. Then by combining photographic painting with filmed live-action, these scenes appeared realistic. These elements provided for a seamless backdrop for a foggy London park at night (*Mary Poppins*), or for a dynamic sense of scale of a dormant volcano (*20,000 Leagues Under the Sea*). The effect was simple in concept, but required an artist's eye for detail, the ability to match or augment lighting in a particular scene, a sense of scale, composition, and lighting. Both Day and Ellenshaw were the masters of this craft.

When Walt decided to use untapped funds to shoot in Britain, he called upon Ellenshaw to paint mattes for his version of Robert Lewis Stevenson's *Treasure Island*. The entire production was shot in England, but Ellenshaw's matte paintings made it seem like some scenes were shot in the Caribbean. His matte paintings were exquisite. One of the shots involved one real ship in a harbor (the budget would not allow for more ships) and Ellenshaw painted in the rest. Walt was pleased with the work Ellenshaw had done. Walt told him if he was ever in California, he would have work for him.

Ellenshaw packed up his belongings and with his wife, Bobbie, and young son, Harrison, sailed to America. After taking a train cross country, Ellenshaw showed up at the Disney Studio and asked for Walt. The studio guard let him in. He walked into Walt's office, surprising him.

"What are you doing here?"

"You said when I came out to California, you'd have work for me." Ellenshaw beamed.

Walt raised his eyebrow. "Peter, I don't have work for you, but we'll find you something."

Walt called down to the soundstage where they were shooting some miniatures for *20,000 Leagues Under the Sea*. The crew was having a difficult time getting a shot to look real. Ellenshaw suddenly found himself in the middle of a group of seasoned movie veterans without much patience to listen to the newly arrived Englishman.

But Ellenshaw took some of the production's visual effects problems, such as lighting and staging, and re-worked them into a stunning palette. He had a gift for lighting, a crucial talent to have as a matte painter. In creating a new lighting scheme, he gave the film believability and also helped to make the miniature effects of the Nautilus more plausible and elegant.

One of Ellenshaw's signature shots was of Vulcania, an island housing Nemo's secret lab. Credit is due to the visual effects artists who worked with Ellenshaw. The film was awarded an Academy Award for Best Special Effects, but in those days, the Oscar went to the studio, not to the individuals responsible for the effects.

In 1959, the studio embarked on an ambitious tale with leprechauns and magic in *Darby O'Gill and the Little People*. Ellenshaw ingeniously employed the concept of split-scale set to create the illusion of little leprechauns mingling with real humans.

Sometimes called forced perspective, split-scale makes the camera and the audience see both the leprechaun and human in the same shot. They appear to be talking to each other in real space and real time. The key, especially in this film, was how well they interacted. Actor Albert Sharpe (Darby O'Gill) and Jimmy O'Dea (King Brian) were filmed standing several feet from each other on the soundstage. The camera sees them in close proximity to each other. Once the film is projected on a screen, the audience thinks O'Gill is actually talking with a real leprechaun. To this day, many people and some visual effects veterans cannot figure out how this was done!

"Remarkable, actually. I don't know how the hell we did it," teases Ellenshaw.

Ellenshaw continued to work his magic on a number of Disney projects through the 1950s. He had done the famous large-scale painting of Disneyland, which Walt featured on his first *Disneyland* show to sell the public on his bold project. He directed one of the park's first major filmed attractions, *Circarama,* and painted mattes for a number of Disney's features and television shows, including the *Davy Crockett* shows.

It was *Mary Poppins* that cemented Ellenshaw's reputation as a master of the matte. The film, directed by Robert Stevenson and produced by Bill Walsh, was a landmark for every technique Walt Disney Productions had used since the days of the *Alice Comedies*. The film was strong in so many ways. Its acting (barring a few sniggles about Dick Van Dyke's Cockney accent), story, production design, music and visual effects were superb.

Ellenshaw created a fantasy London town that was rich with texture and life from the strokes of his painting brush. The opening shot of Julie Andrews sitting on a cloud above London is the perfect introduction to this magical nanny. Ellenshaw's other key shots include the sun setting on London with twinkling lights down in the city and a simple, yet wonderful matte shot with Mr. Banks (David Tomlinson) walking through a foggy London park at night. For his work, Ellenshaw received an Oscar.

He retired from the Disney Studios shortly after Walt Disney's death in 1966, and continued his fine art career until his death in 2007 at the age of 93.

## HARRISON ELLENSHAW

Though not born into the Disney family, Harrison could easily have been. He arrived with his parents in California when he was nine years old, and he spent a lot of time running around the Disney studio lot while his father worked. There were times he was on the set as Kirk Douglas or James Mason walked on by. To keep busy and out of trouble, Peter gave his son a paint brush and he would paint a small corner of a matte for *20,000 Leagues Under the Sea*. Just as children of the 1950s saw Walt Disney as their uncle, Harrison was fortunate enough to have Walt in his real life. He is proud to say that he was the first kid to ride the train at Disneyland with Walt personally conducting.

Harrison clearly had talent to paint and possibly enter the visual effects field, but did not want to necessarily follow in his father's footsteps. He went to college and got his degree in psychology, then joined the Navy during the Vietnam War. His service as an officer gave him plenty of training and experience in later dealing with Hollywood personalities.

After the Navy in 1970, Peter convinced his son that there was work on the Disney studio lot and Harrison might be a good fit. It was on *Island at the Top of the World* (1974) that Harrison got his first taste of filmmaking glamour. He assisted matte department head, Alan Maley, in washing his paint brushes.

But the experience of working under Maley's supervision helped Ellenshaw understand the rigors and complications of creating visual effects. As he worked on numerous Disney features during the early 1970s, his reputation for mastering the art of the matte painting and being able to solve visual effects problems with finesse, earned him the nickname of "The Crown Prince."

"I was called the Crown Prince basically because of my father's legacy," says Harrison. "I'm sure in many people's eyes I was considered the idiot son that got a job there because my father was so well respected."

Whether or not the nickname was given to him out of respect or jealousy, Ellenshaw certainly knew his craft and did it well. But life around the Disney effects department was becoming repetitive and at times boring.

Though Harrison worked on projects outside of Disney, he had a good gig at the studio. It was steady work and he eventually became the head of the matte department. Much of the visual effects department, in general, was getting on in years. Harrison was the young guy, constantly improving his own matte painting while honing his skills on practical visual effects. If anyone was an heir apparent to the Disney way of making magic, he was it. Yet the studio continued with its safe slate of silly-yet-cute Disney productions.

"I yearned to do effects for outside films," says Harrison. "In 1975, I got my first chance to work on a non-Disney film, *The Man Who Fell to Earth*, directed by Nicolas Roeg and starring David Bowie. This was followed by an incredible bit of luck as I was asked to do some matte paintings for a highly speculative science-fiction film called *Star Wars*."

Ellenshaw's mattes in the original 1977 version of the film were stunning. His signature matte was the Death Star's tractor beam chamber placing Obi-Wan Ben Kenobi (Alec Guiness) perilously miles above the Death Star's core. His other signature matte is of the space port of Mos Eisley and the Yavin Rebel chamber in the film's climatic scene.

"I was asked to do the matte paintings for *Star Wars*," recalls Ellenshaw. "ILM was a new facility struggling to build equipment AND do shots for *Star Wars*. I would leave Disney at 6 p.m. at night after working on *Pete's Dragon* and drive over to Van Nuys and work on paintings for *Star Wars*. They had built a matte stand on the second floor of a warehouse. But it was a very primitive bi-pack camera that had some limitations. I was paid $500.00 for each matte shot. I had to share the money with my cameraman (only fair). After we struggled to get six or seven paintings composited at ILM, I finally gave in and did the remaining six or seven at Disney. So Disney then got the $500.00 per shot. That might seem unfair, but after all I was using their equipment, which was much better. The key is that Disney (technically) was NOT contracted to do the matte paintings for *Star Wars*—I was."

*Star Wars* firmly established Harrison as one of the best matte painters in the business. It gave him a taste of the possibilities of state-of-the-art visual effects. Along with his young colleagues at the Disney studio, he wanted to work on something spectacular and groundbreaking.

# Chapter 5

# *WHAT WOULD WALT HAVE DONE?*

There were high hopes for Walt Disney Productions by 1979. By the looks of it, the year was already off to a promising start. *Big Thunder Mountain Railroad*, a multi-million dollar thrill ride, was opened at Disneyland. Originally designed by Imagineer Tony Baxter, the attraction replaced one of the park's earliest rides, *Nature's Wonderland*. The new thrill ride was an instant success, putting guests on a wild mine train ride through Disney's version of the wilderness. The company's WED Imagineering division was hitting home runs during this time, keeping the company afloat with the additions of "weenies" such as *Space Mountain*. Walt used that term for attractions that caught visitors' eyes, drawing them to an attraction like bees to honey.

The company's management team under Walker was intent on completing Walt's final project, EPCOT. Before his death in 1966, Walt had ambitious plans to build a Utopian city of the future in Orlando, Florida. He had a number of his employees secretly buy up thousands of swampland acreage in the middle of the state. His dream was to build a vacation kingdom that dwarfed the Disneyland Anaheim property.

The centerpiece of Disney World was EPCOT. It was every bit an idealized vision of a futuristic city. Many cities around the United States were in decline, with urban decay and crime. Disney's vision of Utopia abolished the woes of traffic, crime and grime infecting many major cities of the 1960s. Major corporations would be encouraged to fund some of the city's major office buildings and research laboratories. Disney had years of experience in having major companies sponsor many of his Disneyland attractions. It was a win-win for both parties.

In the 1970s, by the time EPCOT received the green light for construction, and due to political pressure and legal concerns, it turned into a permanent world's fair rather than a real working city. An adult version of Disneyland's Tomorrowland, if you will. Because of the immensity of the project, much of the company's talent and resources were poured into the new theme park. It was scheduled to open in the fall of 1982 and would be renamed EPCOT Center. The company seemed to be firing on all cylinders.

But there was a huge shake up at the studio in 1979. Animator Don Bluth was considered by some people at the studio to be Disney's new leader in the Animation Department. After animating a number of films during the 1970s, Bluth led a group of young animators out of Disney. He felt, as many did, that the magic of Disney's older animated films was gone.

"We felt like we were animating the same picture over and over again with just the faces changed a little," said Bluth, according to Leonard Maltin's *The Disney Films*.

Bluth's departure was a huge publicity mess for the studio. Just two years after Roy E. Disney's resignation from the board, it seemed that Walt Disney Productions was losing momentum.

## THE BLACK HOLE

Though children during the 1970s mostly enjoyed films with the Disney name on them, the films themselves felt as though they had been done before. After Walt's triumph with *Mary Poppins* in 1964, much of the studio's product after his death was fairly predictable. Almost every movie had the same title sequence, same forgettable music and songs, same cast and crew. One could watch a Disney film from 1967 or 1977 and get the same vibe. The vibe was not necessarily bad. It was just dull.

There were finally rumblings that the studio was willing to try a new course of action. The biggest film on Disney's radar was a science fiction adventure years in the making. *Space Station-One* was originally going to be produced by studio stalwart, Winston Hibler. He was perhaps best known for his folksy voiceovers on the studio's *True-Life Adventures* series.

The idea for *Space Station-One* (also called *Space Probe-One*) was ambitious in scope. The plot involved the crew of the spaceship Palomino coming across a huge, seemingly derelict ship, the U.S.S. Cygnus. The film was planned as early as 1974, but production problems put it on hold. That is until *Star Wars* came out a few years later and changed the Hollywood movie business forever. Disney figured there was no better time than the present to produce its science fiction epic. By July 1977, writer Jeb Rosebrook had written what would essentially become the basis for the film's story structure. He introduced the plot device of a giant black hole.

The production was immediately put on the front burner and renamed *The Black Hole*. It was more gutsy than any other Disney film in years, and would feature mind-blowing visual effects. Peter and Harrison teamed up for the first time. Peter did the exquisite production design and supervised the miniature effects, while Harrison supervised the matte paintings.

Rumors of the film flew around science fiction circles. Could it be that Disney was finally making a film that everybody would want to see? The film had high anticipation by audiences, especially those who had experienced *Star Wars, Superman: The Movie* (1978) and *Alien* (1979). Science fiction and fantasy had finally gained respect by both audiences and critics. Anticipation was high waiting to see the next big sci-fi blockbuster. *The Black Hole* was an expensive gamble for Disney. The budget was $20 million, which in the late 1970s was considerable. It was one of the most expensive movies of 1979.

Tom Wilhite was still cutting his teeth at Disney when he was put in charge to find a way to market *The Black Hole*. The film really did not have big-name stars, nor did it have a young cast.

Audiences were used to the faces of Harrison Ford or Christopher Reeve, not Ernest Borgnine or Anthony Perkins. The cast of *The Black Hole* featured Robert Forster, Maximilian Schell, Yvette Mimieux, Roddy McDowell, Slim Pickens and Joseph Bottoms. A fine cast, but not enough to draw in people to the theater.

Wilhite saw to it that the real stars of the film were the visual effects and Peter Ellenshaw. Ellenshaw, after all, was a solid link to the Disney fantasy legacy.

"The thing I found very refreshing about Tom Wilhite was that he brought a new perspective of how to market this film," says Harrison Ellenshaw. "He had enough insight to understand that *The Black Hole* was not a very good story. Rather than market it as a science fiction film, he decided to market the visual effects Academy Award winners, of which there were four, working on the film."

Art Cruickshank, miniatures cameraman, had won his Oscar for *Fantastic Voyage* (1966) at 20th Century Fox. Eustace Lycett, composite optical photography, had won his Oscars for *Bedknobs and Broomsticks* and *Mary Poppins*. Danny Lee, mechanical effects supervisor, won his Oscar for *Bedknobs and Broomsticks*.

Released on December 21, the film was one of the big movies of the Christmas season and it opened to good box office. It just did not do great box office like *Star Trek: The Motion Picture*. That film had opened a few weeks earlier to a large audience made up of fans of the original television series. It was one of the top-grossing films the year, and was commercially successful enough to launch a sequel in 1982.

According to Box Office Mojo, *The Black Hole* pulled in almost $36 million and managed to stay in theaters for months. It was later rereleased in theaters with *Sleeping Beauty* on a double-feature billing, and became a big seller on videocassette in the early 1980s. The problem was that *The Black Hole* was not cool enough for science fiction junkies, it was too juvenile for adults, and it was too scary for smaller children. It had the dated elements of a Disney film, especially in the robot designs, which appeared staid and clumsy.

Producer Ron Miller, who would later head Disney, recalls, "Intentionally done that way, believe me. I think it could've been better, but there we go again."

Though it was loosely based on the studio's own *20,000 Leagues Under the Sea*, it jettisoned some of that film's strengths like a strong story and strong characters. *The Black Hole* was not a bad film, yet its flaws undermined what could have been a big hit for the studio.

The film's main spaceship, the U.S.S. Cygnus, was unlike anything seen before in a science fiction tale. The Victorian influence gave the ship dimension and regality. The star fields, hand punched into a large velvet canvas, were not made of just white stars and a black background. Instead, they were colorful and dimensional. Other scenes featured seamless matte paintings that made the interior of the Cygnus appear awe inspiring. The only real flaw in the effects were the live-action effects showing the robots of V.I.N.cent (voiced by Roddy McDowell) and Maximillian flying around with wires holding them up. Today those wires would be digitally removed.

There were grumblings that Disney still did not "get it." The visual effects, though impressive as any in *Star Wars* or *Star Trek: The Motion Picture*, had a reputation for being clunky in how they were made. One of the aspects of Wilhite's campaign was his focus on Disney's innovative, yet humongous, Automated Camera Effects System (A.C.E.S.). This system, similar to the Dykstraflex computer motion controlled camera system used on *Star Wars*, yielded impressive camera moves in, under, above and around the U.S.S. Cygnus. But the system was gigantic and not seen as cool and lightweight as John Dykstra's rig.

Motion control was designed to perfectly maneuver a camera around a model of a spaceship, for instance. It created the illusion that a spaceship is flying though space, or past the camera. In reality, the ship is stationary and the camera is doing all the movement.

"When they came up with *Black Hole*, Disney didn't have motion control," recalls *Tron* animation compositing cameraman, Glenn Campbell. "They went out to every studio in town on a fact finding mission. They took pictures and measurements of everything we did. I said get motion control. They went back and they built A.C.E.S. It was the epitome of everything motion control should not have been. Everybody else had fast flexible systems that could move around and do blur. They took great pride in the fact that ACES was strong enough to jack up a car."

The visual effects and cinematography were impressive enough to warrant the production two Academy Award nominations. Frank Phillips, ASC was nominated for his cinematography. Peter Ellenshaw, Art Cruickshank, Eustace Lycett, Danny Lee, Harrison Ellenshaw, Joe Hale were nominated for their visual effects work. The film did not win any Oscars, and amazingly, John Barry's eerie score was not nominated for Original Score.

*The Black Hole* had been a modest success, and it symbolized a major change for the studio, though no one knew it then.

What *The Black Hole* did for Disney was threefold:

First, it established that the studio, though reluctantly, was willing to branch away from its traditional family fare. It was the first studio produced film to receive a "PG" rating. Earlier in 1979, Buena Vista Distribution picked up an independent film called *Take Down* for distribution. That film was rated "PG."

Second, it represented a changing of the guard. Peter Ellenshaw came out of retirement to not only create exquisite production design, but also work with his son Harrison on the film's spectacular effects. Peter passed the visual effects baton to Harrison.

Third, the film used both computerized and analog visual effects. The opening title sequence and some of the video displays on the spaceship Palomino used computer vector graphics by John Hughes (no relation to the late writer/director of numerous 1980s teen movies). The work was done on an Evans & Sutherland Picture System 2 computer. Hughes would eventually co-found the visual effects and animation studio, Rhythm and Hues.

## RON MILLER

Ron Miller, on the surface, was the ideal person to lead Disney from its complacent spot in the film industry to prominence. Tall with a handsome all-American look, his image was confident and reassuring. Disney was a reflection of clean-cut looks and bright smiles, and Miller fit right in. He was polite and seen as a nice guy who was very likable and used words like "gosh."

In the 1950s, he married Diane Disney, one of Walt's two daughters. Walt and his wife Lillian had adopted a second and younger daughter, Sharon. Walt himself was fond of Miller, seeing him as the son he never had, and someone who could possibly lead his company after he was gone. Miller was an offensive end for the Los Angeles Rams football team. During one game, he was knocked unconscious. Walt convinced Miller that working at the Disney studio was a much safer line of work. After one season of professional football, Miller joined Disney. He worked on many of the studio's television shows as an associate producer. Later, after Walt's death, Miller took the mantle of producer on most of the studio's feature films.

When Disneyland was being built on a former orange grove in the sleepy farm town of Anaheim, Miller drove blueprints from Burbank to Anaheim daily. By the 1970s, he worked in the executive offices at Disney. A rift had been developing for years between Roy E. Disney and how Miller and Card Walker handled the company. Roy held a significant amount of stock in Disney and eventually left the Disney studio in 1977, but he remained a shareholder. Miller stayed and worked for Walker.

Beginning in 1960, Miller produced a number of films. His first official producing credit came on *The Beatniks* (1960), a low budget independent film written and directed by none other than actor Paul Frees. Disney fans know Frees as the voice of the Doom Buggy narrator on *The Haunted Mansion* attraction.

Miller continued to co-produce and produce many of Disney's films through the 1980s. Most of the films he produced carried his own trademark of making them Disney friendly. The films tried to stay on the safe route, never wavering from the supposed philosophy of Walt.

"Calling up the image and philosophy of Walt was commonplace: 'Walt would have done such and such,'" says Wilhite. "I'm sure it happens everywhere that has an imposing founder who's suddenly gone. They no doubt did it with Gandhi; I'm sure they'll do it with Bill Gates. I had a friend who worked in another department who found that she could get more things accomplished if she started her memos with a quote from Walt: 'As Walt once said…' After a while she just started making up the quotes to suit her needs."

Having been close to Walt for many years, Miller realized that the Walt Disney brand name meant family entertainment. Disney films were seen as mostly wholesome. Yet many of Disney's films did take on touchy subject matters. *The Parent Trap* (1961) used divorce, then a fairly taboo subject, as part of its plot. *Old Yeller* (1957) tackled the idea of growing up into adulthood. Some of Disney's films were also scary and challenging to young children. Who can forget when Bambi's mother was shot?

"If *Bambi* had been released in the 1970s, it would've never gotten a 'G' rating," says Harrison Ellenshaw. "Bambi's mother getting shot is something that still impacts the psyche of Baby Boomers everywhere, and has caused them to spend thousands in therapy."

Walt knew how get an audience reaction, and those reactions were forever planted in people's minds for years. He wished he could shed his image as a maker of family films, though. He once confided in Miller that he wanted to make more adult-themed films.

"My wife and I and Walt were looking at *To Kill a Mockingbird* out in his screening room," recalls Miller. "When it was all over, Walt looked at us and said, 'God, I wish I could make a film like that.' And obviously he couldn't. He felt that would go beyond what Disney would be associated with and make and produce. He felt frustration, too."

Miller was soon in charge of the studio's production slate and could finally decide what kinds of films to release. Miller did not live in a box. He saw that the industry had changed. Younger audiences accepted more violence and profanity in movies. They liked high concept movies that took them to places they had never been before. The other studios, even if they were hopping on the *Star Wars* bandwagon, recognized that young audiences were the key to getting butts in seats. They also recognized that young audiences and word-of-mouth could reach older film goers, as well. It was once said that *Star Wars* was the kind of movie Disney should have made. Walt undoubtedly would have approved.

The myth about Disney at this time says the studio was only good for theme parks and the occasional re-release of its classics. But that does not paint an accurate picture of it. The company was big and had numerous corporate divisions.

"We tend to think of the old Disney as just being a maker of family films and animation," says Ellenshaw. "But somehow, the idea of a large corporate entity having theme parks gets a little bit forgotten. They didn't just make movies. They marketed movies. There was a whole division of the company devoted to Imagineering. It was very busy expanding Walt Disney World. EPCOT was in development at that time. That was a huge and probably greater capital investment than the entertainment division."

The company also ran a successful record division and its merchandising division that was second to none.

By 1980, the studio was at a crossroads. *The Black Hole* was not the hit the studio had hoped for, and the upcoming releases of *Herbie Goes Bananas* and *The Last Flight of Noah's Ark* were not impressing many around the studio or within the film industry. It did have an ambitious horror film on the slate called *The Watcher in the Woods*. But the studio needed shaking up. Miller saw an opportunity in Wilhite and promoted him, giving him the title of Vice President in Charge of Development.

"I was looking for somebody who had a good story mind and who could recognize good properties at the time, and Tom did a good job," recalls Miller. "God, there was a number of films that he brought to our attention. *Tex* and of course, *Tron*."

Miller also stepped up in the Disney ranks, taking over as president and Chief Operating Officer of the company.

Promoting Wilhite was perhaps one of Miller's strongest decisions he made as president. It was a signal to the studio and the rest of the film industry that Disney was finally catching up with the times. Wilhite was young. He was hungry. He was smart, yet foolish enough to take chances on risky projects. His promotion would affect Disney for years to come.

# Chapter 6

# SETTING UP SHOP AT DISNEY

Lisberger was desperate to find a home for *Tron*. He and Kushner continued to bring in various studio executives to Venice Beach for pitch meetings. The executives were impressed with the artwork and storyboards.

"Many times these execs would reply 'What is this thing?' or 'This thing is really out there, but I like where you're going,'" recalls Lane. "So it was exciting to see that we were onto something, even though some of the studio people really didn't fully understand the vision, or the huge jump in visual technology that we were trying to make."

Nobody was signing a deal to make *Tron* a feature film reality. Through MacBird's contacts at Universal, the film was pitched there. But the studio passed. Hearing about an executive who was hungry for new projects over at Disney, Kushner picked up the phone.

"I first called Tom Wilhite to go to Disney, because that was our first choice," says Kushner. "We had actually gone to two other studios. They were both interested. We had the script and had done storyboards."

But Kushner said in an interview in the 1980s, "Disney was one of the last on our lists. The reason is that we felt they were the vanguard of traditional animation, that they would probably not be interested in computer simulation. Or if they were interested in computer simulation, they would probably want to develop something in-house."

Regardless, it was Disney that made the most sense for the *Tron* project. The concept involved heavy use of animation and visual effects. It was trippy and psychedelic. Many of Disney's past achievements involved trippy animation like the pink elephants in *Dumbo*. In some ways, with the combination of live action and animation, *Tron* fit in the tradition of Disney's own *Mary Poppins* or *Song of the South*. But it would break away from those films with something entirely new to feature filmmaking—computer animation.

"At this time the pressures were intense for Steven to keep his company alive, and to make the next deal," recalls MacBird. "I think the pressures got to him, and contributed to the souring of our relationship. Whereas one moment he loved my script and was ready to roll, the next moment he changed his mind and wanted rewrites. These lightning shifts of direction became quite puzzling. I'd done eight drafts by then. We began to disagree heartily about the direction of the script. The computer science ideas, which Steven once welcomed, were mostly cut. Alan withdrew from the project."

Lisberger was under tremendous pressure. The studio, with its small and talented staff, was in danger of shutting down. The *Animalympics* debacle was a huge blow. As owner, he had already spent hundreds of thousands of dollars on developing *Tron*. His livelihood, and the livelihood of his staff, depended on a project like *Tron* to be picked up by a major studio.

By the time Lisberger and Kushner took the script to Disney sometime in 1980, the script probably resembled what showed up on screen in 1982. Disney made a deal on Lisberger's script. But even that script would continue to change right up until the time the film went into production in 1981.

"Somehow one of my drafts was shown at Disney, then Donald negotiated a deal there with himself producing with Steven—and me nowhere in sight," says MacBird. "To this day I consider this dirty pool. Now, I had a contract to co-produce. It was legal and binding, and as such, had the ability to force my inclusion on the film. I went to one meeting at Disney with Tom Wilhite, Steven, Donald, and others, and Disney was like 'who are you?' I explained to them who I was, but Donald (I guess) had laid tracks before me and they weren't buying it."

By this point, Lisberger and Kushner felt good about the script they had, and so did Disney. Lisberger and MacBird had split up creatively months before. They did not want to go back to earlier drafts and neither did Disney.

According to the U.S. Copyright Office, there is a record of the *Tron* screenplay credited to Steven Lisberger and Bonnie MacBird. The screenplay had the additional title of *Futurebowl* with the words of "underlying original concept & story. By Steven Lisberger." The date of November 22, 1980 is listed as the date of execution, which most likely means the date when the script ownership was transferred to Walt Disney Productions. In the notes section, it states: "Agreement re screenplay, story & related materials. Tron & 1 other title." The credit for screenplay and story changed again during negotiations. MacBird ultimately received a "Story by" credit shared with Lisberger. He received sole screenplay credit.

During a meeting between MacBird, Lisberger and Kushner, she accepted a buyout. They offered her an associate producer credit, but she refused it.

"I took a 'buy out' and used that money to produce a musical I wrote and directed," says MacBird. "It was a success, garnering good reviews and delighted audiences. I subsequently wrote spec screenplays for some time, and every one of them was optioned or sold. I have not spoken to Steven or Donald since that meeting."

Lane also felt slighted by the sale of *Tron* to Disney.

"I had worked on *Tron* for a long time and was all set to jump to Disney when Donald took me aside," recalls Lane. "He said that the Lisberger Studio couldn't pay the balance of my salary that they owed me, nor the compensation of the bonus for being the *Tron* production designer that they were supposed to pay whenever they sold the project."

Lane explains that he got his lawyer involved to settle the pay dispute. He was eventually paid in part for his work, but he lost the production design credit as a result of Kushner's negotiations with his lawyers. Since *Tron* would be made by union members from all branches of the film industry, the production designer credit had to go to an Art Director's Guild member.

"I told Steve I was leaving because of their tactics," says Lane. "I passed on the name of Syd Mead to Steve. He had never heard of the guy before. I told Steve to go and contact him. They did and were knocked out by his designs too and hired him as the production designer of *Tron*. And what a job this guy did!"

Whatever was going on regarding the credits and contracts probably did not concern Wilhite. What concerned him was getting Disney a moneymaking film on the lot, and fast.

"At the time, *Tron* seemed like a perfect bridge between the Disney legacy and the present," says Wilhite. "It was technologically innovative and adventurous. It introduced an imaginative and wholly new mythology and adventure. What I attempted to do at that particular time was look for projects that embodied what I believed was consistent with the Disney image and name, and then hopefully build upon and perhaps expand on that foundation."

Wilhite loved the idea of taking what was essentially *The Wizard of Oz* mashed up into a modern fairy tale. There was huge potential for a movie that imprisoned the hero Flynn inside a computer in a world he created. Video games were becoming even more popular in arcades and at home with Atari dominating both markets. Kids now expected their summer movies to have great adventures, hot girls, and mind-blowing visual effects. *Tron* had it all and Disney would be cutting edge once again.

## FROM LISBERGER STUDIOS TO DISNEY STUDIOS

There was a buzz of activity occurring in Orlando with the construction of EPCOT. In Japan, Disney focused on building Tokyo Disneyland for the Oriental Land Company. Meanwhile, the studio lot back in Burbank was quiet as a college campus in summer.

In 1980, the Disney studio lot seemed as though Walt had never left. The soundstages he commissioned were quiet after *The Black Hole* was finished. Old back lot sets, which were built for the 1950s television series, *Zorro*, still stood. The Animation Building was still open and animators continued work on *The Fox and the Hound* and *The Black Cauldron*. The studio commissary still served hot lunches. Yet it was not the same vibrant place that thrived back when Walt was alive.

When Lisberger and his select group from Venice Beach came to set up shop, it was as if the hippies and punk rockers invaded Harvard. Bill Kroyer, Michael Fremer, Darrell Rooney, Arne Wong and John Norton were some of the Lisberger Studio vets who came to Disney. Nearly everyone on the Disney studio lot adhered to the Disney dress code of suits, nice shirts and slacks, or nice dresses for the ladies. Kroyer, Fremer, Rooney, Wong and Lisberger wore jeans, black T-shirts and tennis shoes.

"I remember seeing people dressed in patent leather white shoes, with matching belt, Ivy League pin-striped shirt, crew cut hairstyles, etc.," recalls Wong. "We came in with Mohawk haircuts, long hair, punk fashion, tattoos, etc. It was a culture clash, and to top it off, we were not home bred in the studio system."

"The Disney Studios had no connection with what Disney Studios became under Michael Eisner," recalls Lisberger. "It was the studio that time forgot. It was 'Dinosaurville' out there. There was no energy."

Fremer recalls, "It was like a little college of all old people. Nothing much was happening there at all. It was dead. You just couldn't believe how dead it was."

The studio lot may have slowed down, but retired Disney veterans still came to the studio often. It was not unusual to see animators Frank Thomas and Ollie Johnston, Marc Davis, or Ward Kimball walking around the studio lot to visit friends, or to sit down in the Animation Building to draw. They held onto a sense of magic and respect for Walt's studio. It was home.

Lisberger and his staff respected the old Disney veterans.

"A lot of those people from the old days, they're so classy, it's amazing," says Lisberger. "They have knowledge. They have a way about them. They used to say to me that things hadn't been that exciting since Walt was gone. They felt for the first time in a long time like the studio felt when Walt was around, that they had felt that energy. I never really understood this until some of them told me that when Walt was there everything was always cutting edge."

## JERRY REES

On the Disney studio lot were some young animators who had graduated from CalArts. Jerry Rees was among a group of CalArts graduates that included John Musker, Brad Bird, John Lasseter, Joe Ranft, John Van Vliet and Tim Burton. At the age of sixteen, Rees' father drove him up to the Walt Disney Studio. With a portfolio in hand, he entered the Disney studio lot and before he knew it, he was being mentored by Eric Larson and Milt Kahl.

Rees was a natural animator with a keen eye. He had a sense of scale, composition, and a way of making characters come alive. He had a good sense of directing and staging a scene. He was smart. During high school, he happened to enroll in math as an elective in high school. He took computer programming working with wall-sized computers.

"This was in 1974 or 1975," recalls Rees. "I took FORTRAN computer language and I had no idea why."

He immersed himself into the Disney studio culture shortly after high school. But like other young animators such as Kroyer, the young Disney artists were frustrated with the lack of ambition in the Animation Department. The place did not even have electric pencil sharpeners. It seemed as though cobwebs had started forming on the pencils and paint brushes. The young animators were dying to prove their mettle and still carry on the Disney tradition.

Rees was restless. He was getting paid a good salary and got to go to art class once a week, but there was really nothing to do. Kroyer eventually abandoned ship and went to Lisberger, only to come back on *Tron*. Rees wanted work and he got his chance on *The Fox and the Hound*.

"I remember it was Art Stevens and Ted Berman directing at the time," recalls Rees. "They gathered several of us in a room to start this film, *The Fox and the Hound*. They said, 'Well, if it was up to us, we would just keep re-releasing stuff from the library because we got enough films. But they want us to make another movie.' So that's how we started the movie!"

Rees enjoyed bucking Disney tradition. Many times he animated by looking outside the box. Berman and Stevens did not like what they saw and told Rees he could not do it that way.

"Eric was on my side and he goes, 'That's how we used to do it. We used to go out and look at nature and study and just invent new things.' It was in that environment I started to hear about this film that had come in upstairs."

Rees went to Wilhite's office.

"My savior in all of that was Tom Wilhite," says Rees. "He was really trying to stay connected. I went and asked him, 'Can I look at the project?' He said sure, come and take a look around."

Going up to the third floor of the Animation Building, Rees found a lot of activity. Fantastic *Tron* storyboards and concept art dominated the room. The drawings were cutting edge and cool. This was not the same work being done downstairs. This stuff had life and ambition. Rees' eyes lit up.

"The rest of my animation friends stayed downstairs and were waiting for the next movie. I told them, 'I gotta make something. I have to be part of something. I don't want to be paid to sit on my ass.'"

Rees was quickly hired to do storyboards with his old pal, Bill Kroyer.

## SYD MEAD AND MOEBIUS

Lisberger and Kushner had a production deal in place, but they had a lot of pre-production work to do. The storyboards they brought over from Lisberger Studios needed to be re-worked and refined. The duo started the hiring process to expand their production team.

Syd Mead is best known today for his fantastic futuristic designs in both *Tron* and *Blade Runner*. Both films were to be released in the summer of 1982. When Mead came onboard the *Tron* production, he had just finished work on *Blade Runner*. He had already established himself in the film business with his design of V'Ger in *Star Trek: The Motion Picture*. Long before his foray into Hollywood, he was considered to be one of the best designers in the world.

From his own fascination with cars, Mead learned how to draw at an early age. In the mid-1950s, he was stationed as a sergeant in the Army in Okinawa. By 1959, he worked at the Ford Motor Company's Advanced Styling Center in Dearborn, Michigan, designing future Ford automobiles and getting paid little. It was at the Hansen Company in Chicago where Mead got his first taste of real income by producing stunning books for U.S. Steel. He became one of the most sought-after designers, or futurists, in the business.

Mead's art featured cars with beautiful lines. He was as good a designer as he was a salesman. His futuristic designs were alluring, yet functional. Some designers created future products that became dated in no time. Mead's work never seemed dated. He designed everything from kitchen gadgets to 747 airplane interiors. His reputation was of a high caliber individual who was not accessible by most people, including the young team making *Tron*.

"We had no real expectations he would even answer the phone, much less talk to us," says Ellenshaw. "But he is a remarkable man. Very personable. Was then, is now, and was happy to come in and contribute. His contribution cannot be underestimated."

Mead got a call from Kushner to have lunch with him and Lisberger on the Disney studio lot.

"Lisberger had stuff already that he brought with him from Boston," recalls Mead. "He had some kids doing drawings for him. I took a look at the script and started to do some work. I redesigned the aircraft [Sark's] Carrier, the tank and Light Cycle. He had sketches on those three key transport items before. I don't know if he didn't like them or what the deal was. And with my design background, I think I had a better handle on theorizing what these theoretical machines would look like given the premise of the story."

Because of Mead's limited schedule and other commitments, he could only give the production a limited amount of work. It took him only two-to-three weeks to create a huge portfolio of the vehicles and costumes. He also had designed the iconic logo that would be used for the film.

Lisberger and Kushner then looked up French comic book artist Jean "Moebius" Giraud. He was legendary in France and in the comic book world for his extraordinary style and technique. His vision could vary. He could create a standard looking comic strip, or he could draw pictures of dark and scary characters. His comic strip, *Frank et Jérémie*, was made when he was still in his teens. He later created the legendary comic book character, Blueberry. By the 1970s, he was involved with an aborted attempt to bring Frank Herbert's epic novel, *Dune*, to the big screen with director Alejandro Jodorowsky. With his work in *Metal Hurlant*, he had a huge following with American artists. The electronic world of *Tron* only seemed fitting for an icon like Moebius.

Rees was one of the lucky ones to work directly with Moebius.

"Here I am just practically two years out of college, jumped to the studio with three of my friends and we'd quickly done that one feature, then jumped up there and the guy sitting across the table from me was Moebius," says Rees. "Talk about intimidation. You're covering your drawings. He was the nicest guy you'd ever meet. Just really supportive and creative."

The hiring of Mead and Moebius was not lost on Rees.

"I thought that was so brilliant on the part of Steven and Kushner to really bring in industrial designers and conceptional people and people like Moebius. You go to somebody who is kind of a futurist and designer in a legitimate realm of architecture and design, and see how that real stuff affects your story."

Ellenshaw was also impressed by Moebius. The famed artist contributed his time to draw storyboards, as well.

"Here you have Moebius doing storyboards," says Ellenshaw. "It's like having Michelangelo come and do storyboards. 'I'll take a little break from doing the Sistine Chapel ceiling and I'll tell you what. I'll do some storyboards.'"

Both Mead and Moebius refined the artwork and costume design that was already done by the Lisberger Studio artists. Mead's work brought not only form, but function, to the "Electronic

World." The film's vehicles like Sark's Carrier, the tanks, and Light Cycles, were all functional. If a human being was bolted into the "Electronic World," they would easily adapt to the environment.

Moebius defined the look of the costumes. He also drew up his own version of the Solar Sailer, which became one of the film's signatures vehicles. Instead of the hard gladiator look Lisberger and his artists initially developed, the costumes became more streamlined and in some cases, elegant. This was not a fully animated feature anymore, so some practicality had to be considered. Actors would have to wear these costumes, after all.

## TESTING THE NEW KID

Still hesitant about Lisberger's directing abilities, Miller and Wilhite needed to feel more comfortable with Lisberger's ability to direct.

"I liked Steve and Donald personally. I believed they could pull it off," recalls Wilhite. "I admit that I called their agent, Jeff Berg, and asked if someone like Walter Hill, who I knew, might come on as an executive producer to keep an eye on things—as Walter had done on the first *Alien* movie. After all we were committing $12 million to a first-time director. I know this seems like small change today, but at the time it was a big number for Disney."

Lisberger was one of the young directors coming up in the film business in the ranks that included Randal Kleiser (*Grease*), George Lucas (*Star Wars*), Steven Spielberg (*Jaws*), Walter Hill (*The Warriors*), Martin Scorsese (*Taxi Driver*), and Francis Ford Coppola (*Apocalypse Now*). He had never directed a live-action feature film before.

"I think Wilhite got that, and I think he was really impressed with how much pre-production work we had done," says Lisberger. "And he was also intrigued by computer animation. He wasn't sure I could pull all of this off. He didn't say that bluntly, in retrospect."

Wilhite relented. "Berg wasn't enthused about the idea of another director looking over Steve's shoulder, and, frankly, I never pursued the idea any more. I felt they could do it."

Wilhite commissioned a test to see if Lisberger could make *Tron* come alive. On a Disney soundstage, Lisberger and crew set up a blue screen and a mock jail cell. An actor was hired to be a video game warrior, and another actor was hired to play a guard.

After rummaging through the Disney costume department, someone found one of the sentry robot costumes from *The Black Hole* was found. This was worn by an actor playing the guard. The scenes were shot in black-and-white 35mm with a VistaVision camera and 35mm camera with an anamorphic lens. Each frame of the footage was blown up to a Kodalith cel. Each cel, which looked like a large transparency, measured approximately 16x20-inches. Each one of those frames was painted by hand later on by artists. This technique gave the test footage a "candy apple neon" glow Lisberger was seeking.

Another short test was done with professional Frisbee champion, Sam Schatz. Dressed in clothing and gear raided from a sporting goods store, Schatz threw a Frisbee around as the camera filmed him. These tests proved to Wilhite and Miller that Lisberger was on to something very innovative and very cool. The result of both screen tests convinced Wilhite and Miller that Lisberger was capable of directing a major $12 million motion picture.

# Chapter 7

# *ON THE HORIZON*

Contrary to popular mythology, Walt Disney Productions was actually doing well in 1980. In fact, the company had been healthy during most of the 1970s. With income from Disneyland in Anaheim, Walt Disney World in Florida, its regular rerelease schedule of its classic films, and various merchandise properties, the company was financially solid. The company virtually had little or no debt on the books.

Many books written about Ron Miller's eventual successor, Michael Eisner, make Miller out to be an incompetent leader. One simply needs to look at the numbers to see that he was beginning to lead a company turnaround. Unfortunately, the numbers were not as high as those at other major companies during the "go-go" '80s. The cost of EPCOT hovered around $800-to-900 million. The company had an ambitious plan on getting into the cable television business with the Disney Channel. To some, however, the company looked soft in the middle.

Revenues for the company reached nearly $1 billion in 1980. Its theme park division recorded record income. EPCOT was finally under construction, while a giant landfill was being graded in Japan for Tokyo Disneyland. Disney would be a partner in that project, while the Oriental Land Company would own a majority of the new park.

Disney's film division, surprisingly, increased revenue over 1979. Miller partnered with Michael Eisner at Paramount Pictures to co-finance and distribute more adult-oriented films. First on the slate was a live-action version of *Popeye* (1980). Ironically, the creator of *Popeye*, Max Fleischer, was Walt Disney's major competitor in animation for years. Fleischer's son, Richard, directed *20,000 Leagues Under the Sea*. Paramount distributed the live-action version of *Popeye* domestically, while Disney distributed the film internationally. This same co-finance/co-distribution arrangement was done on *Dragonslayer* (1981).

Disney had distributed its own films with other studios in the past. When the studio was smaller, it had distribution agreements with United Artists and later R.K.O. Radio Pictures. Roy O. Disney formed the studio's own distribution arm, Buena Vista Distribution Company, in 1953. That division of the studio would become a powerhouse. It even released films made by outside producers including Walt's friend, Rowland V. Lee (*The Big Fisherman*—1959). Yet by the 1970s, Disney needed more clout with exhibitors. The old Disney films and formulas were no longer popular.

Miller talked to Eisner and suggested he come over to Disney to run its film division. Eisner, already very successful over at Paramount, declined because he also wanted to run more of Walt Disney Productions.

## RAIDERS OF THE LOST ARK

Directors Steven Spielberg and George Lucas were two of the hottest and highest-grossing filmmakers of all time. Lucas and Spielberg, with writers Phillip Kaufman and Lawrence Kasdan, devised an ingenious story about an intrepid archeologist named Indiana Jones who searches the globe for mysterious treasures and battles Nazis. Lucas came up with the hero and idea while vacationing with Spielberg in Hawaii.

Not everyone in Hollywood was sold on the concept. Spielberg, after directing two hugely successful films, *Jaws* (1975) and *Close Encounters of the Third Kind* (1977), directed a flop, *1941* (1979). The film still made money, but the production costs outweighed any profit. Spielberg's clout, as hard as it to now believe, fell flat. *The Empire Strikes Back*, the follow up to *Star Wars*, had budget overruns which were turning the film into one of the most expensive films of the year. Despite their success, Lucas and Spielberg had trouble finding a home for Indy. One of the only studios to express interest in *Raiders of the Lost Ark* was Disney.

Miller knew that by landing the duo at Disney, it would signal a change that the studio was back in the film business. He courted Lucas and Spielberg and expressed intense interest in making *Raiders of the Lost Ark*. Though the film was violent and scary, it was still a property that could show Disney could play with the bigger studios. Disney, after all, scared the daylights out of children with some of its past films. What harm would a little Nazi face melting do?

Ultimately, it was the deal Lucas and Spielberg were demanding that spelled doom for Miller and Disney. They wanted to take a huge chunk of the profits to the eventual Indiana Jones franchise. Card Walker balked and the duo walked.

"When I was making the picture deals," says Miller, "Card said 'Ron, I don't know why you're giving away the store.' We got off to a slow start that way. It was there. We had to live with it. You weren't going to get good writers, good directors, and in some cases good actors, if you weren't going to go there along with it."

Lucas and Spielberg took the film to Paramount, where it found legendary status. After Michael Eisner read the script, he apparently found it to be the most amazing script he had ever read.

Harrison Ellenshaw recalls being in the screening room viewing dailies with Miller for *The Watcher in the Woods*. Miller was grumpy and was not liking what he was seeing. Staring at the screen, Miller uttered, "Why can't this be *Raiders of the Lost Ark*?"

## THE SHAPE OF THINGS TO COME

By the end of 1980, Walt Disney Productions was doing good business at the box office. The studio's financial success was due to the rerelease of some of its catalog titles during the year. *Lady and the Tramp*, *Song of the South*, and *The Aristocats* proved that the Disney name brought audiences into theaters.

On the flip side, the income from those rereleases offset mediocre returns of the studio's newer films. *The Last Flight of Noah's Ark* did not cause kids to beg their parents to take them to see it. *Herbie Goes Bananas* earned a decent profit. The *Herbie* movies always did. But the box office returns were not anything to crow about. *Popeye* did well domestically for the studio's partner, Paramount, but it is not known how the film did overseas for Disney, according to Box Office Mojo.

Still in his twenties, Wilhite had the maturity and drive of a corporate CEO. Seeing Disney's rough box office ride through the 1970s and 1980, he eagerly went to work in finding new properties and new talent to bring to the studio. He wanted to keep Disney's family image alive, but he also wanted to update it.

Before Wilhite's promotion, a film was green lit to capitalize on the *Animal House* (1978) craze. The studio tried jumping onto the raunchy teenage comedy bandwagon with *Midnight Madness*, which starred a young Michael J. Fox and Paul Reubens. The film was rated "PG" and only grossed approximately $2.9 million. The film suffered from being too innocent and not raunchy enough. Over the years, it ultimately became a cult hit.

The studio's supernatural horror film, *The Watcher in the Woods*, had a great and mysterious poster and a spooky premise about a missing girl. Yet when it was released in April of 1980, the audience was dumbfounded on the "other world" ending.

Vincent Canby, the famous movie critic for *The New York Times*, panned the film. "I challenge even the most indulgent fan to give a coherent translation of what passes for an explanation at the end."

The film was released wide in June, but suffered poor box office and the studio withdrew it immediately. Harrison Ellenshaw, having just finished working on *The Empire Strikes Back*, came back to Disney to help salvage the film. A new ending was devised and shot with improved visual effects that Ellenshaw supervised. But after it was rereleased in 1981, it still bombed. People began wondering what was wrong with Disney.

Looking inward, Wilhite encouraged the development of experimental short films by some young animators already on staff. Tim Burton was one of those animators. He was a scrawny and strange kid with a lot of talent. He eventually directed *Vincent* (1982) and *Frankenweenie* (1984), two short films whose whimsical Gothic elements found themselves in Burton's later films. Another young Disney animator, John Lasseter, worked on *The Fox and the Hound*.

Wilhite solicited other scripts and sought directors who would ordinarily not even think of working at Disney. One of his biggest triumphs was getting the rights to film *Tex*, based on the best selling youth novel by S.E. Hinton. Her books had a resurgence in popularity by the 1980s, and other studios were jumping on the band wagon to adapt them for the big screen. Wilhite beat them. The film would be directed by Tim Hunter, co-written by Charlie Haas, and star Matt Dillon. For Disney, it was a major break from the teen comedies it thrived on during Walt's era. The innocent Annette Funicello and Tommy Kirk comedies were updated to brooding teenage dramas of the 1980s. For Wilhite, it was only the beginning.

Another coup was hiring Carrol Ballard to direct the film *Never Cry Wolf*. A close friend of George Lucas, Ballard took years to make his films. He had directed the critical and box office hit, *The Black Stallion* for Francis Ford Coppola and United Artists. It was released in 1979. *Never Cry Wolf* would take a few years longer than expected to make, but it would turn out to be a gorgeous and touching film.

Wilhite found a charming script from writers Lowell Ganz, Babaloo Mandel and Bruce Jay Friedman called *Splash*. Work continued on *The Black Cauldron*, *The Fox and the Hound*, and the live-action adventure, *Condorman*. Wilhite put into development plans of bringing the world of Frank Baum's *Wizard of Oz* books back to the big screen. Walt Disney bought the rights to the remaining *Oz* books in the 1950s. *Return to Oz* was going to be directed by Walter Murch.

Perhaps Wilhite's biggest purchase was the rights to Gary K. Wolf's book, *Who Censored Roger Rabbit*. Director Robert Zemeckis had been attached to direct it in the early 1980s.

"At the time Zemeckis was not a particularly hot director, although he had powerful friends," says Wilhite. "He'd only made *Used Cars* and *I Wanna Hold Your Hand*. He had a chance to direct *Cocoon* and he came to me to ask to be let out of his *RR* contract, which we did. At that time we were making *Splash*. Zanuck-Brown [producers Richard D. Zanuck and David Brown] asked to screen the picture before it was released and they replaced Zemeckis with Ron Howard. Then Zemeckis directed *Romancing the Stone* (1984), which was a hit in its own right. After I left Disney in 1984 to start Hyperion, the whole thing came full circle and Zemeckis again became *RR* director (in 1988)."

*Tron* was Wilhite's riskiest gamble. As the production team was being put together on the Disney studio lot, Wilhite was busy soliciting scripts and trying to hire outside film directors. He did not have time to contemplate the risky venture about to unfold on the Disney soundstages. Here was a film with a first-time feature film director and a crew of non-Disney animators and visual effects wizards. To top it off, the film was going to use groundbreaking computer animation. An older studio executive might have pulled the plug.

"I was a young executive. Maybe naïve. Maybe a bit more self-confident because I was young and naïve," recalls Wilhite. "I certainly wasn't computer literate—after all, the PC hadn't really become the ubiquitous thing it eventually became. *Tron* just seemed unique and exciting to me and perfectly suited to Disney."

The production of *Tron* was ready to roll.

During the construction of Disneyland in 1954, Walt Disney took
Harrison Ellenshaw for a ride on the park's railroad. (Courtesy of Gregg Shay)

Harrison Ellenshaw works on a matte painting for *No Deposit, No Return*. (1976—Courtesy of Harrison Ellenshaw)

Lisberger Studios, Inc. staff. (Courtesy of Darrell Rooney)

Chris Lane's early concept for the "Electronic World"
battle arena. (Courtesy of Chris Lane)

(Left-to-right) Peggy Flook (Lisberger), Steven Lisberger and
Roger Allers celebrate at the Venice studio. (Courtesy of Darrell Rooney)

(Left-to-right) *Animalympics* art director Roger Allers and producer Donald Kushner. (Courtesy of Darrell Rooney)

*Animalympics* music editor, writer and voiceover artist Michael Fremer and Roger Allers.
(Courtesy Darrell Rooney)

Bonnie MacBird was hired early on in the
development of *Tron*. (Courtesy of Darrell Rooney)

Animator Darrell Rooney was the first live-action model for *Tron*.
(Courtesy of Darrell Rooney)

Rooney plays a cowboy in the "Electronic World." (Courtesy of Darrell Rooney)

Richard Winn Taylor II was a prolific television commercial director before entering the world of computer simulation. (Courtesy of Richard Taylor)

Writer/Director of *Tron*, Steven Lisberger, addresses the crew on the
Walt Disney Studios back lot. (Courtesy of Darrell Rooney)

Lisberger was adept at putting together talented teams for his films.
(Courtesy of Darrell Rooney)

*Tron* film editor, Jeff Gourson. (Courtesy of John Van Vliet)

Co-visual effects supervisor and associate producer, Harrison Ellenshaw, on the set of *Tron*. (Courtesy of Harrison Ellenshaw)

Ellenshaw playfully expresses his frustration over explaining Kodaliths to everyone.
(Courtesy of Harrison Ellenshaw)

Computer image choreographer, Bill Kroyer. (Courtesy of Bill Kroyer)

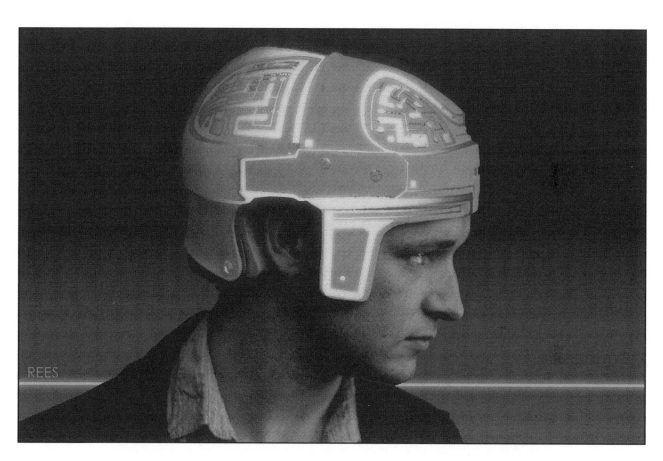

Computer image choreographer, Jerry Rees. (Courtesy of Jerry Rees)

The effects animation crew. (Courtesy of John Van Vliet)

Drawing of Flynn getting derezzed into the "Electronic World."
(Drawn by Darrell Rooney)

All the work on *Tron* was not always serious. To let off stress,
animators drew cartoons spoofing *Tron*. (Drawn by John Van Vliet)

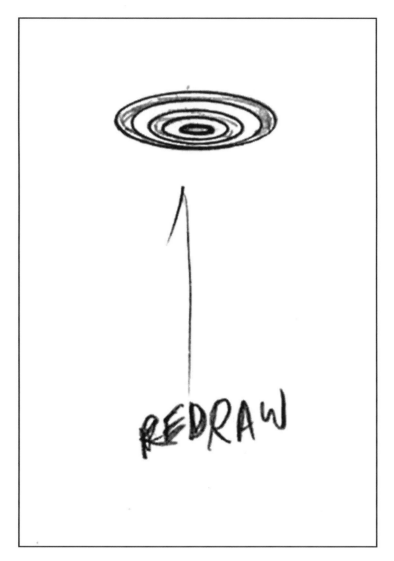

Animators on *Tron* had to make sure their work was precise. (Drawn by Peter Gullerud)

Lynda Ellenshaw was one of the youngest crew members on *Tron*.
(Courtesy of Lynda Ellenshaw Thompson)

Jesse Silver paints the elaborate background for the holding cells in *Tron*.
(Courtesy of Jesse Silver)

Animation compositing cameraman, Glenn Campbell. (Courtesy of John Van Vliet)

A Kodalith blow-up from the 65mm original negative. Featured are
Jeff Bridges and Cindy Morgan. (David Arnspiger Collection)

Robert Abel and Associates crew (left-to-right) featuring Bill Kovacs, Kenny Mirman, Richard Baily, and Frank Vitz. (Courtesy of Kenny Mirman)

The *Tron* crew takes a break from filmmaking. (Courtesy of Steven Lisberger)

(Left-to-right) Richard Taylor, legendary newsman Walter Cronkite, and Harrison Ellenshaw. (Courtesy of Richard Taylor)

The *Tron* crew portrait on the *Something Wicked This Way Comes*
set in Burbank, California. (Courtesy of the *Tron* crew)

Sound effects designer, Frank Serafine, works on the elaborate
*Tron* soundtrack. (Courtesy of Frank Serafine)

(Left-to-right) Bobbie, Harrison, Lynda and Peter Ellenshaw celebrate after the premiere of *Tron* at the Walt Disney studios. (Courtesy of Lynda Ellenshaw Thompson)

Effects animator, John Van Vliet, arrives at the Samuel Goldwyn Theater in Beverly Hills, California for the crew premiere of *Tron*. (Courtesy of Peter Gullerud)

Animators Peter Gullerud and Maureen Trueblood celebrate at the
"Tron Prom." (Courtesy of Peter Gullerud)

The Bally's arcade video game of *Tron* was immensely popular.
(David Arnspiger Collection)

*Tron* fan and memorabilia collector, David Arnspiger,
shows off a vintage 1982 Halloween costume. (Photograph by William Kallay)

Actress Cindy Morgan (Lora/Yori) and author William Kallay.
(Photograph by David Arnspiger)

The 2007 American Cinematheque 70mm screening in Santa Monica, California. Double-billed with *Star Trek: The Wrath of Khan*. (Photograph by William Kallay)

Actor Bruce Boxleitner shares a *Tron* memory with futurist, Syd Mead,
at the 2007 screening. (Photograph by William Kallay)

Bill Kroyer and Dan Shor discuss the finer points of animation and acting at the 2007 screening. Background: Georgia Scheele, daughter of John Scheele, effects technical supervisor. (Photograph by William Kallay)

Richard Taylor and Harrison Ellenshaw at the Visual
Effects Society Awards in 2008. (Photograph by William Kallay)

(Left-to-right) *Tron* publicist Mike Bonifer, *Tron: Legacy* producers Sean Bailey & Steven Lisberger, and Bill Kroyer at D23 in Anaheim, California in 2009. (Photograph by William Kallay)

(Left-to-right) Bill Kroyer, Steven Lisberger, and Richard Taylor gather outside the Aero Theatre in Santa Monica, California after the 2011 screening of *Tron*. (Photograph by William Kallay)

*Tron* effects technical supervisor, John Scheele, and Richard Taylor after the 2011 screening. (Photograph by William Kallay)

The audience's reaction to the 2011 screening of *Tron* was electric.
(Photograph by William Kallay)

# Chapter 8

# *CASTING AND CHARACTERS*

One of the first orders of business in getting *Tron* into production was casting. And it was not going to be easy.

With few exceptions, Walt Disney Productions was not known for hiring big name stars for its films. Walt tended to feel more comfortable in hiring actors who, though very talented, were lesser known. Unlike today where animated films feature big stars, Disney preferred radio stars and actors whose names were not familiar with the public. Pinto Colvig (Goofy), Cliff Edwards (Jiminy Cricket) and Clarence Nash (Donald Duck) were popular radio stars. The stars of Walt's animated films were the characters.

On the live-action side, Disney usually stuck with character actors and actors he had nurtured under contract. Tommy Kirk, Annette Funicello, James MacArthur, Kevin Corcoran and Fess Parker were studio staples. Hayley Mills, daughter of British actor John Mills, became one of Walt's favorite young actors who went onto stardom. Actor Brian Keith was a dependable star of Disney films like *The Parent Trap*. Dean Jones was a reliable actor in a number of Disney productions. Sean Connery acted in *Darby O'Gill and the Little People* and went onto a successful career playing the original James Bond and other characters.

Walt spent the necessary money if he wanted a blockbuster cast. He hired Kirk Douglas, James Mason and Peter Lorre for *20,000 Leagues Under the Sea*, and he went out of his way to sweet talk young actress Julie Andrews to star as *Mary Poppins*. But the studio generally did not attract big name stars. Fred McMurray, who was a big star in the 1940s, hit a rough patch during the 1950s with his career. Disney hired him for a light comedy, *The Shaggy Dog* (1959), and McMurray found himself starring in other Disney productions. During his career revival at Disney, he starred in director Billy Wilder's *The Apartment* and the popular television show, *My Three Sons* (both in 1960).

By the 1970s, the Disney studio was the last stop on most actor's career paths. Jodie Foster and Kurt Russell were young actors at the studio. Foster acted in *Candleshoe* (1978), while Russell voiced the adult character of Copper in *The Fox and the Hound* (1981). Once Foster and Russell grew up, they went onto successful careers at other studios.

Don Knotts and Tim Conway, with their silly dialogue delivery and funny facial expressions, were a perfect match for *The Apple Dumpling Gang* (1975), *Hot Lead and Cold Feet* (1978), and *The Apple Dumpling Gang Rides Again* (1979), but they were not enough of a draw for a blockbuster. The studio's big gamble with *The Black Hole* brought in older talent such as Maximilian Schell and Ernest Borgnine. But they were not box office draws to a generation weaned on Robert DeNiro, Al Pacino or John Travolta.

"People who might have had properties felt that maybe Disney could make a fine film out of it," says Miller. "They never submitted it because they knew the philosophy of the company was not to give 'points.'"

"Disney had a problem back then," says Lisberger. "The agencies that controlled most of the talent in town had sort of a proprietary attitude about finding films for their actors other than Disney films. Our initial casting list was pretty much summarily rejected. We really didn't get too far into it before we realized once we said it was for Disney, and I was a first-time director coming out of animation, and once we mentioned it was about video games that pretty much ended most of the conversations."

In order for *Tron* to gain credibility outside of being a visual effects groundbreaker, and for Disney to finally signal it was serious in hiring big name actors, a credible lead actor was needed. The film also required the leads of the film to play dual roles. One role had their "Real World" character (i.e. user) living and breathing among us. The other role had their alter ego, or their program, living in the "Electronic World."

## JEFF BRIDGES: KEVIN FLYNN/CLU

"It was [writer] Charlie Haas, who did one of the polished re-writes on the script, who suggested Jeff Bridges to me initially," recalls Lisberger.

Son of actor Lloyd Bridges and younger brother of Beau, Jeff was part of a respected Hollywood acting family. During the 1970s, he won accolades for his acting in films such as *The Last Picture Show* (1970) and *Thunderbolt and Lightfoot* (1974). His acting skill was excellent and he was nominated for an Oscar for Best Supporting Actor in both roles. He was very credible and held the screen with his likable presence and seemingly ageless looks. He acted in the big budget films *King Kong* (1976) and in the box office flop, *Heaven's Gate* (1980). He received word about a new movie in pre-production at Disney.

"Jeff was sort of in a lull, and he cruised in from Malibu one day and he and I sort of struck it all off," recalls Lisberger. "And he was like, 'This sounds really far out.' He got that it was far out. He got that."

"I remember first hearing about it about a guy who gets sucked inside a computer," recalls Bridges. "They were going to use all this technology that hadn't been used before. It kind of got explained to me in sort of a rough way, and I didn't understand what was going on. The thing that really got me was Steve's enthusiasm. He had such a vision and such a can-do attitude. And there's probably a good dose of kid in me that likes to do things like getting sucked inside computers."

Continues Lisberger, "We had a meeting and we talked about the script and it never occurred to me to offer him anything other than the part of Flynn. I was a little surprised how big Jeff is. He's a tall guy, very physical and athletic. But he read the script for the part of Flynn, and then in the meeting he said to me, 'I really want to do this. Do I have the gig?' I was so impressed with him that we had such a good meeting that I agreed to it on the spot."

Bridges was an inspired choice for the role of Flynn. The character was a grown-up adolescent who was admired by the arcade kids, respected by peers of his own age, and popular with the ladies. As an actor, Bridges was instantly recognizable by audiences. He seemed old enough to gain respectability for young kids and teens who would see the film. They would see him as "the cool older guy" who not only owned an arcade, but who designed the games in it. Older audiences, those in their 30s and 40s, liked Bridges because he was just plain cool. Casting Bridges gave some much needed clout to Disney. This was the first time since Julie Andrews was cast in *Mary Poppins* that the studio had a young certified superstar.

The character of Kevin Flynn was way ahead of his time. He was a "hacker" before audiences knew what a hacker was. Flynn was the dude with looks, charm, guts, a sense of humor, and brains to get him through any bind. He was part California beach bum and part Steve Jobs. In other words, he was an idealized version of an early 1980s computer geek.

## BRUCE BOXLEITNER: ALAN BRADLEY/*TRON*

The role of Tron, who Lisberger characterizes as the film's Dudley Do Right character, was the most difficult to cast. In the production's storyboards and drawings, Tron is seen as a chiseled, physically perfect specimen. In the early 1980s, muscle-bound movie stars had not become popular as they would later in the decade. Sylvester Stallone was busy making *Rocky* sequels. Arnold Schwarzenegger had not yet broken through in mainstream feature films.

"One of the things I regret about the casting was originally when we boarded the picture, Flynn was going to be more of a brainiac, a little more nerdy," recalls Lisberger. "He was going to be smaller physically. Tron was going to be more massive and more of the sort of strong silent nerd."

In casting Bridges as Flynn, Lisberger got a tall and athletic actor who was not nerdy. Yet, with Bridges' acting range, he could pull off being the cool nerd. As for the role of Tron, that was going to be more difficult. That is when Peter O'Toole came into the picture.

O'Toole was a classically trained Irish actor whose most famous role was that of T.E. Lawrence in director David Lean's 1962 epic, *Lawrence of Arabia*. During the 1960s, he was one of the most reliable actors the era's epic films such as *Becket* (1964), *Lord Jim* (1965), *The Lion in the Winter* (1968), and *Goodbye, Mr. Chips* (1969). By the 1970s, O'Toole took fewer roles and faded into the background of Hollywood. It was not until he played the role of a crazy director in the *The Stunt Man* (1980) where his stock rose again. He wanted to play Tron.

"That's a myth that Peter O'Toole was offered the part of Tron," says Lisberger. "Peter was offered the Sark part."

Sark was the main villain in *Tron*.

"I met with him at the Beverly Wilshire and he was very energetic and he loved the script," continues Lisberger. "He actually ended up coming to my house. We went over a whole bunch of aspects. He really wasn't interested in playing Sark. He wanted to play Tron. He was obviously too old for it at the time and it didn't make any sense anyway, really."

Clearly, as good an actor as O'Toole was, there was no way he would be cast as Tron. He would have made for a great villain as Sark, but not as one of the film's heroes. Lisberger wanted someone who was younger and who could pull off the alter egos of Alan Bradley, the computer wizard in the real world, and of Tron, Alan's electronic do-gooder. In a sense, he had to be like Clark Kent/Superman.

Who could have played Alan Bradley/Tron? Since *Tron* was being filmed at Disney, there were not very many choices. While the studio did have Kurt Russell under its wings in the early 1970s, he had sought more mature fare at other studios. He began to collaborate with writer/director John Carpenter (*Halloween*—1978). By 1981, Russell had worked with him on the "R" rated *Escape from New York* and firmly established himself as an action hero.

Looking at the star roster of the day, other theoretical choices could have been Sylvester Stallone, Harrison Ford, Treat Williams, Barry Bostwick, or Harry Hamlin. Stallone and Ford were huge stars and they would not dare step foot on Disney's studio lot. Their salaries were incredibly high and Disney would not pay them anyway. Williams, Bostwick and Hamlin were not big stars, but they were reliable actors. But even they would not go into a Disney film.

It was suggested by the head of Disney casting, Pam Polifroni, that Lisberger look at a young actor named Bruce Boxleitner. By his early thirties, the actor had already amassed an impressive list of credits, mostly in television. Born in Elgin, Illinois in 1950, Boxleitner was a tall and dark haired actor who had done a number of television shows in the 1970s. His most notable role during that time was in *How the West Was Won*, a mini-series on NBC. He played Luke Macahan.

Boxleitner was sent the *Tron* script while on location for a TV movie for NBC. The script perplexed him.

"I didn't understand the script," recalls Boxleitner. "It looked like some kind of *Star Wars* type of thing. I guess my mind wasn't there at that point. I was reading it out in the middle of Arizona on location during a TV movie for NBC. A western. It just wasn't there. That's what I find so funny. I was sitting out there on a horse. I think I left the script in a saddle bag. I don't even know what happened with it until I got back to Hollywood a week or so later."

He told his agent he did not understand what *Tron* was about. His agent told him the film was being made at Disney.

"Bruce Boxleitner had a promising career ahead of him," says Lisberger. "He was really not interested in working for Disney. That was for has-beens. He was 'No. No. No.' We couldn't get anybody interested in this movie. NOBODY! NOWHERE!"

However, for Boxleitner, Disney and Bridges were huge selling points.

"I'm the original Disney kid," says Boxleitner. "We were the kids who grew up when *Disneyland* first came on. When I knew that Jeff Bridges was attached to it, I took another look."

He was invited to Disney to watch the test footage that Lisberger had done. Although it was still difficult to comprehend the overall concept of *Tron*, Boxleitner's interest began to grow.

"It was really a hard thing to visualize it at that time," recalls Boxleitner. "What is *Tron*? I dug that he was kind of a Spartacus of the Game Grid. But what was that? Once I saw the visuals, it was an absolute. Absolutely exciting. It was like something that no one had seen."

Boxleitner, like Bridges, was the anti-geek hero. Sure, he could put on a pair of oversized 1980s glasses to look nerdy, but it did not work. He still looked too cool. The character of Alan Bradley/Tron was an intelligent computer whiz like Flynn, but he was written as straight-laced, by-the-numbers kind of guy. MacBird says that the original drafts had more of Alan Kay's personality traits than what appeared in the completed film. Lisberger was aiming for more of a computer-smart Boy Scout.

"The idea of playing two [characters], sort of the Clark Kent and Superman, was kind of fun," says Boxleitner. "And Jeff was somebody that I admired the movies he was in. I wanted to work with him."

Four days before the film was to go into production, Boxleitner signed on. For him, there was no stigma of working at Walt Disney Productions.

"I wasn't really aware of any kind of a real stigma about it," recalls Boxleitner. "But I can see where that probably existed. There was this band of young rebels over there. I was with a group of young visionaries."

## CINDY MORGAN: LORA/YORI

The only female role in the film belonged to Lora/Yori. Lora was a nerdy counterpart to the "Real World" Alan, while Yori was a counterpart to Tron in the "Electronic World." Both females were written as stilted, almost robotic characters, though Lora had a little bit more warmth. Casting the right actress still provided a good counterbalance to Bridges and Boxleitner.

Singer Debbie Harry, who fronted the band Blondie, was very interested in the role. Blondie was one of the most popular bands in the world with songs like "Tide is High" and "Call Me." Harry was instantly recognizable on album covers, and was one of the pioneers of early music videos that appeared occasionally on late-night television. MTV was not on the air yet when *Tron* was being cast. Her striking looks and punk rock attitude might have been a boon for the film, but she had not really acted outside of a music video and a few low budget films.

"We screen tested Debbie Harry," says Lisberger. "She really wanted to do it. She gave it her best shot, but it didn't work out."

Michelle Pfeiffer's name came up as an option. At this point in time, she was unknown, but she had been cast in the sequel to the 1978 megahit, *Grease*. The sequel came out a few weeks before *Tron* in 1982 and bombed, but Pfeiffer's career eventually flourished.

It was then that another beautiful actress came into the picture named Cindy Morgan.

A native of Chicago, Cynthia Ann Cichorski was striking, intelligent, and witty. An all-girl Catholic school graduate, she initially wanted to follow in her father's footsteps to become an engineer and work in audio. She had been accepted to the Illinois Institute of Technology, but had instead gotten into work as a disc jockey.

"I worked for several years in Milwaukee and Chicago and couldn't get a job to make commercials," says Morgan. "Nobody would hire me in commercials because everybody knew me as the radio personality. I left my radio job because they gave me the morning drive, the big shift, took away my overtime and gave it to some guy. Literally I got a cut in pay. So I logged off the air and did five minutes of modeling at an auto show."

That exposure led her to pack her bags and head to Los Angeles.

While in L.A., she took comedy improvisation classes and dated Larry Anderson, the comedic actor who had helped out at the Lisberger Studios in Venice Beach. At one point she and Larry had lunch with Lisberger and some other people involved with *Tron*, but none of this particular meeting gave Morgan an inkling she would be cast in the film. After going to auditions around Hollywood, Morgan landed a gig as the Irish Spring Soap girl. Being in a national television spot not only brought her great exposure, but it provided steady income. Morgan seductively mimicked an Irish accent and television screens lit up. Proctor & Gamble, the maker of Irish Spring, sold millions of soap bars.

She was then cast in an "R" rated comedy for the fledgling studio, Orion Pictures called *Caddyshack* (1980). The film was a moderate box office hit and it gained an audience on the fledgling home video format. Directed by newcomer, Harold Ramis, and starring 1970s comedy icons Chevy Chase, Bill Murray, Rodney Dangerfield, and Ted Knight, the film was a true guy's film. It had quick jokes, witty comebacks, a sports theme and a rollicking theme song from Kenny Loggins. The film was raunchy, but it fit in the era of *Animal House*.

The film's production was known for its party atmosphere.

"Everything you've heard about it was true and more," says Morgan. "It was 1979. That was the year that people thought drugs were good for them and not addictive and not harmful. As much fun as we had and partook, people died very soon after."

One of the writers of the film, Douglas Kenney, died shortly after the film was released.

Morgan was cast in the role of the risqué girl of the country club, and it forever cemented her in the minds of guys everywhere. She played a character named Lacey Underall. A blonde vixen with dynamic looks, she was every guy's ideal fantasy woman. Before so-called political correctness, Lacey Underall was sublime to most guys.

Looks aside, Morgan was not the flirty girl seen in the film. She had her morals. During the production of *Caddyshack* in Florida, she had a run-in with one of the producers.

"One of the producers said I'm sending a photographer from *Playboy*," recalls Morgan. "I said I'm really flattered. I'd love to do it. I can't. I was the Irish Spring girl at the time and Proctor and Gamble won't have it. 'I'm sending him.' I called my agent and I said, 'Help me.' And my agent said, 'Honey you're not a doe-eyed girl from the Midwest.' Of course, I fired my agent subsequently. I had to throw the photographer off. The producer called me from L.A. between takes and said you're fucked in this business, you'll never fucking work again. And I said so be it. Because I used to run camera and sound, I cleared the set. I said I need four people. That's the director of photography, the director Harold Ramis, that actor and me, and until then, you're not getting a shot off."

Her stance won respect from her peers on the set, but that moment of defiance temporarily hurt her. As a result, her likeness was not seen on posters, video cassettes or later, DVDs. Morgan did not work for almost a year after *Caddyshack*.

Then she auditioned for a sci-fi fantasy film called *Tron*.

"The first interview was really with Jeff Bridges," says Morgan. "It wasn't like I went to a casting session and met the casting director. I was called in the first time to meet with the director and Jeff Bridges. I read a scene with him and it seemed to go okay. The next thing I knew I was called up to one of the heads of Disney's office. I went up there thinking I'd be auditioning again. He asked me what my political affiliations were and like any good blonde actress, I told him I had none. I got the job."

## DAVID WARNER: ED DILLINGER/SARK/MASTER CONTROL PROGRAM (MCP)

In most modern films, bad guys were played by British actors who acted snarky and snide. Audiences could always count on a British actor to play bad guys with pride. Most of the James Bond films always had a British bad guy. Steven Spielberg and George Lucas' *Raiders of the Lost Ark* featured British actors Paul Freeman and Ronald Lacey as Nazis. Darth Vader was played by tall English actor David Prowse (though he was voiced by American actor, James Earl Jones). British actors seemed to be key to having a great villain.

*Tron* required the lead actors to play duel roles. For the villain, the actor playing that part would be playing three different characters—Dillinger, Sark and the Master Control Program (MCP).

Dillinger was Kevin Flynn's arch nemesis in the "Real World."

The Master Control Program, also known as the MCP, was originally written as the main villain in *Tron*. The cylindrical, spinning device ruled the "Electronic World" like a Roman emperor. He took satisfaction in sending warriors to the Game Grid for battle. Although the MCP was a major character, he was not fully developed in the film. It was his lieutenant who was a far more imposing figure.

Sark was an unflinching and cold-hearted version of the MCP who stalked around, pushed his minions to the floor, and challenged lowly programs to Light Cycle races. Although he followed the MCP's orders, Sark also played by his own rules.

Peter O'Toole would have been perfect for the roles of Dillinger/Sark/MCP, but the actor had no interest in playing them. Lisberger was desperate with only two weeks before the production began. As luck and timing would have it, British actor David Warner was available. Lisberger immediately hired him, never having met him before. Warner was a brilliant and classically trained actor. He was tall and immediately imposing when the role called for it. Born in Manchester, England, he acted on stage in the Royal Academy of Arts as a member of the prestigious Royal Shakespeare Company. He soon found himself working in film, acting in *Tom Jones* (1963) and *The Omen* (1976).

By 1981, Warner appeared in an obscure British film by director Terry Gilliam called *Time Bandits*. The film featured a boy, played by Craig Warnock, and a group of time traveling dwarfs. Warner played the Evil Genius, a sly and devilish villain. Warner seemed to have fun in this scene-stealing role. The film was a surprise hit, earning approximately $42 million. Disney actually considered picking the film up for distribution, but did not.

"When he walked on to the Disney lot, it was probably two weeks before we started," says Lisberger. "That was the first time I'd ever seen him. I was a little taken aback with how skinny he was. The storyboards had a very sort of heavy, muscular guy. So we got involved with padding all that out. Certainly David was great."

## BARNARD HUGHES: DR. WALTER GIBBS/DUMONT

The character combo of Dr. Walter Gibbs/Dumont required an older actor. According to Lisberger, Gibbs was not modeled after anyone in particular. Yet he can reasonably be compared to a visionary like Bill Hewlett or David Packard who started a business in their garage. Only years later, after technology has surpassed their visionary achievements, is a guy like Gibbs seen as a relic.

Gibb's alter ego resides, like the rest of the cast, in the "Electronic World." Dumont is an old program who has the power to communicate to the users in the "Real World." As technology advanced, he and his fellow programs were relegated into the far reaches of the "Electronic World" and forgotten. Dumont was the film's Obi Wan Kenobe, a wise sage who gives advice and help to the young programs when they need it.

One of the film's inspired casting choices for Dr. Walter Gibbs/Dumont came down to veteran actor, Barnard Hughes (1915-2006). His sweet demeanor and his grandfatherly appearance were suited for these two roles.

Hughes was a veteran and distinguished stage actor on the New York City stage. He had acted in a number of television shows including *All in the Family* (1971) and *Doc* (1975). By the late 1970s, he had won a Tony Award for his role in the stage play, *Da*. Young audiences probably were not too familiar with Hughes, but he would cement his reputation with them in the roles of Gibbs/Dumont.

## DAN SHOR: POPCORN CO-WORKER/RAM

The last major role of the film fell to Popcorn Co-worker/Ram. The Popcorn Worker, hiding out in the maze of ENCOM's cubicles (further enhanced by Harrison Ellenshaw's amazing matte painting) was a quick gag that still elicits laughs from audiences today. It was the role of Ram that added much-needed spark and emotion to the "Electronic World" scenes.

New York City-born actor Dan Shor was cast. He had parts in films like *Wise Blood* (1979), directed by John Huston, and *Back Roads* with Sally Field (1981), directed by Marin Ritt.

"I was doing a play [in Los Angeles] called *The Sport of My Mad Mother*," says Shor. "It was a punk rock musical. It starred all of my friends. One of them was Peter Jurasik. In it we were a pair of punk rock gangsters whose names were Fak and Cone. Somebody from Disney saw the play and we were both called in to read for *Tron*, and we both got Ram and Crom. We were Fak and Cone one day, and the next day we were Ram and Crom. It was really bizarre."

Shor was instantly intrigued by the concepts of *Tron* after reading the screenplay. He saw the potential of being in a truly fun film.

"I was a cartoon fan and a comic book fan," says Shor. "I was still a kid then, so I was a Marvel comics fan. It wasn't a bizarre script to me at all. It was a comic book. We thought of it as a comic book. It was presented to us like a comic book. It was easy to understand. We didn't understand computers. I never had a computer and I didn't understand the concept of users. But once you did, you went with the gang, with the flow, and went with Steven Lisberger who was the visionary behind this whole experience."

# Chapter 9

# *THE CREW OF TRON*

Being a film that took place inside a computer, *Tron* needed someone who was versed in computer animation. Unlike today where a kid can create digitally animated movies on a laptop, the art form virtually did not exist back in the early 1980s. There were only a select few companies in the United States, and a few experimental laboratories on various college campuses, that could produce a few minutes worth of computer animation. *Tron* needed someone who was not only computer savvy, but who was creatively brilliant.

By the time *Tron* went into pre-production, visual effects artists were featured in the pages of science fiction movie magazines. What are now known as "fan boys" ate up everything they could about their visual effects heroes. John Dykstra, Richard Edlund, Douglas Trumbull, Harrison Ellenshaw, and Dennis Muren were familiar names in visual effects geek speak. Although Richard Taylor was not a household name, he was certainly one of the visual effects industry's most gifted artists.

## RICHARD WINN TAYLOR II

Richard Winn Taylor II seemed like an unlikely guy to make mind-blowing graphics and visual effects. Tall, with a kind grin and humble tone in his voice, Taylor was one of the most innovative minds around. A former merchant marine, Taylor earned a Bachelor of Fine Arts degree at the University of Utah and then earned his Masters Degree in Photography and Printmaking at USC. Taylor's talent as an artist was incredibly deep. Not only could he paint nearly anything that came to his mind, but he also knew how to use and manipulate light to make stunning art.

Early in his career, Taylor founded Rainbow Jam with his partner Kenvin Lyman. The pair designed psychedelic light shows for The Grateful Dead and toured with the band. Their mind altering light shows fit right in with concert goers who loved The Dead and questionable substances. Lyman also created some of the famous Led Zeppelin posters of the era.

Taylor's honed his mastery of light and how to manipulate it into dynamic imagery at Robert Abel and Associates. A small independent studio in Los Angeles, "Abel's" specialized in dazzling television commercials. The studio was on the cutting edge. Their ability to catch a television viewer's eye and make the viewer remember the ad *and* product being sold was ingenious. The firm specialized in streak photography, a process that made light streak across the screen, made famous in *2001: A Space Odyssey*. The company was founded by Robert Abel and Con Pederson. Taylor joined Abel's in the early 1970s. It was during this era that Harry Marks (of Marks and Marks) pioneered dazzling television graphics and logos, as well.

While at Abel's, Taylor invented the "candy apple neon" look. This was a startling new method in animation. In standard animation, animation cels are lit from above with studio lights and filmed with a camera. Cartoon characters like Mickey Mouse are evenly lit with pleasing light. With Taylor's method, animated characters were lit from behind. The term "candy apple neon" was coined because the animated characters, when backlit, appeared dreamy, electric and luminous.

One of Taylor's famous ads was for the 7-Up Bottling Company called *See the Light*. True to his Rainbow Jam roots, he directed one of the most psychedelic commercials ever made. It featured women dressed in bathing suits dancing with 7-Up bubbles. Animated bubbles float up the television screen while a woman with butterfly wings gracefully flies. Taylor even managed to mix in catchy Roaring '20s style music with an Elvis Presley sound-alike on the soundtrack. All of this amazing imagery was backlit. Steven Lisberger and John Norton were so inspired by the "candy apple neon" look that they based the electronic warrior (i.e. Tron) on Taylor's technique.

By the late 1970s, Taylor worked on the ambitious *Star Trek: The Motion Picture*. Paramount poured money into the film in the hope it would surpass *Star Wars* with superior visual effects and box office grosses. The studio hired Robert Abel & Associates. Taylor, Syd Mead, and the staff of Abel's designed the miniature spaceships. After working extensively on the film, Abel's was fired.

"We had a big falling out with Paramount Studios," says Taylor. "We eventually got replaced by Doug Trumbull. And it was a big disappointment to me. We did scenes in the film. We designed the models. It was a big political hot potato over why that happened. After that film had been taken out of our hands, I felt like it was time for me to leave Abel's. I'd been working toward that."

Taylor received a call from director Terrence Malick, who had recently made *Days of Heaven* (1978) for Paramount. Malick, who was known for his long delays in making his next film, told Taylor of a new science fiction epic he was developing based on the Big Bang and the evolution of Earth.

"I knew that the only way to possibly do that was with computer simulation," says Taylor. "I had my eye on computer simulation all along, any form of it."

Taylor got Paramount to pony up some development money for the visual effects, and for six months, he worked on and developed some tests on making the Big Bang work on a computer. Suddenly, Malick pulled the plug.

"He kind of put everything on hold," says Taylor.

Taylor had known Gary Demos from the days of Rainbow Jam. Demos had worked for a company called Triple-I, also known as Information International, Inc. Both he and John Whitney, Jr., whose father John Whitney, Sr. was a computer animation pioneer, started a film division at the company. Jim Blinn, a pioneer of computer animation at the Jet Propulsion Laboratory (JPL) was also involved with the division's foray into the movie business. One of the company's earliest visual effects came in the form of European television logos, as well as the creation of logos for Mercedes-Benz, ABC television and the computer rendering of actor Peter Fonda's head for *Futureworld* (1976). They also did a computer-simulation visual-effects test for Steven Spielberg's *Close Encounters of the Third Kind* (1977). The footage was not used.

"I saw the potential at Triple-I to really turn it into a film production company," says Taylor. "I had some meetings and said I would like to come out here and start directing and put together a real film production company. All it really was John, Gary and a Moviola and this film recorder. It was all disorganized."

Taylor saw an opportunity to not only spread his wings, but to jumpstart Triple-I's film division. It was nice and dandy to have slick computer graphics, but the graphics had to eventually tell a story if they would work in movies. He worked with Art Durinski, a tall and likable fellow, who digitized solid objects into a computer at Triple-I. Those objects were formed into a polygonal shape on the computer.

"Where on each point on a surface of an object, you would have to define to the computer the coordinates of that space—x, y and z space," explains Durinski. "Then point-by-point you would have to show how those points connected up to form lines, and then how those lines connected up to form surfaces."

Interestingly enough, Lisberger had scoped out Triple-I some years before. While working on *Animalympics*, he stopped by the fledgling company to see what kind of wonderful things they could create.

"At the time that he came, he basically just came to see what we could do," recalls Taylor. "*Tron* at that point was going to be entirely an animated film. It wasn't going to be live-action. It was going to literally be an entirely animated film. He wanted to do a test that he paid us for the MCP. Very simple test. Really just a simple geometric thing that rotated. So we did this test for him then he went away to keep working on the picture. I didn't see him for a long time."

More work poured into Triple-I with Taylor actively seeking more projects. The company produced a number of computer graphics for print ads, logos and commercials. But Taylor desired to work on feature films. Producer Howard Jeffrey approached Taylor to do the visual effects on a new film called *Looker*, which would be released in 1981. Taylor jumped at the opportunity. The film was directed by Michael Crichton (*Westworld*—1973).

One of the biggest achievement's of *Looker* was to scan actress Susan Dey into a computer. The only way the visual effects team could this was by drawing precise intersecting lines on her skin. Durinski used a huge mouse device to tell the computer which points were being scanned. The computer rendered a simulated image of her body. For the time, this was quite a breakthrough in filmmaking. Unlike *Tron* where computer animation would be fully rendered as a scene, the imagery of Dey's computerized avatar was used only on computer monitors within scenes.

To further expand the business image of Triple-I, Taylor saw to it that the company should have an incredible demonstration film. The result was a short demo reel that combined Triple-I computer animation from its archives with footage of new character called Adam Powers. This was one of the earliest computer simulated human characters known to have been put on film.

Though it might be lost on today's technically sophisticated audiences, the Adam Powers demo was quite revolutionary. The tuxedo wearing juggler was articulated, where just a few years before, digital characters had little movement. He was dimensional like a real human being.

"That was really the first mo-cap, by the way," says Taylor. "I shot a real juggler in leotards with black spheres with all these different points on the body. We shot him with three cameras simultaneously. Front view, side view and top view. Then we made prints of every frame. Those were put on a big digitizing tablet and those points were digitized in. We had these points to animate the skeleton of the character."

Motion capture has since been used extensively on films like *The Lord of the Rings* series and in a number of films by director Robert Zemeckis like *Beowulf* (2007). Director James Cameron put his own spin on mo-cap in *Avatar* (2009).

What set the Adam Powers demo miles above almost any computer simulation of the time was its camera movement. With computer simulation, a theoretical digital movie camera within the computer had no limitations. Jim Blinn's NASA Jupiter fly-by simulations, and even those from MAGI Synthavision, had impressive camera movement. But in Triple-I's demonstration reel, camera movement became more refined and smoothly rendered. The short impressed attendees at that year's SIGGRAPH convention and placed Triple-I at the forefront of computer simulation.

Lisberger, who had long admired Taylor's work and remembered what he saw at Triple-I, came back with a proposal.

"He had already made a partial deal with Disney," says Taylor. "They were telling him they liked the project and it was moving along and they were doing script rewrites. Steve had already made the decision that it was going to be a live-action film."

Over dinner to brainstorm ideas for *Tron*, Lisberger hired Taylor as the film's co-visual effects supervisor. The film was such a large-scale production that it required the expertise, patience, and visual effects knowledge of two supervisors. Taylor brought his "candy apple neon" look to the film, as well as his expertise on computer simulation.

Taylor's visual effects partner had three major jobs—supervision of the film's practical visual effects, making sure the practical visual effects matched the computer simulations, and to make sure that over 600 people working on the production were happy.

## HARRISON ELLENSHAW

Harrison Ellenshaw had just finished work on *The Empire Strikes Back* and was back at Disney to help fix the studio's embarrassing headache, *The Watcher in the Woods*. The "new Disney" began to have a reputation for not knowing what it was doing. Ellenshaw, who was now known as one of the industry's top visual effects wizards, was thrown into reworking a new and improved ending for the film.

Though he had left Disney to work on occasional outside productions like *The Empire Strikes Back*, Ellenshaw had his finger on the pulse of the studio. While working on *The Watcher in the Woods*, Ellenshaw heard rumblings of *Tron* being made on the Disney studio lot.

"Every studio turned it down," says Ellenshaw. "But Disney had, a little bit reluctantly but not too much, embraced this idea. Disney wanted to take these chances. Ron Miller and Tom Wilhite, the two people responsible for films at Disney, decided to take probably one of the biggest gambles they could."

Lisberger and Kushner hired Ellenshaw to co-supervise the visual effects and to be the studio liaison between the young outsiders and the Disney veterans.

"Part of my job was to bridge the gap between the old timers and these new kids who all seemed to wear black leather jackets and were hugely mistrusted," says Ellenshaw. "They talked about backlight compositing and glows and doing things on animation stands that weren't done."

The film was as intriguing to Ellenshaw as it was to everyone else coming on board. After viewing the extensive storyboards and reading Lisberger's script, he was overwhelmed by the scope of *Tron*. It was a new frontier that even this *Star Wars* veteran could not fathom at first.

"I can't even remember if I asked specific questions like, 'How does it get from the computer onto film?'" says Ellenshaw. "It was so compelling. It was just like this was going to be a lot of fun and a lot of work. But I was young and I didn't mind that."

As pre-production moved forward, Lisberger and Kushner gave Ellenshaw an additional credit as "associate producer."

"They were good enough—I don't know if was a reward or punishment—to call me an associate producer, which these days is a rather disingenuous title."

The reason for this elevated title for Ellenshaw was due to the studio's reluctance to hire outsiders to work inside the studio. Much of the studio staff, especially in camera, effects and animation was older than the outsiders coming into work on *Tron*. Many of the old timers were very much set in their ways.

Making *Tron* was something almost alien to the older staff at the studio. Disney, like most animation studios, placed their backgrounds and cels on an animation stand. A camera was mounted above the animation cel and lit from above. In *Tron* most of the animation was going to be lit from behind and special filters were to be inserted in front of the camera lens. This was Taylor's "candy apple neon" backlight compositing method and it was unheard of at Disney.

"I remember one of the executives at Disney saying to me in a very patronizing manner, *Tron* was nothing new," recalls Ellenshaw. "'We know how to make things glow and we always have.' I thought, well, that's an interesting statement. Then why am I having to go and hire a lot of people to make things glow if you have people who can make things glow? But that was the attitude."

Ellenshaw did not have the opportunity to raid other departments for assistance, even if he wanted to. Many of the resources were taken up on completing films for EPCOT. That was okay with Lisberger and Kushner. They wanted hip animators to create the world of *Tron*. They did not necessarily need animators steeped in Disney tradition.

The hiring of Ellenshaw was ingenious on the part of Lisberger and Kushner. Ellenshaw was the key tie to the studio's past, recent past, and future. Only in his mid-thirties, he was already an experienced visual effects artist. By the time he worked on *The Empire Strikes Back*, he was considered by many who worked with him to be a natural leader.

In keeping the Ellenshaw family tradition alive at Disney, Harrison hired his younger sister, Lynda.

"It was my first job on a feature film and I was merely an assistant scene coordinator (working directly with scene coordinator, Don Button.)," recalls Lynda.

The experience of working not only on *Tron*, but with her big brother, would become an invaluable experience for her.

"The funny thing I remember is that I was working in Disney's Sales Processing Department after graduating from U.C. Irvine," continues Lynda. "It was a clerical job processing orders for 8mm films. I had been at the job about a year when I asked (begged) Harrison if he had any jobs available on *Tron*. He told me he wouldn't hire me. When I asked why, he said 'Because if you aren't any good, I won't be able to fire you!' (He denies this story.) Well, I guess they were desperate as I got the job and I became the youngest salaried employee on the lot. I worked for eight months on the film—never did get fired!"

Ellenshaw's personality showed confidence and likability. With his charming demeanor, both subordinates and high ranking executives found they could trust in him to lead the massive project. He could be a lot of fun to work for, but he was a professional who knew that time equaled money.

His ties with Disney went back to his childhood. He had grown up during Walt's time, and learned the craft of visual effects in the decade after Walt's death. Although there was life being infused in the studio with the arrival of *Tron*, there was still a lot of apprehension. Many who had been at Disney were scared about the studio's future.

"You had studios that were starting to make films reflective of the times," says Ellenshaw. "Disney and Walt himself probably wouldn't have gone in that direction. People didn't want to go to Disneyland, for God's sake, in the 1960s and see a ride that included hippies and a love-in. That's insanity. That's crazy. People would've walked away. They went to Disneyland and they went to Disney movies as escapism. So the studio had no real motivation to change, nor should they."

Ellenshaw was certainly one who admired the past accomplishments of the studio. He held high regard for Walt and Roy in what they accomplished. He had known Roy E. Disney, Diane Disney and Ron Miller for years. He knew most, if not all, of the original animators and artists on the lot. His father was close friends with Walt. Disney was a huge part of Ellenshaw's life.

But like many of his peers at the studio who grew up with Disney, he wanted to do something grand. *The Black Hole* only gave him an inkling of what the studio could do. Working on *Tron* was the perfect opportunity.

## BRUCE LOGAN, A.S.C.

To film *Tron's* live-action scenes and extensive visual effects sequences, which would be added in later in post-production, the film required an accomplished cinematographer.

Born outside of London, Bruce Logan had grown up by the seaside making short cartoons in his room. He used an unusual French-made camera that shot film on 9.5mm film stock. Most

American amateur/semi-professional film gauges (the size of the film) were 8mm, Super 8mm and 16mm. With his experience in animation and film gauges, he became proficient with film cameras.

Logan was hired to shoot visual effects in Kubrick's *2001: A Space Odyssey*. He worked alongside Douglas Trumbull for about two-and-a-half years creating the film's elaborate and groundbreaking visual effects. Logan then decided to join Trumbull in the United States. Their first major project together was an elaborate visual effects scene for director Michelangelo Antonioni's *Zabriskie Point* (1970). The scene took place in the desert.

"The end of the movie is probably in this guy's [lead character] imagination, but the whole world blows up," says Logan. "We did all these destruction shots of Los Angeles. We let off thousands of pounds of napalm and shot them with high-speed cameras. I believe the shot never got used in the picture. I went to a screening of *Blade Runner* that Doug Trumbull was speaking at, and he told me then the footage we'd shot of *Zabriskie Point* ended up being the explosion at the beginning of *Blade Runner*."

Logan's cinematography skills got him behind the camera as the director of photography on *Big Bad Mama* (1974), *Jackson County Jail* (1976), *I Never Promised You a Rose Garden* (1977), and *The Incredible Shrinking Woman* (1981). In that time span he was in charge of second-unit photography (miniature and optical effects) on *Star Wars* and additional photography on *Star Trek: The Motion Picture*.

"I don't know where Steven got my name from, but I got the call," says Logan. "I think Steven really wanted me. I guess we really hit it off and there it was."

Logan's expertise in various lenses, lighting and film formats came into play on *Tron* in more ways than one. It was such an unusual film that it required unconventional ways to bring its effects to life. No other film in history used so many different filmmaking formats as this film did. If ever there was a hybrid of analog and digital techniques, *Tron* used them.

By the time Logan had been signed on to shoot *Tron*, a decision had to be made in how to shoot the film. The characters of the "Electronic World" were supposed to glow with energy coursing through their digital circuitry. This is where Taylor's signature "candy apple neon" glow was to be implemented. How could this be accomplished? There was no such thing as Photoshop or After Effects to simply add in the glow to the live-action characters.

The only way to feasibly perform this task was to optically enlarge (also known as blow-up) the "Electronic World" footage to Kodaliths. Each frame of that footage would be inked and painted by artists to give the characters their "candy apple neon" glow. The footage being shot for *Tron* had to be ultra sharp and bright in order to create healthy Kodaliths.

There were four choices in which to shoot *Tron*.

Method one was to shoot on conventional 35mm film. The problem was the live-action footage that had to be blown up to the Kodaliths would be very grainy. In addition, the amount of composites needed would eventually degrade the film's quality even more.

Method two was to shoot the "Electronic World" in 65mm, and the "Real World" scenes in standard anamorphic 35mm. That could create an uneven final print where the 65mm footage would look super sharp and clear, while the 35mm footage would be less refined. Not a deal breaker, as *Close Encounters of the Third Kind* used this method with excellent results. But Logan and Lisberger were looking for a consistent look.

Method three could use anamorphic lenses and shoot in 35mm for the "Real World" scenes, then film the "Electronic World" scenes in VistaVision. But VistaVision cameras were noisy. The blow-up to the Kodalith cels could still utilize a sharp and fine grain image, but not as good as 65mm film could offer.

"I used the VistaVision cameras on *Incredible Shrinking Woman* and it really wasn't something you could make a movie with," says Logan. "The [film] reload was so hard. You have to shoot inside this huge blimp. Shooting in 65mm was a much more friendly format for a live-action motion picture, and that's what basically what we were shooting."

Thus, method four was to shoot the entire film in 65mm.

"The studio was pushing to shoot the live action in 35mm, and just shoot the stuff that we needed, the effects, in 65mm," says Logan. "Both Steven and I pushed really hard to shoot the whole picture in 65mm just so that it had a consistency of a really fine high-resolution look."

Logan decided to shoot the film on soundstages with black backgrounds rather than white backgrounds. The backgrounds were to be "keyed" out later and the computerized world of *Tron* would be inserted later behind the actors. The white backgrounds were originally used on the screen tests at Disney with Frisbee expert, Sam Schatz. But Logan felt that lighting white backgrounds would take too long.

It was also decided to shoot the film in both black-and-white and in color. The "Real World" scenes would be shot in color, while the "Electronic World" scenes would be shot in black-and-white. Shooting in black-and-white gave the effects crew the ability to add the "candy apple neon" glow to the "Electronic World" in post-production. VistaVision would also be used in compositing the Kodaliths.

Logan chose to shoot with Super Panavision 70 cameras, which he had been familiar with since he used them on *2001: A Space Odyssey*. There have been rumors that these were the same cameras used on *Lawrence of Arabia*, but even Logan is not sure.

## ROSANNA NORTON

The beautifully drawn costumes by Moebius (Syd Mead also did a number of sketches for the production) required a costume designer to bring them to life. By the 1980s, fashion made it possible to create costumes that hugged the body. Clothing and fabrics in the early 1980s had advanced so much that it was not unusual to see women dressed in Spandex leotards at the gym.

Rosanna Norton was a rebellious blonde-haired UCLA student who protested the Vietnam War during the 1960s. After signing petitions, as many college students did back then, she ended up on Richard Nixon's infamous "list." That did not stop her film career from flourishing.

After being the costume designer on Brian DePalma's mid-1970s films, *Phantom of the Paradise* (1974) and *Carrie*, (1976), Norton went onto work on *Airplane!* (1980). She had finesse and talent to design almost any kind of costume, from funky 1970s threads for the high school kids who tormented Sissy Spacek, to the period costumes in Robert Zemeckis' directing debut, *I Wanna Hold Your Hand* (1978). *Tron* was the most unique and challenging job of her young career.

"When I was brought in, I was like a technician," says Norton. "They had the drawings of all the characters. They were line drawings. They weren't colored or anything. I had to figure out how to make those things work on real people. Very difficult thing to do."

Moebius had done a terrific job in streamlining the look of the "Electronic World" beings. There was fluidity in the lines of the clothing they wore. There was a mixture of elegance and future punk. Envisioning the costumes was one thing. Actually making them to form-fit on actors was not that cut-and-dried. The costumes needed to be made from scratch and the "circuits" had to be silk screened on the costume. These faux circuit lines acted as guides for artists to later paint on the "candy apple neon" glow in post-production.

"The people who worked in the paint shop at the Disney studios helped me," says Norton. "We had to build forms to stretch the leotards on. We invented ways to make these wire forms that wouldn't snag the leotard and make them flat. We had to print one side, then we had to carefully print the other side. It had to be able to stretch. If you ever see a leotard, it's like pantyhose. It's got to stretch out on the person's body. It was technically very, very difficult."

The early stages of development on *Tron* included helmets on the "Electronic World" characters. Norton looked at different alternatives. Initially, helmets were sculpted at the Disney studio, but nothing seemed to work. Motorcycle helmets were tried, but they were too bulky and you could not see the actor's faces. It was decided to use hockey helmets. They were light weight, the actor's faces could clearly be seen, and they could be bought in any sporting goods store. To emphasize the imaginary circuitry coursing through the helmets, Taylor took each helmet home at night and painted and applied black circuitry.

## JEFF GOURSON

The production of *Tron* required someone with a good eye for cuts, as well as a person who could edit while the effects were being done. They found the perfect person to do it in film editor, Jeff Gourson.

He started as an assistant editor going back to Alfred Hitchcock's *Topaz* (1969). Eventually he found work on Steven Spielberg's *The Sugarland Express* (1974) and *Jaws* (1975) with famed editor Verna Fields as his mentor. His first major feature to edit for Universal Pictures was on *Somewhere in Time* (1980) and then he moved onto *The Incredible Shrinking Woman*. It was, according to Gourson, Bruce Logan who might have recommended him to edit *Tron*. Fields also gave him a high recommendation.

"Reading *Tron* for the first time was very interesting because the movie was practically all visual effects," says Gourson. "I did like the script and I knew that nothing has ever been done like this before on such a large scale. There were hundreds of storyboards that I would look at as I was reading to help me understand a lot of the visuals, since most of them were created during post."

He was hired about a week before production. Editing *Tron* was very different from editing a conventional film.

"On a normal production I would start receiving my dailies the next day," says Gourson. "This film was completely different. During pre-production, Bruce was doing a series of black & white developing tests. When they started production Bruce still wasn't satisfied with the look, so he wouldn't release the exposed negative to be developed or printed until he was satisfied, which was weeks into the production. I was able to spend a lot of time on the set which really helped me later on in the cutting room."

Set up in a large trailer on the Disney studio lot next to Lisberger's office, Gourson set to work for the next fourteen months. Usually films take between nine-to-eleven months to complete. Gourson was also the first editor on the Disney studio lot to use a KEM editing machine. Before digital editing, KEMs were state-of-the-art editing machines and many film editors used them. Disney's resident studio editors, like Cotton Warburton (*The Love Bug*), had been using the reliable, but old-fashioned Moviola for years.

## HIRING ARTISTS AND A PUBLICIST

Despite being funded and made on the Disney studio lot, most of the people who worked on *Tron* were hired from the outside. This was unprecedented for the studio, as it normally relied on inside artists, craftsmen, animators, directors and actors to make its films.

However, this was not the first time the studio hired or relied on an outside company to do work for them. It just was not preferred. In 1938, Walt hired his old animation friends, Hugh Harmon and Rudolf Ising, to make a *Silly Symphonies* short called *Merbabies*. In the late 1950s, Disney's distribution arm, Buena Vista, distributed a few films made by outsiders, including *The Big Fisherman*.

*Tron* required many talents that Disney, even if it wanted to at the time, could not and would not give up for the production. Disney animators were busy working on either completing *The Fox and the Hound*, or were toiling away on the seemingly endless production of *The Black Cauldron*. John Lasseter was one animator who wanted to dive into the world of the computer world of *Tron*. But he was so wrapped up in working on other Disney projects, the studio would not let him go.

Much of the studio staff concentrated on EPCOT. *Universe of Energy*, The American and French pavilions, *Spaceship Earth*, *World of Motion* and other attractions featured some type of film-related show. Some of the park's films were made independently, like the 70mm *Symbiosis*. In addition, films were being made and edited for Tokyo Disneyland, which was set to open in 1983. On the Disney back lot, a huge turn-of-the-century set was built for the film version of Ray Bradbury's work, *Something Wicked This Way Comes*.

Staff needed to be hired on *Tron*, and that meant hiring outsiders. Lisberger, Kushner, Taylor and Ellenshaw were the main guys doing the hiring. Taylor was responsible for coordinating the individual computer effects companies, Triple-I, MAGI, Digital Effects and Robert Abel and Associates. He also hired a number of outside people do perform various animation and background painting tasks. Ellenshaw also hired a number of animators, background artists, scene coordinators, and visual effects wizards.

## PETER LLOYD

To fill in the massive requirements of the effects animation department, Taylor looked up his old friend, Peter Lloyd. Lloyd was a renowned graphic artist who created some of the 1970s greatest album covers, including Rod Stewart's *Atlantic Crossing* album. Just like Taylor, he was adept in painting with near-transparent glows and striking color schemes.

"Richard knew Peter Lloyd and loved his work. I was very glad we got him," says Lisberger.

Because the film required teams of different artists and animators, they needed to get an idea of how the film would look as a whole. Lloyd's expertise came into play on the film's backgrounds and storyboards.

"No one had ever attempted backlit composting on the scale we were about to undertake," says Lisberger. "Richard and I knew the only way it was going to be possible was to turn it into a manufacturing system, that is standardized so teams of people would all be using interchangeable techniques. Creating this backlit schematic was a huge job in and of itself. And it meant it would be several months before finished backlit frames would be ready to look at. We needed to dial in our look beforehand and the only way was to do production paintings that mimicked backlit art. Peter's job involved taking art from Syd and Moebius and the storyboards, and sometimes his own, and using airbrush to render the look of the final scene. We called these paintings 'colorizations.'"

At this point in time, *Tron* had the equivalent of an all-star artistic line-up—Jerry Rees, Bill Kroyer, Richard Taylor, Steven Lisberger, Syd Mead, Moebius, Harrison Ellenshaw, John Norton, Jesse Silver, John Van Vliet and Peter Lloyd.

Lloyd's contribution to the look of *Tron* was not lost on those who worked with him. His airbrush paintings of the Solar Sailer, the tanks, Light Cycles and the MCP were mesmerizing. Much of the look of his work found itself into the final film.

"What Peter did was beautiful, sometimes too much," recalls Lisberger, "because the mass production techniques required to backlight hundreds of thousands of frames in the 'Electronic World' could not always match Peter's individual paintings, even when that was our intention. Peter would ask me why I changed this or that decades later."

"Peter did the original drawings then passed them on to the Background Department have the lines inked," recalls Taylor. "Then other airbrush artists added the grads. He also worked with Steven and me on the layout of many of the posters, especially the one with Jeff in the Light Cycle in the foreground with Tron and Yori standing in the middle with the Solar Sailer in the background. Peter was extremely prolific. The amount of colorizations he'd do a day was astounding. As an illustrator, his technique was flawless."

Lloyd passed away in 2009.

"Even though we didn't see each other much over the last years, we got to talk," says Taylor. "And through the years we'd have some long catch up phone calls. It's amazing how much you can miss a person you don't really get to see much. I truly miss the guy. He was a hero to me as an artist but even more as an example of a really good man."

## JESSE SILVER

Many of the people who worked on *Tron* attribute Ellenshaw for giving them a break in the first place. One of them was background artist, Jesse Silver. A rather tall, burly individual with a penchant for smoking a classic pipe, he was a gentle giant with amazing artistic talent, but had not found much work in film.

"I first met Harrison about two years prior starting work on *Tron*," says Silver. "I was making the rounds trying to get started in the film business. I went over to Disney. At that point I didn't have a reel. I didn't have a portfolio. I just had some of my original easel paintings. Harrison took a look. He said, 'I believe you have the makings and I think I could use you, and I'll give you a call when something comes along I think I could use you for.'"

Silver had a hard time finding work after that meeting. For two years, he toiled on occasional assignments, but finding steady work was tough. He was down to his last $30 when he decided he was going to quit his dreams of painting for movies. He was going to call his former boss in the jewelry business to see if he could get work. Just as he was about to pick up the phone, it rang.

Silver recalls, "I pick it up and the voice at the other end said, 'This is Disney Studios. Would you hold for Harrison Ellenshaw?' I thought it was a joke. I was about to slam down the receiver and I said wait a minute. It was Harrison! He asked if I would be available to come and work on this picture. Of course! I didn't tell him I was dying. 'Yeah, absolutely. Sure I think I can manage it.'"

## JOHN VAN VLIET AND GLENN CAMPBELL

John Van Vliet was another CalArts graduate who was beginning his career in the film business during the late 1970s just as the visual effects industry began taking off. He was at the school, for a time, with John Lasseter, Jerry Rees and Tim Burton.

"I was at CalArts during the same time period and shared many of the same instructors, but those guys were a year or two ahead of me," says Van Vliet. "I was a freshman when they were (I believe) juniors and seniors. But it's a testament to the quality of those early teachers in that so many movers and shakers came out of that school in a short time span. I believe it was the academic version of the perfect storm."

Van Vliet's first credit was a big one, animating laser beam shots in *The Empire Strikes Back*. Van Vliet was not just an animator who clocked in and clocked out. He genuinely had a creative drive to embellish or "plus" his animation. Working at ILM gave him freedom that he later found lacking at Disney.

"Way back when I worked on *Empire*, I was doing the laser scenes," recalls Van Vliet. "[He said to other ILM animators] 'You know what would be really cool is when he does this thing with the laser, why don't we use this glow trail like a video burn?' It was like yeah, we can do that! [Disney] was like no, no, no. We know what we want, just do it like it's been. I was like, 'Aw man, this would look great!'"

He was hired on *Tron* to perform effects animation, which gave the film its streaking glows and cool animated effects.

Glenn Campbell was another young man getting his start in the visual effects industry by performing photographic effects on *Star Trek: The Motion Picture*. His specialty was operating an effects camera that shot plates, cels and composited effects. Peter Anderson, a renowned cinematographer and visual effects genius, called Campbell to lead the camera department on *Tron*.

"I jumped at the chance when I got called," recalls Campbell. "They said we're doing this movie called *Tron*. By default, *Tron* means electronic. Sounds cool whatever it is. The place that did *Mary Poppins*? Count me in! I didn't even blink. Didn't have a script. He didn't even have to describe the movie to me."

Both Campbell and Van Vliet arrived on the lot around the same time, eyes wide open and jaws agape at their good fortune of working on the magical studio grounds. Just as the Lisberger Studios crew found out, the visual effects crew stepped into a time warp.

"I walked in like John and was given the grand tour and said, 'Gee, I was kind of expecting blinky lights and guys in white lab coats doing the latest stuff that even ILM doesn't have!' recalls Campbell. "We're Disney and we're innovating! Instead, it was 1967. It was just frozen in time."

"They had the resources," says Van Vliet. "They had people. They had it all. There was so little communication going on that's where the big problem was. And that was part of the frustration. When I got the call to come down there, Disney, my God, I'm going to the Holy Grail and I was really excited. This is the place that did *Mary Poppins*, the film that made me go crazy."

## MICHAEL BONIFER

Michael Bonifer was another young person with enough crazy ideas and passion to do something spectacular once he arrived at Disney. Born in Indiana and raised with strong family values, he went to Notre Dame, graduated and went into freelance writing.

"I had been living in Chicago and I had written a book, a funny history of Notre Dame football called *Out of Bounds*," says Bonifer. "I was pretty much broke in the worst winter in history. There was a reception for my book in Chicago. Celebrity writer, Aaron Gold, who wrote for the *Chicago Tribune*, was there. He did some voodoo horoscope thing. I said I was going to move to New York or L.A. He would ask me, 'What do you drink? Beer drinker, right?' Yeah! 'What's your sign?' Capricorn. He goes, 'L.A.' I packed up and got the hell out of Chicago."

With his portfolio of clips that he had written in Chicago, Bonifer had a hard time getting work once he was in Los Angeles. When Wilhite was still Head of Publicity, he hired Bonifer and the two Midwesterners hit it off.

"We both had this love of the entertainment business and infatuation with movies, sort of this special place for Disney. Really believed in it," recalls Bonifer. "A lot of our friends in the business would make fun of Disney. Wilhite's friend, David Clark, used to rag our asses. He would call it the studio that time forgot. Meanwhile, we were having the time of our lives. The young people ruled the fucking studio."

Bonifer was soon shown the fantastic presentation of *Tron*. He was immediately hooked on Lisberger's vision.

"I don't think there was any doubt that I was going to be the publicist on this," says Bonifer. "We were all getting our first computers at the time. Nobody wanted to know about computers. Everybody was scared of computers, a little bit I think. I started trying to figure out what the hell computers were doing to make graphics."

Bonifer loved the fact he was in the presence of greatness. Truth be told, almost everyone working on *Tron* had deep respect for the old timers at Disney.

"Nobody was thumbing their noses," says Bonifer. "We were celebrating. We loved it. We couldn't explain it to our hipper-than-thou friends. We knew it was really cool."

# Chapter 10

# *PRODUCTION BEGINS*

When Kushner and Lisberger negotiated the film with Disney, the original budget was not anything to brag about. Ideally, Lisberger was looking to make an avant-garde experimental movie that would not require a lot of money.

"Originally it was pitched as a four-and-half million dollar movie and it increased as it went along," says Kushner. "We used the old adage, get them to spend more. Once the studio starts spending money, they're making a movie. At that point in time, they see something they like, they're going to spend more money."

As the production neared, the budget shot up. The need for hiring animators, effects experts, and computer wizards required a lot more capitol. The techniques of backlight compositing and the use of computer animation had never been done on this scale.

Wilhite approved a budget of $12,388,000 for *Tron*. It may seem low by today's standards, but back in 1981 this was a considerable sum, especially for Disney. The studio spent far less money on its films, with the exception of its animated features and *The Black Hole*.

The budget for *Tron* was not huge compared to what other studios had been spending over the last few years. Between 1979 and 1980, there were hugely inflated budgets on a number of film productions. *The Empire Strikes Back, Raise the Titanic! The Blues Bros., Popeye, The Shining, Flash Gordon, 1941, The Wiz, Apocalypse Now, Xanadu, Star Trek: The Motion Picture*, and *Heaven's Gate* had huge cost overruns in the range of $25 million to over $40 million. By 1981, most studios had scaled back after a number of those films flopped. The average budget for films going into production in 1981 was between $10 million and 17 million.

## SCREENPLAY

Lisberger's *Tron* script was constantly revised before production and during production. The script was considered cold and lacked basic human emotion. Much of the dialogue was infused with technical terminology and computer gags that ultimately went over the audience's head. The only people who understood the terms were those steeped in computers. Screenwriter

Charlie Haas (*Tex*—1982) was hired and added humor to the script, but the story was still considered convoluted.

Seen in 1982, the screenplay was confusing, but it had many merits. Lisberger always considered the script and film as an avant-garde piece, rather than a commercial film.

"The movie is, and I think, remains in terms of the electronic look, avant-garde," says Lisberger. "Who back then expected avant-garde or experimental from Disney Studios No one. And they still can't get over that. There's still a misconception of what that movie was. They still somehow think Disney tried to do 'just a video game movie.' No! No! No! The corporate types at Disney had no idea what the actual artists who were making the film were attempting. They had no clue. They do now."

For a first-time writer/director, Lisberger was given considerable leeway in the production, especially with the script. Though it was far from perfect, the script was brave in its attempt to create two worlds, the "Real World" and the "Electronic World." In these two different worlds, Lisberger's script has considerable themes throughout.

## USERS, PROGRAMS AND DUALITY

"Users" are real living people in the "Real World." They have created the beings inside the computer's "Electronic World." These beings are a human's alter ego called "Programs." The programs carry our identity. This could be our driver's license number, our Social Security number, or our credit card number. The programs, the good ones and the bad ones, are mostly indebted to their user and want to do everything they can to please him or her.

"Americans struggle with duality all the time," says Lisberger. "Duality has traditionally never been easy for an American audience. The American audience tended to be very linear. Look, *Wizard of Oz* was no hit when it came out. If you look at every movie, every story like *Alice in Wonderland*, a story that says there is one world, and then there is another world, people have had a problem with it. The digital world has changed all that."

In the early 1980s, computer experts and hobbyists understood the concept of users and programs. They programmed their computers to tell them what they wanted them to do. As computers became more user friendly over the years, human users did not have to think about programming to get their programs to do tasks. Programs eventually became smart enough on their own to handle most mundane jobs. But in the early 1980s, this was something very new and intimidating to most people. The only mainstream computers people used were simple arcade machines or calculators.

Today it is not uncommon for people to carry a personal computer in their pocket or purse. An iPhone is not only a phone but a personal computer that handles a person's information, phone numbers, addresses, emails, etc. It is a super computer. What is making the iPhone tick? Programs. Who makes the programs work? Users.

Lisberger's script also delves into spirituality. The programs are consistently looking for clues and messages from their users. According to Kushner, Ellenshaw, and Lisberger on the 2002 DVD, a scene was added later. In one of the film's significant scenes, Tron has fought hard to reach the I/O Tower to send a message to his user, Alan Bradley. Once he has snuck inside Dumont's cathedral within the I/O Tower, Dumont the shaman prays with Tron and Yori before he lets Tron send his message. Inside of the I/O Tower, Tron uses his "Identity Disc" to receive instructions on taking out the MCP. As he stands ready to send his message, Tron is bathed in a powerful heavenly ray of light from above.

"Technology has divided our reality in the digital realm and the real world, so we seek wholeness and unity," says Lisberger. "The image of the disc held overhead is that symbol of the new unity."

The film, on the whole, touches on what human life means in the realm of our own universe. The programs within in the "Electronic World," like most humans, ask themselves why am I here? Who created me and this reality?

"I guess the underlying ethos for that is that we haven't been able to resolve the mysteries of this reality," says Lisberger. "We construe all sorts of religions, suspicions and scientific theories to try to explain that which really doesn't want to be explained so easily in this reality. And I think we find that really frustrating."

He continues, "We're not really even sure who we're supposed to thank for this heaven of a planet that we've been given. When we build an exact copy of this world in cyberspace, there won't be any mysteries because we will have rendered every bit and written every goddamned zero. And we'll know exactly how it works, and we'll know exactly who to thank and who to blame. But the downside is that cyberspace makes us feel we know everything when we don't. I really believed in cyberspace as having to do with the future and the unknown, and therefore being a mirror of the best and the worst in us. That was all in there. And the years that have gone by, people come up to me and say, 'Are all those spiritual concepts in there intentional?' They really are."

The screenplay and film touch on the frontier of computers and cyberspace. Both were meant to help humans and make the world a better place. Ideas and methods of helping each other out were some of the promises of this technology. Instead, the Ed Dillingers of the world got their hands on the electronic frontier. Where computers were meant to educate, entertain and create, they have become, to a degree, corrupted with pornography, slander, and viruses designed to destroy.

"The amazing thing, if you look at American history, it goes through these cycles and it takes a long time," says Lisberger. "But in cyberspace, we did it in record time. We found a frontier. We made it safe. We corrupted it. And we turned it into a fool's paradise, in what, fifteen years?"

## THE HACKER, VIOLENCE WITHOUT GUNS AND A LOVE TRIANGLE

In another one of Lisberger's prognostications, we see perhaps for the first time in a feature film a computer hacker. Only in this story, Kevin Flynn is a good guy. He is out to prove he created *Space Paranoids* and other games that Dillinger stole from him. In later films that came out after *Tron*, audiences became more privy to computer hackers in movies such as *WarGames* (1983) and *Die Hard* (1988). When *Tron* was released in 1982, the idea of a hacker was alien.

The concept of the boomerang-like "Identity Discs" came from Lisberger's knowledge of the mandala. Although beings in the "Electronic World" are derezzed (i.e. zapped out of existence), Lisberger was keen on keeping the violence down.

"I love the idea that there were no hand guns in an action-adventure movie," says Lisberger. "I don't think there's been too many action-adventure movies without guns. The only personal weapon is a glowing Frisbee. And that Frisbee is a symbol of self. It is Jungian icon. A mandala. What you know and what you are is your mandala. The disc has become the icon of our age."

The love triangle between the three leads, both in the "Real World" and the "Electronic World," was later criticized for not being developed enough. Love triangles had been used for ages in plays, books and films. In *Tron*, Flynn used to be Lora's boyfriend and now she is dating Alan. Once Flynn is beamed into the "Electronic World," he recognizes Lora's virtual twin, Yori, and creates friction between him and Tron.

Flynn, while in the "Electronic World," notices Yori and her resemblance to Lora. Tron steps between them and Flynn playfully backs away. We see a twinkle in his eye. In the final act of the script, as Flynn is about to jump into the energy beam of the MCP, he gives her a passionate kiss goodbye. Yori certainly likes to play the electronic field. Unfortunately, the love triangle is not played up much more than in those scenes.

"I thought it was one of the things that could've been better in the script," recalls Bridges. "There could've been more love triangle I think between, Flynn, Yori, and Tron. I think that could've been more fleshed out."

## THE INVENTION OF ENCOM

The concept of the corporate video game giant, ENCOM, emulated some of the companies like Atari. By the time *Tron* was in pre-production, Atari had invaded arcades with *Asteroids*, *Centipede* and *Battlezone* video game machines. Perhaps an even larger impact came from their invasion of the home video game market. Since 1977, when the company introduced its "Video Computer System" (VCS, later known as the 2600), Atari was clearly the market leader in home video games. By 1980, the company was a part of Warner Communications and now had the marketing muscle to get its games into the public's eye.

Atari founder Nolan Bushnell ruffled the feathers in the company's upper management, leading to its sale to Warner Communications (now Time/Warner). There were other unhappy people at Atari who shook up the establishment, as well. At issue for some game designers at Atari was their lack of getting recognition. They spent countless hours developing games for the company for very little money and no recognition. The company was raking in millions and took the credit for creating those video game hits.

Tired of feeling neglected, designers David Crane, Alan Miller, Larry Kaplan and Bob Whitehead, known as the "Gang of Four," founded Activision. Taking their considerable talent with them and thumbing their noses at their former employer, they created some of the era's most popular games for the Atari 2600. Games included *Freeway*, *Dragster*, and *Kaboom*!

Flynn's fight against ENCOM somewhat parallels the Activision story. Here was a brilliant guy who created some of the world's most popular video games, only to have his ideas stolen from him. Not that Atari stole from the future Activision gang, but the company certainly took the credit.

What really blew fans of *Tron* away, years after it was released, was the fact that ENCOM's name sounded like modern company names like 3-Com. In the original scripts by both Lisberger and MacBird, the company was called AIC.

"I ask myself how did I stumble upon calling the corporation in that movie ENCOM? Like 'dot com?' There was no 'com.' Dot com hadn't been invented yet. And that corporation is called EN-COM. That one even freaks me out!" exclaims Lisberger.

## PRODUCTION BEGINS AT THE LAWRENCE LIVERMORE LABORATORIES

Production began on April 20, 1981 at the Lawrence Livermore Laboratories. The facility is located in the scenic hills of Livermore, California, approximately forty-three miles east of San Francisco. This might seem like an unlikely place to shoot a movie about being sucked into a computer. But it was actually perfect for it.

"The big set we had, the big location, was the Lawrence Livermore Lab," says Kushner. "That was very difficult. Really, we didn't have that secured up until three weeks before we went up there. Somehow they changed their mind. We had a lot of trouble. First they said yes, then they said no. We started making some friends."

Rather than build a huge set, or possibly have Ellenshaw paint mattes, Kushner negotiated with the powers-that-be at Lawrence Livermore to shoot there. The laboratory was a top-secret government facility, specializing in laser technology, nuclear arms, and computers for various government projects for national security. The biggest and most secretive device at Lawrence Livermore was a state-of-the-art and powerful laser nicknamed "SHEVA." The lab was also one of the early computer pioneers in the world, having once housed a Univac computer and Cray Computer.

One of the earliest scenes in the film takes place inside the ENCOM laboratory. It opens with a spectacular shot of a multilevel maze of staircases and bridges that go several stories high. This is where the characters of Alan, Lora, and Gibbs meet for the first time in the film. This sequence sets up what will happen to Flynn a short time later.

Both Gibbs and Lora, donning lab coats and safety goggles, use a huge laser device to "derezz" an orange as part of an experiment to turn matter into anti-matter, then back to matter again. The laser flares up and the fruit, via computer monitor, is virtually sliced into pieces, disappears, then reforms perfectly within seconds. It is reminiscent of science fiction films where people are teleported or beamed to another place (i.e. *Star Trek*). Later in the film, Flynn hacks into the MCP and then is beamed into the computer by the MCP to battle for his life. This scene in the film was shot in part of an actual laser bay called NOVA at Lawrence Livermore.

Each member of the cast and crew had background checks done before they could set foot in Lawrence Livermore. Everyone was cleared, except for Norton. Because of her involvement with the UCLA protests, being on Nixon's list caused her some problems in getting into Lawrence Livermore. Security eventually figured out she was an upstanding citizen and she was cleared to work.

Logan did not have any trouble getting into Lawrence Livermore. Once he was inside during production, he had some issues with security.

"I'm a British citizen," chuckles Logan. "The first time I went there I didn't have any trouble just scouting the location. But when it came to shooting, I had a guy who was assigned specifically to me to watch me the entire time I was there. So this guy followed me to the bathroom. It was pretty interesting."

Along with security clearances, all of the production equipment had to be cleaned before entering.

"Every light that came in there had to go through a surgical process," says Logan. "It had to go through the cleaner room. It had to be sucked and scanned before it entered the area."

Once inside, Logan figured he would use the fluorescent lighting already installed in the lab. On shoots with that type of lighting, it can be necessary to use filters to correct the color of light coming into the camera lens. Shooting without a filter on a film camera ellicits a blue tone to the film, which can look unacceptable to a cinematographer. Logan chose a different route.

"I let them go blue and I lit with orange light," recalls Logan. "By using the orange light, then correcting out the orange light, the fluorescents went kind of a dim blue which gave it kind of a really nice kind of rich fill light to it."

According to Kushner, the shoot at Lawrence Livermore only lasted about five days, but it would turn out to be memorable. Morgan decided she did not want to waste time in getting to the make-up room. She took a short cut.

"I think so far outside the box, I don't see the box," says Morgan. "There was this roped off area and I just cut right across it. Suddenly everyone says STOP! FREEZE! I froze. I had walked into what apparently was a bit of a spill or a leak or something. Somebody came over, very carefully, and cleaned whatever was on my shoes and got me the heck out of what I stepped into. It was roped off for a reason."

## NOW THAT'S A BIG DOOR!

Flynn hacks a security panel to get Alan, Lora and himself inside the lab. Flynn, with his playful demeanor, watches a gigantic door slowly open as he grins at Alan and Lora. To Lisberger's dismay, Bridges improvised one of the film's famous lines.

"Now that's a big door."

This line gets one of the biggest laughs in the film. Lisberger was shooting for a straight forward approach to his lines of dialogue.

What audiences also could not help but notice was the giant ENCOM security door. It opens very slowly and seems to take forever. Many wondered if it was a real door. Turns out it was. The 97,000-lbs. door was located at the Lawrence Livermore's Rotating Target Neutron Source II facility.

"Its purpose was to provide high intensities of 14 MeV neutrons for materials studies in the fusion energy program," says Don, a physicist who worked at the lab during the production of *Tron*. His last name was not given due to security purposes.

Despite the size and weight of the door, it was built on a special hinge that allowed for one person to open it. The door could also be opened via remote control.

After sneaking into ENCOM's lab, Lora leads Flynn upstairs to her desk where there is a computer hooked up. She tells him not to screw up her life's work, the derezzing laser, and leaves him alone to hack into the MCP. Instead of listening to Lora's request, he enrages the MCP and is beamed into the "Electronic World."

# Chapter 11

# *IN THE ZONE*

After completion of filming at Lawrence Livermore, the production moved south to the Burbank Disney studio soundstages. Interestingly, *Tron* was shot on Stage #4 where *Darby O'Gill and the Little People* was filmed.

There was no precedent on building an "Electronic World" set because there really was no set. Bridges, Boxleitner, Morgan, Hughes and Shor had to rely on minimal props, their imagination, and Lisberger's direction to make believe they actually lived in the "Electronic World."

"Big black soundstage, which was just basically a big black warehouse," recalls Morgan. "Empty. Complete black, empty studio. Black, black, black."

Normally, visual effects of the 1980s required the use of large green or blue screens. Visual effects, sets, and animated characters were superimposed behind or with the actors later in post-production. Disney had used forms of "keying" out blank backgrounds for years in the *Alice Comedies, Song of the South* and *Mary Poppins,* for example.

*Tron* was to use a similar principle of placing the actors into the "Electronic World." Instead of using blue or green screens on the soundstage, set builders erected giant swaths of black material. The actor's costumes were white with black circuitry taped on their costumes. As the actor stood against the black background, he or she would stand out completely as a result of the color differences. The black circuitry on their costumes was to be painted with neon color in post-production.

The choice of black material for the soundstage was not so cut-and-dried.

"Most black cloth, if you put it at angle to the light, it has a sheen to it," explains Taylor. "We needed to have material that absorbed light so we didn't get a lot of reflections."

"For the black we used two types of paper," recalls Ellenshaw. "One was matte black and one was paper with a peach fuzz-like black side to it—very much like velvet. This was the preferred material since it absorbed light better than just matte black paper. But the manufacturer ran out of the good stuff and for some reason couldn't make more. Black velvet was not used—too expensive, as I recall."

Since black soaks in so much light, Logan had his crew light up the soundstage with nearly every available light he could get his hands on. Not only that, Logan had to consider other potential problems that could come up once the 65mm footage was blown-up to the Kodaliths.

Logan explains, "When it came to shooting the electronic stuff, we'd have to have a really high f-stop. The bottom line is that shooting something photographic and you have all these very fine lines, any time you have motion blur, those lines just disappear as far a graphic image goes. They start blurring. We had to shoot not only a large depth of field between foreground and background objects, but also we had to shoot at an extremely narrow shutter angle. Something that was moving very fast, we'd have to go down to twenty-two degrees on the shutter. Each image is totally sharp, so when you make the Kodalith, there was no blur involved on the Kodalith. That would be an ugly artifact."

The production's use of electricity caused brown-outs in parts of the city, putting the City of Burbank on alert. The city could not at first figure out what was causing it. Tracing their grids pointed them directly to 500 South Buena Vista Street. This was the third time in Disney Studio history that either the Burbank Fire Department or power company had to intervene. *Darby O'Gill and the Little People* used up so much juice that the fire department had to be called. *The Black Hole* also used so much power that the city was in danger of a going into a brown-out.

"The City of Burbank shut us down twice during the production," says Logan. "'No more. Gotta shut you guys down.'"

"Because the set was so dark, all black, they were literally blowing out the transformers at the Burbank power station," says Fremer. "The only solution was to go to AC lighting, which would apparently not tax the grid as much. But no one's dressing the wires! The first I look at the dailies, I go in and I'm listening, there's a sixty-cycle hum!" exclaims Fremer.

That hum, along with many other production sound problems, cropped up and drove Fremer crazy.

The amount of lighting required on the film made the sets hot. Burbank gets cooking once spring and summer roll around. For the actors wearing the skintight costumes and hockey helmets, it became a struggle both on the set and off.

"The other thing I'm remembering that was very tough were the helmets, especially for me because Steve wanted the hair long and curly for Flynn," says Bridges. "We would shoot sometimes in the regular world, then we'd go back to the *Tron* world. So I would bleach my hair. Bleach continues to work on your hair after you do it. I would have my helmet on and the bleach would get so hot that my hair would break off."

Morgan had a different issue with the costume. Early during production, she had to wear a skull cap for her costume.

"That skull cap!" exclaims Morgan. "First of all, who looks good in something like that? Nobody. Secondly, that thing was fitted tight to my head. When it shifted, they [costume department] would yank on it. Now of course there are blisters after hours and days of this. And at one point, they started yanking on the goddamned blisters. That was the day I said I'm not wearing this damn thing one more minute. I grabbed one of the hockey helmets and I said we're doing the scene in this today."

With the costumes being skintight, Cindy Morgan's costume was more complimentary to her already fit body. Still, she wanted to make sure she fit into it perfectly.

"When I got the job," says Morgan, "I remember the second assistant director called me and left a message. She said, 'Where are you?' [I replied] 'I'm at the gym and I'm not leaving until I lose five pounds!'"

Bridges and Boxleitner, on the other hand, had their own issues. The costumes did not leave much to the imagination when it came to dealing with the male anatomy. Indeed, the film did have a major love scene in the script, but it was still under the guise of "PG" rated romance suitable for kids to watch. This was a Disney production, after all. In order to conceal the naughty bits, Norton resorted to dance belts. Male ballet dancers usually wore these uncomfortable devices to support their manhood while jumping around *Swan Lake*.

"I never got used to the dance belt," recalls Bridges. "It's like a jock strap that's two straps under your ass. You have one that goes right up your ass. Girls apparently enjoy that. They wear those thongs all the time."

Besides the dance belt, Bridges was not keen on the costume as a whole.

"You feel very exposed, the next thing to being naked, I guess. You kind of got used to that."

"There were no pants!" exclaims Boxleitner. "Where are the pockets? Where do I put my little script sides? It was about as close to being naked as you could be. It hid nothing. Thank God we were only thirty or thirtyone years-old and in good shape. I think there was a situation where we had to wear bathrobes if we went outside or to the commissary. The old secretaries were having the vapors with these young butt cheeks standing there."

The roles were reversed for Morgan. She got a kick out of watching the male actors twist and wriggle in their costumes.

"We have to wear crap like that all the time," says Morgan. "Welcome to my world."

One of the myths about Disney was a policy to make every one of its movie sanitized. While most of that is true, the studio did allow some nudity in at least one of its films, *Fantasia*. Centaurettes (half human, half horse) are easily seen strutting around the screen with bare topsides. In original sketches, the centaurette breasts are fully formed. In the film, they were brushed out, leaving just the shape. Morgan's costume and the way it was padded helped her character fit right in with the Disney female characters of the past.

"Now this is Disney," says Morgan. "Again we're making this perfectly formed woman. So they're getting me the bra, the perfect shape, and I'm looking in the Disney costume department. There's drawers and drawers of bras that have padding this and that and the other. [The costume department lady] took me in and said, 'Honey that's nothing. Let me take you on the guy's side.' They have drawers and drawers of padding, if you understand what I'm saying. It was easier for me than it was for them."

Morgan kept cool with her professionalism, as did Bridges, Boxleitner and Shor. But it was difficult not to notice Morgan in her skintight costume.

"Cindy Morgan would walk by," recalls Shor with a grin. "This is Lacy Underall. Cindy Morgan was stunningly beautiful. I mean ridiculous, and she was one of those beauties that was more beautiful in real life than on film. And she was wearing a skin tight pajama. Oh my God."

## PRETENDING

Sets for the "Electronic World" were built to give the actors some reference points. But even these were minimal. Sark's war room set consisted mainly of his control panel in which he talks to the MCP, and a rig hung from the soundstage rafters that held an actor above. The Solar Sailer consisted of a wooden control panel, steps, and a narrow walkway. The Game Grid set, in which Flynn battles an opponent with an "Electronic World" jai-alai scoop, consisted of giant white circles of white tape on the floor of the soundstage. The famous Light Cycles were not even built for the actors to use as references. Their cycles consisted of a wooden crate on which to stand or sit, and a piece of wood to use as their handlebar. With such minimal set dressing, it was sometimes tough for the actors to figure out what was going on.

"That was kind of a downside," says Bridges. "It sounds great, but once you get out there, the level of pretending that you have to do is quite immense. There is no big Master Cylinder [Master Control Program]? What's it called? None of those things. Basically you have some black velvet things and white adhesive tape around it to mark what you're looking at."

Acting in this environment of black space challenged Morgan. Lisberger did his best to direct her.

"Okay Morgan, you're on the Solar Sailer. You're crossing the Game Sea. Go!'

Morgan's eyes fixated blankly on the blackness of the set.

"What the hell are you talking about?" she questioned.

Lisberger took out sketches of the Solar Sailer and showed her where to go.

"And you're flying the ship," directed Lisberger.

"Another question—what the hell are you talking about *flying the ship*?" asked Morgan.

"That table there, that's the control panel," said Lisberger.

"You know Steven, there's nothing here," said Morgan.

"Just do anything and the artists will paint it in."

"There was concern you're either overacting or under acting," says Bridges. "You never really got a feeling of being in any sort of reality. So that was kind of tough. It was all going to be done after the fact. I remember we were all encouraged to wear colorful clothes, because for months we were all locked inside this big soundstage and everything was black and white."

As for Morgan, she needed more guidance from Lisberger.

"We're walking back from lunch one day," says Morgan. "I said, 'Steven. I was a sound engineer, and I worked a lot with computers. I don't understand what I'm saying a lot of the times. And if I don't know what I'm saying, how is anybody else going to know what I'm saying?' And Steven said, 'If they don't get it, then the movie's not for them.' And I said, 'But then Steven, they may not come to the movie.' And he said, 'That's okay.' So Steven stayed true to his dream which kept it standing the test of time."

As Morgan became more comfortable with Lisberger's vision, she realized how fun it was acting with Bridges and Boxleitner.

"And what a cool job to get two absolutely great-looking leading men," says Morgan. "This was like a dream job! I found nothing wrong with this job."

Lisberger, with his direction, was encouraging his actors to use their imagination, something that Morgan also appreciated.

"When you're a little kid and you're playing a game and you're riding an elephant, you don't have to see the elephant," says Morgan. "You just know you're riding the elephant. You have that sense of play. That was available to us. If nothing else, there was no reality."

Boxleitner had to deal with reality when it came to throwing a Frisbee. Effects animation would be added in post-production to give the Frisbee discs, or "Indentity Discs," their glow and streaks. Still, he had to train vigorously to make it look like he had been throwing Frisbees for years. He trained with Sam Schatz and became very proficient.

Boxleitner recalls, "Everyone thinks, 'Oh wow! Throwing a Frisbee, so what? What do you need training for that for?' I did. I had to do all these jumps and moves. Overhand and sidearm. Also, I had to deflect the ones that Schatz was throwing at me. Often times it was an actual Frisbee striking off of mine. And this guy was like lightning. Accurate! So I was really defending myself."

## VIDEO GAME CHAMPION

Movie sets are not always the beehive of activity seen in old 1940s movies. There can a lot of down-time. To counter boredom, and to get the everybody in tune with his vision, Lisberger had the latest arcade games installed on the set. This was brilliant, as it got the actors and crew addicted to what kids and teens were already addicted to—mind-blowing video games.

"Steve was kind of a big kid himself," recalls Bridges. "There wouldn't be too many directors or experienced directors around that would allow three video games on the set!"

"I didn't play games much then," recalls Taylor. "I got involved with them because of Jeff Bridges. We all started playing. And we had contests between ourselves. Bridges was really good. Everybody got really competitive."

Bridges schooled nearly everyone on the set with his game skills. On Atari's *Battlezone* he ran up the score and set the record. This got everyone else pumped up to take on arcade champion, Kevin Flynn.

Bridges says with a smile, "I encouraged that to happen. I've got to prepare as an actor. I need these games to get in the mood. So we would all have tournaments. We had a great time with that. Shots would be held up while somebody was in the zone."

"We were competing and Jeff Bridges would somehow always beat the high score," says Rees. "So one of us would go in and go, 'Aha, I got the high score.' Then Jeff would come in the *Tron* outfit and he'd get into the thing then he'd step away. Then you'd go look at the score. 'DAMN! He beat the high score!'"

Shor adds, playfully, "He got to steal and hog the machines because he was Jeff Bridges. Big star asshole. I love the guy! I was a better Frisbee player, I guarentee it. I practiced with the experts because I was supposed to look really good. So did he. I'll go [on record] that I was the better Frisbee player. I'll give him the computer game."

Bridges was such a tough and determined video game warrior that Lisberger wanted to study Bridges' intense facial reactions to the game play. He asked Ellenshaw to lie on the soundstage floor and videotape Bridges playing. Lisberger used those intense game-playing expressions of Bridges' face in the final film. Bridges was undeterred and still managed to hold the set record on *Battlezone* until he was dethroned by veteran make-up artist, Gary Liddiard.

The activity on the set was not constrained to video game playing. Boxleitner was an accomplished rancher and knew how to lasso. Bridges had a close friend and stand-in named Loyd Catlett, a veteran stuntman, who worked on *Tron*. While Bridges was off somewhere on the soundstage playing video games or listening to his Sony Walkman, Boxleitner and Catlett were busy causing their own mischief.

"Loyd and I would be standing there in our *Tron* outfits roping at chairs, practicing rope tricks," says Boxleitner. "We were hellions running around roping people by the legs and stuff."

But on quite a few occasions, it was Bridges who held up the production playing video games. He was still trying to break his scoring record.

"We had all these arcade games on the set, even when were doing stuff on the Grid," recalls Boxleitner. "The crew guys would be playing. I think it later proved to be a mistake, because there were too many people off playing these arcade games instead of paying attention to what they should be doing. They're calling for Jeff. 'Where's Jeff?' And Steven goes, 'Jeff! Where the heck are you?' You hear off in the distance, 'I'm over here! I'm preparing for my role!' He was on *Battlezone*. I know he took one machine as far as the people who invented the thing further than they thought it could go. He was the real deal."

## THE MEANING OF *TRON* AND RAM'S DEREZZ SCENE

For Lisberger, *Tron* was really about Flynn and his "Electronic World" creation.

"The story really is about how he doesn't take this world of these characters seriously because he built it all," says Lisberger. "It's just a bunch of bits and bytes on the Game Grid. What happens is after awhile he comes to appreciate this world and the people in it more and more. Then eventually he ends up being a hero there."

The most faithful program in the film was Ram. He is truly dedicated to serving the commands of his user. To round out his character, Shor channeled three different personalities.

"I think Ram is a little bit of me and a little bit of Lisberger," says Shor. "Lisberger was an incredibly positive guy. Ram is a love dog. He's like a spaniel who just is a lover and that's his gig to be of service. I thought of him as a dog the entire time. My relationship to all the characters, especially Flynn, was that of a dog. I approached it with that same zeal."

But Lisberger regretted not adding certain bits of dialogue to flesh out the film. After both Flynn and Ram are blasted out of their Light Cycles by a tank, Flynn takes Ram to a broken down Recognizer. In the completed scene, Ram dies. His death is taken seriously, then sadly, and then humorously by audiences. As he dies, he says to Flynn, "Oh my User. Users are users..." Even though Ram is stunned to realize Flynn is his creator, some of that is lost in Flynn's reaction.

"The scene where I'm dying, where I'm derezzed, and Jeff and I are looking into each other's eyes, it's like a silent love scene," recalls Shor. "The audience started laughing and I'm going, 'They're laughing at this? Oh I see why.' It's because it's romantic. It's a romance. It's not a gay romance. It's a computer romance."

"I wasn't sophisticated enough, in a couple places, to know what I had," laments Lisberger. "It might've been a good thing if Flynn said to Ram when he was dying, 'In my mind, you're just as great a warrior as Tron.' Little things like that," says Lisberger.

## GETTING ALONG…MOSTLY

By most accounts, everyone got along on the set. There were not many, if any, huge star flare-ups or battles to get more screen time. Lisberger, despite his relative inexperience directing live-action, got along splendidly with most everyone and proved himself to be a good director. One day during production, Lisberger wanted to see how good Boxleitner's Frisbee skills were.

"Steven was great," says Boxleitner recalls with fondness. "I love the guy to death. Think about this. He's a first time director on a big [studio] lot. He had this vision. He could be a little dictator, too. He was so focused and so driven. Some days you said, 'Ah, F-you.' I remember he brought me in one time during lunch. Everybody else went to lunch. He had to see what I had learned with Sam."

Boxleitner stood on the set alone in costume. Lisberger climbed to the top of a tall ladder, Frisbee in hand, and fired a direct shot at Boxleitner's head. Sam Schatz watched. The actor, without looking, immediately reached back behind his head and caught the Frisbee. This was caught on film and used in the final cut.

"We had long hours on *Tron*," says Boxleitner. "I was tired and probably a little grumpy myself. That's who I was looking at so defiantely. I'm very proud of that shot."

Morgan was impressed with Lisberger as a first-time feature film director.

"Everybody has a first time," says Morgan. "I'm not worried about that. I always get nervous when I'm working with a director who's also a writer, because they fall in love with every word they've got on the page. That was the only thing. This was his baby."

Her main beef was with one particular line in Lisberger's script.

"I said don't make me say this line," she begged. "My friends are coming to the movie."

Lisberger, with his stern gaze, told Morgan to say the line. She paused, took in a deep breath, and sighed. She looked at Lisberger signaling she was ready.

"Action!"

"'I knew you'd escape. They haven't built a circuit that could hold you.' The audience still laughs. I choked on that line," says Morgan.

Bridges cut both the dialogue and Lisberger some slack.

"I've had very good luck with working with first-time guys or people haven't done too much," says Bridges.

Bridges had worked with writer/director Michael Cimino on *Thunderbolt & Lightfoot*, as well as Cimino's epic, *Heaven's Gate*. He also acted in Peter Bogdanovich's second feature film, *The Last Picture Show*.

"We haven't done too much better than *Citizen Kane*," says Bridges. "That was Orson Welles' first movie. When you're a novice like that, you don't know what you can't do, so your imagination is just wide open."

It has been noted over the years that Bridge's alter ego in *Tron*, Clu, sounds quite a lot like his alien character in *Starman* (1984).

"When I was doing *Starman* I really didn't think of it in that way. I didn't think of Clu," clarifies Bridges.

As Flynn, Bridges gave the character a boy-who-refuses-to-grow-up mentality. Bridges is humorous in the film with a constant Cheshire Cat grin on his face. Yet the actor infuses his character with the smartness of a real computer programmer. Many of the young game programmers of the era, like those who worked for Atari and Activision, were brilliant programmers with a sense of what it was like to be a teenager.

One of the memories Bridges has of the production is his use of a Widelux camera. The Japanese-made camera allowed a photographer to take sharp panoramic pictures.

"[*Tron*] was probably one of the first films I did a lot of photography on," recalls Bridges. "I took a lot of pictures. The Widelux, for my money, gives you a photograph that's more how the human eye sees. The lens has peripheral vision. I think it's particularly cool to take it on a movie set. To me it really seems like a sort a link between still photography and moving pictures because the lens itself moves."

In stills taken on the set by Disney's official photographer, it is easy to see the enjoyment the actors were having. The actors were given the chance to be kids again.

"There was a lot of laughter going on," says Shor. "There was nothing about changing the world in this movie. It was about having fun and creating a comic book for an audience to enjoy."

Shor was also impressed with Bridges from the beginning of production.

"Jeff Bridges, he was like a friend within thirty seconds," says Shor. "Jeff is exactly as you think he would be. He is that nice. He is that cool of a guy."

David Warner, who was considerably intimidating on screen, was considered a true gentleman on the set. Shy and quiet, he kept to himself until he was ready for his take. That is when he let his evil acting persona out as Sark.

"David, specifically, when he would walk in, he didn't talk a lot," says Morgan. "We didn't do a lot of chumming around with David. I did that scene with David, and he said you're going to die, there was no acting going on. I believed everything that came out of his mouth!"

"I loved David Warner," says Rosanna Norton. "Poor David. To put him into that costume, he couldn't take it off. It was almost like a set piece."

However, Norton's working relationship with Lisberger had gone from great to sour.

"I think Steve Lisberger got angry at me for some reason or other," recalls Norton. "When I first started working on the show, he was so friendly with me. I had two young children at the time, and he would call me up every night. As soon as I got home, the phone would ring. He wanted to discuss more things on the phone at night. He was just obsessed."

During production, according to Norton, Lisberger asked her for her opinion on aspects of the film.

"I assumed he wanted my opinion when he would ask me something, but really I was naïve," says Norton. "I think he just wanted me to agree with him. He would ask me questions about the script. I really didn't think that it was dramatic to reveal these characters in this other world right away. He really got really angry and said I'm completely wrong. I said okay I'm wrong. You asked me and I'm telling you."

She argued with Lisberger repeatedly over the choice of using leotard-type costumes opposed to costumes that were tailored to the actor's body. The rip in their relationship became larger.

"If people get mad at me, tough shit. I'm going to tell my story, goddamn it," says Norton. "It almost ruined my family life. It was so hard on my family to have this guy calling me every single night. I was trying to work with him as a colleague, as his underling. He wanted to be my friend. He wanted to talk to me a lot and get my input. Then he got so angry if I didn't agree with him."

With about a week to go before production ended, Norton was fired.

"I was fucking fired and that was really not right," says Norton. "I wasn't given any notice. I was fired. I was just there trying to make something come together."

"Necessity was the mother of creation," says Lisberger. "The artists and crew on the film often were upset that what they had come up with—be it designs, storyboards, layouts, computer anima-tion, backgrounds, backlit concepts, stunts, costumes, camera, sound effects, music, editorial, the mix, actors performances—only saw the film from their own perspective. Many times I tried to explain that compromise involving their efforts was the only way we would finish the film, but I stopped doing that when I found it usually led to a lecture about me not 'fighting for art.' I can't remember any department head fighting for the department across the hall or in the next building to get more time or money."

Norton was replaced by veteran costume designer, Eloise Jensson (*I Love Lucy*). One of the final scenes filmed was the ending where Boxleitner and Morgan wait for Bridges' helicopter to land on top of the ENCOM tower. Each actor was wearing what was in style at the time.

"She went and purchased the clothes the actors wore in the 'Real World,'" says Norton. "I had nothing to do with that. We have to remember when that was. I wanted to do sort of a punk thing. I thought why can't this be cool? Why do these guys have to be 'nerdos?' She went to J.C. Penneys and bought those clothes."

## THE SETS: DILLINGER'S OFFICE/ENCOM

The offices of ENCOM were designed by production designer, Dean Edward Mitzner, with art direction by John B. Mansbridge and Al Roelofs. The set was built on one of the Disney sound-stages.

Dillinger's office is quite striking. The minimal design favors Dillinger's cold heart and corporate mindset. The view out of the window behind him, which overlooks the city lights, mimics the "Electronic World" and the film's final shot.

His desk is perhaps the most extraordinary piece of furniture in the office. Predating modern touch-screen technology, Dillinger simply taps the surface of the desk to manipulate whatever he wants to see and hear from the MCP. When these scenes were filmed in 1981, touch-screen technology, at least for the average consumer, was but a dream.

The entire set was built high. This allowed film footage to be projected underneath the desk glass via rear projection. The footage on the monitors was from stock photos and of Bruce Boxleitner walking down the ENCOM halls. When Dillinger touches the keyboard and various buttons, sound effects were added to give the scene realism.

## ALAN BRADLEY'S CUBICLE

When the audience sees Alan Bradley for the first time, he is busy working at his computer in an office cubicle. This was shot in the Roy O. Disney Building at the Disney studios.

On the side of Alan's cubicle is a sign saying, "Gort. Klaatu barada nikto." This was in reference to the classic 1951 film, *The Day the Earth Stood Still*, directed by Robert Wise. As Alan types away on his computer, words appear on the monitor, courtesy of Triple-I.

The scene is short, setting up Alan to have a meeting with Dillinger. The film then cuts to a full shot of the office, causing the audience to say "Wow!" What looks like an endless maze of cubicles is actually the only matte shot in the film. Ellenshaw extended the cubicle maze, which is in reference to the jail cell maze in the "Electronic World." Ellenshaw's eye for detail and visual trickery was tremendous. In one matte painting, he conveys not only the claustrophobic feeling of office cubicles, but of the drudgery of being trapped in the jail cells in the "Electronic World."

Once he gets a message from Dillinger to see him in his office, Alan, in a huff, leaves his cubicle. Just then, "Popcorn Worker" peeks out from his cubicle and meekly asks if he can have some popcorn from Alan's popcorn popper machine. The audience is not aware that this is actor Dan Shor, who also plays Ram in the "Electronic World."

## FLYNN'S ARCADE

After the audience is taken into the "Electronic World" right after the *Tron* title sequence, the first "Real World" shot opens up on Flynn's Arcade. This was shot in Culver City, California, a mid-sized bedroom community near Los Angeles. It is best known for being the home of the Metro-Goldwyn-Mayer studio (Sony bought the lot in 1989). The fake arcade, built inside an old bank, was located on Watseka Avenue near the old MGM studio lot.

The arcade was a video game player's dream back in 1982. If a gamer died and went to heaven, this would have been paradise. The set was dressed with nearly every current video game machine available. The arcade was dominated by fictional games designed by Kevin Flynn. Game titles, lit in neon on the walls included *Astro Gunner*, *Intruder*, *The End*, *Code War*, *Zero Hour*, *Matrix Blaster*, *Vice Squad*, and *Berzerk*. Eighties fashion also dominated the arcade with one kid wearing a headband and red-white-and-blue striped tube socks. The sight of the kid seen today evokes big laughs.

Flynn's most successful creation is *Space Paranoids*, advertised on a giant billboard on the arcade's roof. As Alan and Lora enter the arcade in a long tracking shot, we see a crowd cheering on Flynn as he blasts Recognizers in a *Space Paranoids* video game. The game machine has Taylor's signature "candy apple neon" designs and mazes surrounding the video monitor. The game itself was featured footage from Bill Kroyer and Jerry Rees' computer simulations. The three-dimensional video game graphics, when they were made, predated many real-world video games by at least a year.

Flynn blows away a Recognizer, scoring 999,999 points on *Space Paranoids*. The crowd cheers.

"It's all in the wrists," he says.

Sweaty with Sony Walkman headphones dangling from his neck, Flynn greets Alan and Lora. After some idle chit chat, he asks Alan and Lora to go upstairs to his apartment where he will meet them. Flynn's apartment, located upstairs from the arcade floor, was shot at the location in Culver City. A set was also built on the Disney soundstages for pick-up footage.

As Alan and Lora enter, Brady cannot believe Flynn's stunted growth from adolescence into a grown man. The apartment looks like a true bachelor's pad with simple set decoration. The scene has one of the funnier dialogue exchanges in the film.

"She still leave her clothes all over the floor?" asks Flynn.

"Flynn," says Lora.

"No," says Alan.

"Alan!" exclaims Lora in horror.

"Well, I mean not that often."

"Now you can see why all his friends are fourteen years old."

Flynn smiles. "Touché. Touché."

Flynn plops down on his low-lying couch and plays what appears to be a Coleco electronic hand-held football game. In this scene, we find out why Flynn is hacking into the MCP and why he is running an arcade instead of ENCOM.

He explains that he created some of the most popular video games of all time, and that it was Dillinger who stole them. Alan cannot believe that this overgrown teenager is the guy behind the popular *Space Paranoids* arcade game.

"I still don't understand why *you* want to break into the system," says Alan.

Flynn flies off the handle.

"Because, man, somewhere in one of these memories is the evidence!"

Bridges based Flynn's outburst on Lisberger's impassioned personality. In fact, many of Flynn's body motions and traits came from channeling Lisberger.

"That's an old actor's trick," says Lisberger. "The director loves it. Jeff's doing my hand gestures and talking the way I talk, 'Don't you get it, man?'"

# Chapter 12

# *CREATING THE ELECTRONIC WORLD: PART ONE*

The visual effects on *Tron* were so daunting that Taylor and Ellenshaw divided them into two groups. Taylor supervised mainly the computer effects, while Ellenshaw mainly supervised the practical visual effects. No easy tasks either way.

"It would've been impossible for us to complete *Tron* if there hadn't been Richard Taylor, and hopefully I say, myself," Ellenshaw says modestly. "One person could never have done that job."

Once the production was in full swing, Taylor and Ellenshaw watched dailies everyday, exchanging their notes and ideas, then went their separate ways. Then they came back and met later in the day to discuss how everything was going. It was much like an old married couple's relationship.

Ellenshaw is quick to point out that despite his responsibility as a co-visual effects supervisor, working on *Tron* was a team effort.

"The term supervisor is very descriptive because you don't do it on your own. Far from it," says Ellenshaw. "You have to enable, in the case of *Tron*, over 600 people to create this very unique look. It includes inkers, painters, effects animators, scene coordinators, computer graphics technicians, and artists. One of the biggest considerations is that you want the film to look like it was done by one person, one mind. You don't want each shot to be different and unique."

"We had to imagine what everything would look like a year away," recalls Lisberger. "Our visuals had no precedent or means of comparison. And they all had to mesh and serve the story and characters which in their own way were from another world, too. Harrison and I worked very hard on preliminary work trying to anticipate how powerful or abstract or distracting the visuals and palette might be. And the really scary part was we all knew there would be no time or money for changes. This film was basically locked on a glide path months before it started. The problem was we didn't know where it would land."

*Tron* required extensive computer animation and it was necessary to hire outside companies to do the work. Disney did not have a computer animation department, and in fact, had not considered one at the time. Despite the advances happening outside the studio walls, the studio simply was not interested in computer simulation. Smith and Catmull had been trying unsuccessfully to sell the studio on their ability to do computer simulation and animation.

"Ed and I for years went to Disney on our hands and knees, in an annual pilgrimage starting in the 1970s," recalls Smith. "They could have had us for free!"

There was not a single company that could handle the elaborate simulations that both Rees and Kroyer were storyboarding. Taylor had to find which companies could do the job. His main choices were between Triple-I in Culver City, MAGI Synthavision or Digital Effects in New York, or Robert Abel & Associates in Los Angeles. Lucasfilm up in Northern California, with its fledgling computer division, was never considered.

"A big hurdle we had to get over was convincing the people at Disney that computer simulation could really make something," says Taylor. "[You could] make it do what they wanted, because most people thought somehow you just typed this stuff in and the computer did it."

In the early days of computer simulation, programming was primitive to the point that the computer could not realistically render organic objects. Human figures, like Taylor's Adam Powers, still had a rough quality to them in so far as skin texture and body shaping. Objects like trees and mountains were animated in the early days at Lucasfilm. The renderings appeared somewhat rough, jagged and unrealistic looking by today's standards. But the work that was being done was due to the limitations of the day's computer power, not the humans making them. Even though the world of *Tron* took place inside a computer, and the vehicles were imaginary, the film still required some sort of realism.

It was decided to go with four different companies that could realistically create the vehicles and computer world of *Tron*. Each company specialized in its own computer hardware.

"Every computer company had their own hot rod," emphasizes Taylor. "There's nothing in common between any of them."

*Information International, Inc.* (AKA Triple-I) would animate Sark's Carrier, the Solar Sailer, and the Master Control Program.

*Mathematical Applications Group, Inc.* (AKA MAGI Synthavision) would animate the Light Cycles, tanks, and Recognizers.

*Robert Abel & Associates* (AKA Abel's) would create the opening title sequence and computer simulate Flynn's flight into the "Electronic World."

*Digital Effects* would computer simulate the Bit and Tron's formation in the film's opening title sequence.

On *Tron*, with four separate companies involved with the computer simulation, each company had less than ten programmers doing all of the effects. The trick was to get each individual company's work to match for one uniform look.

## THE VEHICLES OF *TRON*

The film had a number of signature looks that set it apart from any other film ever made. There was Taylor's "candy apple neon" glow. There were human beings who appeared digitized into the

"Electronic World." *Tron* looked like nothing anyone had ever seen before. Then there were the film's vehicles. Though Syd Mead did not initially design the film's vehicles, both he and Moebius certainly embellished them.

## LIGHT CYCLES

By far, the Light Cycles are the most admired vehicles in *Tron*. Light Cycles were made of simple geometric shapes. Mead's design causes the audience want to race these vehicles through the electronic landscape. The Light Cycles also created jet walls that were emitted from the rear wheels.

The walls not only look fantastic on the big screen, but they are deadly for any Light Cycle rider who crashes into them.

"The back of it [Light Cycle] just trails like a rooster tail of a hydrofoil," says Mead. "They used that for the game aspect of the bikes being tracked in these turns."

The Light Cycles, after they are formed, race onto the Game Grid at blazing speeds. The Game Grid itself is made of white lines that bi-sect black space underneath, and the grid appears on-screen as a gigantic arena. The Light Cycles race across this plane as their jet walls line the Game Grid, creating basic color patterns whenever they turn. In the initial stages of pre-production and storyboarding, Lisberger was trying to figure out how to show the jet walls and their patterns.

"I had a meeting with Lisberger and he said, 'We gotta show some way how these bikes do the patterns," recalls Mead. "I said I suspect you can't make a curve frame-by-frame. I said why don't you just snap it. They could do that easy in the graphics."

The Light Cycle's movement was relegated to hard turns, left and right.

The jet wall idea was not necessarily a first on *Tron*, but it would become a signature element in the film. Most likely coincidental, the jet walls were similar to video games made by Atari (*Surround*) for the Atari 2600 game console, and Mattel (*Snafu*) for the Intellivision game console. *Surround* came out in either 1977 or 1978 (various online sources give two different dates), while *Snafu* came out in 1981. Each game was similar. Players run walls around their opponent. Each player has to outrun and outbox their opponent with quick movement. The *Tron* arcade and home video games used the same principles.

In some of the original sketches by Lisberger Studio artist Andy Probert, the Light Cycles were like flying motorcycles with hard geometric lines. In a few sketches, the Light Cycle riders are not riding a Light Cycle at all. This may have been a study on how the rider would sit on the Light Cycle.

Lloyd took the design a step further by enclosing the Light Cycle and making it one form. This made the Light Cycle more streamlined, elegant, and very fast looking. Mead then took his vehicle know-how and crafted the bike into what we see today. His initial designs shows the rider mounting the bike like he would on a regular "Real World" motorcycle.

"The Light Cycle I envisioned originally had the rider wearing this hard shell costume," says Mead. "He'd climb on the bike, put his feet in the foot rests, lean forward and his helmet would match the curve of the bike. There's no way they could do that. Not even close! So that's why when you see the film, they hold this wand in their hand and then in about three frames the bike just snaps over them. It was a steady curve from the front."

In Mead's final version of the Light Cycle, the windshield gracefully rises over the rider, providing him with a jet fighter-like cockpit. The rest of the bike forms immediately around him. Both man and bike are one-in-the-same. Mead made the Light Cycle seem fast and agile, while giving it weight and power by making the tires fat and wide.

"I originally thought of the front wheels as a big ball," says Mead. "After the tank and aircraft carrier, I knew they [MAGI] could do primitives. I said just remove the center of the ball, then it makes it look like a wheel and it's round and that's the energy source of the bike."

## TANKS

Two other signature vehicles fill the Game Grid space; the tanks and Recognizers. The tanks, unlike the Recognizers, are seen in the film carrying "Electronic World" humanoid crews. The lone tank carrying out Flynn's instructions is manned by his alter ego, Clu.

"What I did was design all of the vehicles—aircraft carrier, tank, and bike, and narrow the machines down to their essential recognizable parts," says Mead. "The tank doesn't have wheels. It has two treads. It's fairly wide and low with a rotating turret with a big gun coming out of it. It's instantly recognizable as a tank."

Early drawings by Probert made the tanks look fairly traditional and compact looking, yet still functional in the "Electronic World" environment. Mead took the tanks and stretched them out into longer, yet functional shapes. He replaced the traditional tank treads with metallic covers which blend in with the shape of the vehicle. The gun turret lies flush with the top of the tank, giving the entire vehicle aerodynamic proficiency.

Inside the tank, Mead's imagination went further. In the famous shot of Clu riding inside, the camera slowly dollies into the tank interior as Clu spins around one way, while the bowl-like structure surrounding him spins the opposite way. The interior is neon red and looks almost three-dimensional. What was great about Mead's design was how Clu rides inside the tank. Instead of being crunched inside of tight environment of a normal tank, he can stand or sit comfortably in the vehicle. He can sit down in front of a widescreen video monitor, seeking information and Recognizers. In some ways, the tank's interior resembles a modern video gamer's playroom.

## KROYER AND REES ANIMATE THE "ELECTRONIC WORLD"

The animation whiz kids, Kroyer and Rees, had been elevated from creating storyboards to the newly formed positions of "computer image choreographer." Though they continued to storyboard during production, they had the additional task of being in charge of the computer animation. Using their well choreographed storyboards, plus their traditional animation skills, they could create brilliant scenes of computer simulation. The only problem was that neither animator was versed in animating on a computer.

"Doing computer animation then is nothing like it is now," says Kroyer. "Nobody knew how to approach it. When we started to make *Tron*, there literally was no software at all to make things move. Nobody had really made anything move with sophisticated timing in a computer, because there was no Alias/Wavefront. There was no Maya."

Rees had taken FORTRAN computer programming back in high school, but computer simulation was a giant leap into an unknown world. Kroyer and Rees were not versed in animating on computers, and the computer companies they were going to deal with, in particular MAGI, never had done extensive story-based animation. The computer programmers at MAGI were not, technically speaking, creative minds. They were computer experts who knew more about zeros and ones than how to make Mickey Mouse walk or make a Light Cycle move with fluid animation. Melding Kroyer & Rees with MAGI took some coordinating.

"Steven looked at the two of us as good liaisons with the computer companies," recalls Rees. "We understood movement. Both of us were used to doing our own storyboards and animating. You could visualize something frame-by-frame and making it happen. Even though the computer wasn't anybody's tool at the time in animation or film, we started dividing up sequences and coordinated stuff and following through."

The duo was trained in traditional cel-based animation, as most animators were. This was a method of animation that had been used for years by Disney and all the other animation studios. After storyboards and rough pencil sketches were tested, screened, and finalized, animated characters were drawn onto individual transparent cels, frame-by-frame. These cels, which would contain a cartoon character like Mickey Mouse, were then placed on top of a separate painted background which sat on an animation stand.

The stand was firmly bolted to the floor of an animation department with a 35mm camera (in most cases) hanging above and shooting downward onto the cel and background. Lights illuminated the scenery. Click. The animation cameraman took a shot, then placed another Mickey cel onto the background. The next Mickey Mouse cel had slightly different movement from the last cel. After shooting several of these individual cels, the film was printed and projected. On the screen, the character appears to move across the background. The illusion of animation was complete.

But *Tron* was different. Much different. A lot of the animation would not require pencils, erasers, ink, paper or animation cels. It required bits, bytes, electronic innards and huge mainframes. Animation moved in a digital environment made of numeric data and code. Kroyer and Rees had to devise a system that worked with their animation skills, the limitations of the computers of the day, and the brains at the computer companies.

"The reason that Jerry Rees and I worked was because we were Disney animators," says Kroyer. "We were really skilled guys in envisioning motion. Because when you're hand drawing animation, you have to be able to visualize what you're going to do."

"Perhaps the best thing about Jerry Rees and Bill Kroyer was that you didn't have to supervise them," recalls Ellenshaw. "You left them alone."

To make animation flow, characters and objects need fluid movement. Nearly all of Disney's classic animated shorts and features were very fluid, and in some cases, lifelike. The problem with computer animation, at the time, was that it was somewhat stilted and occasionally jerky. Both Kroyer and Rees insisted that their fluid animation style be intact in the computer simulation. Not only was their reputation as high quality animators at stake, but so was the so-called Disney legacy of animation. The project, as a whole, was primarily done by outsiders who were not versed in Disney tradition and mythology. But at least with Kroyer and Rees' Disney training, the computer simulation would still feel like they were made by Disney animators.

Working out of a trailer parked on the Disney back lot, Kroyer and Rees had to figure out a way to work with the computer programmers. It was decided to break down the animation into coordinates that both the animators and programmers could understand. Animators understood numbers and movement, while programmers understood numbers.

"When we started to make *Tron*, there literally was no software at all to make things move," says Kroyer. "We just had to ask them how do you make things move, and they would say just assign the models coordinates per frame. It's a X,Y,Z world. It's like zero-Z, zero-X, zero-Y on frame one. Frame two, it's plus-two-X. Frame three, it's plus-four-and-X, plus six and X plus eight. That's it! Of course when you're an animator, you understand you've got to make things move with curves and arcs. You got to have variable speeds, smooth motion. So the first challenge was how are we going to make this work?"

Kroyer continues.

"I kind of came up with a breakthrough idea. It was a pretty basic idea. We'll sit down and we'll have graph paper and we'll figure out the coordinates of where the object's going to be on the key frames. And then we'll go down to the computer room and we'll punch those into the computer and it'll generate all the numbers."

"So often, we think that technology and creativity don't go hand-in-hand," says Ellenshaw. "The artists and the computer guys just can't talk the same language, which is insanity. The way they gave instructions to MAGI to create the shots was by animating in X, Y, and Z in a three-dimensional space. People go, 'What? I thought you said they were animators.' They were animators."

Rees, who had done a lot of elaborate storyboards for the film, also thought this task was going be a challenging one. The concept of computer simulation essentially placed a lot of different eggs into one basket. There was the environment, the vehicles, the movement of the vehicles and the virtual computer camera performing the camera movements to consider.

To see the simulations, Kroyer and Rees used the phone lines, via a CRT computer monitor and a clunky modem, with MAGI in New York. The main guy on the other end of this feed was Chris Wedge, who went on to form Blue Sky Studios and create the *Ice Age* franchise. The process was long and laborious.

"We had modems with a telephone that you'd have on a cradle and it would send signals, then it would print out very simple wireframes on the screen," recalls Kroyer. "I think you could put six images at a time, six wireframes. They would just accumilate. It would take ten minutes for everything to get up there. And that was the only imagery we got to see before we saw motion on film."

"It was really kind of working with the guys who were steeped in the construction of the computers themselves," says Rees. "It was funny because it was so user unfriendly at the time. That's 20 minutes of just typing to get that one vector line change or camera angle. I'd definitely bring reading. So it was very, very, very slow. But it was so fun to have that marriage. They seemed kind of stimulated by having people come in who were just not thinking in their particular box. It was kind of the marriage of what both of us needed."

## LIGHT CYCLE BATTLES, RECOGNIZERS AND VISTAVISION

The result of Kroyer and Rees' detailed storyboards and staging resulted in some of the most exciting sequences in the film. The signature scenes are the Light Cycle scenes, followed very closely by the Recognizer chases and formation of the Solar Sailer.

The second Light Cycle chase, in which Flynn, Tron, and Ram escape from the Game Grid, is a cinematic tour de force. Using quick cuts in the staging, plus a variety of fluid camera moves not seen in computer simulation at the time, gave the scene a feeling of rapid movement. The virtual computer camera is not stationary as it follows the Light Cycles from low angles, all the way up to high angles as the Recognizers fly into the Game Grid. The virtual camera flies around the Game Grid as if it is mounted on a virtual helicopter.

The virtual computer camera was not tied down to conventional camera movement or physics. *Star Wars* famously took audiences into the trench of the Death Star. But *Tron* shook things up by thrusting the audience into the "Electronic World." The computer camera could go anywhere it wanted to within the environment. Miniature models and the old methods of visual effects could immerse an audience into a movie, but nothing like *Tron* did.

"Usually Richard and I would go by on a daily basis and just see what they were doing, and see what had come across the phone line from MAGI," recalls Ellenshaw. "You just went, 'Wow! This is really cool!'"

One of the other signature elements was the use of the Recognizers. These guards of the "Electronic World" were menacing gorillas dressed in red neon. Chris Lane was originally responsible for giving the Recognizers their glow. Rees especially enjoyed working with them. He went to Lisberger and asked him if he could see the dailies of Jeff Bridges attempting to drive an outmoded Recognizer. In the black soundstage footage, Bridges jumps around, ducks, bobs and weaves while standing on stable ground.

"I would find little bits of Jeff falling or jumping," says Rees. "He did something spontaneous jump and then landed. I'll have him jump, when it starts to fall, then I'll cut away from him and have it go down and hit, then I'll use the second half of the scene when it hits. I would storyboard and plug it into the reel and show it to Steve and then he'd say 'okay.'"

The scene of Bridges trying to fly the Recognizer is one of the funniest scenes in the film. Rees and the visual effects crew cleverly meshed both Bridges' live-action footage and computer simulations flawlessly. The scene was infused with much needed humor, giving the Recognizer a big, dumb personality in the way it flew around wildly. Another fun personality trait the Recognizer used was during the close of the Light Cycle escape scene. After Flynn, Tron, and Ram escape, a Recognizer pulls his legs together and stomps on the Game Grid so hard, it shakes the screen.

Once the computer simulation footage was finalized and approved by Lisberger, it was transferred to film stock for viewing. That was usually done with a lot of fingernail biting, as the process was not proven to be always reliable.

"Once you've rendered a frame, you couldn't store it.," says Durinski. "You couldn't put it onto a disc because it was too much information for a disc at that time. After you computed and rendered a frame and recorded it, it would vanish. You could save it on film. If you came back the next day and you saw that you had a glitch in your shot, that essentially meant that you'd have to redo it and go through the whole process again, frame-by-frame."

It was Durinkski, point-by-point, line-by-line, who scanned vehicle drawings of *Tron* into the computer at Triple-I.

"MAGI had two 80MB hard drives," recalls Kroyer. "They did the whole movie on two 80mb hard drives. I can't believe it myself when I hear that. In 1987 when I bought my first SGI (a supercomputer), it had four megs of RAM and it cost $57,000. It was as big as a refrigerator. I think the hard drive was something like a 200mb hard drive."

The footage from the computers was then painstakingly rendered onto film. Various people who worked on the film claim the effects dailies were shown either in VistaVision or 70mm.

According to Ellenshaw, "For a time Disney rented a VistaVision projector to look at CGI dailies projected on a temporary screen on one of the sound stages. I recall the very first dailies from MAGI were shown this way. But, if memory serves, we only rented that for a few weeks (or less). After that we viewed 35mm anamorphic reduction prints."

Why is this significant? Seeing the VistaVision dailies made a huge impression on those who saw them. Apparently, the first CGI scene rendered out to VistaVision was one of the Light Cycle sequences. The format, with its high-fidelity image quality and accurate color, was eye-popping. One of the first people to see these scenes was John Lasseter. Right then and there, he knew his future was in computer animation.

Silver's eyes were never the same, either.

"The VistaVision dailies? Those were fucking spectacular! Before they got put onto IP (interpositive) stock and dupe negative, right off the original negative, it was just breathtaking. What the photographers were achieving with backlight effect was nothing short of breathtaking."

"It was jaw dropping," recalls Ellenshaw. "It was unbelievable. It was imagery that we had wanted and had hoped for. And here it was. It was in color. It was dynamic. It worked. We just stood there."

Lisberger watched the amazing footage, but stood there with the gears in his head spinning.

"Steven said something that the grids appear to go backwards and we wanted to kill him," says Ellenshaw. "It was like, 'Shut up! This is amazing!' But that was Steven asking for perfection. Love him to death for that."

Computer resolution also came into play in the VistaVision format. The low horsepower of computer animation of the time rendered "anti-aliasing," or better known as "jaggies." Jaggies were blocky artifacts that could be seen on objects in computer animation.

"That was a topic of discussion—higher resolution versus anti-aliasing," says Rees. "What theoretically would work better on the big screen. The resolution of stuff coming out of the computer, obviously the higher the resolution, the longer it would take to compute all that stuff. There was this whole school of thought on could you anti-alias the lines. It wouldn't necessarily make it crisp but it would keep you from seeing 'jaggies.' I remember there were 'No Jaggies' T-shirts where it would show raster graphics."

Since there was no real-time method to see the computer graphics in full motion, Kroyer and Rees had to wait until the rendered footage came back from the lab to see if their careful plotting and staging worked.

"The very first time we'd ever saw movement was on film," says Kroyer. "There was no way to preview anything. There was no computer that was fast enough to actually show images, even twelve frames per second, let alone 24-frames per second. They literally rendered the frames and put them on a film recorder onto film. If you can imagine going into a theater on the soundstage at Disney and looking at a 70mm [VistaVision] vector pencil test, that's how we did *Tron*. It was eye-popping and pretty humbling. But the amazing thing was we were never really surprised by what we saw, because we were so thorough in envisioning it."

"I remember clearly," says Ellenshaw, "so many times during the production, that I felt like I truly had glimpsed the future. This was the start of something really cool."

Not only were the *Tron* computer simulations remarkable for their then state-of-the-art animation, but Lisberger, Kroyer and Rees' eye for direction and virtual camera movement is all the more astonishing. Considering how limited computer rendering power was, their animation pushed the boundaries and then some.

As Kroyer and Rees were rendering their animation, technology kept racing ahead of them.

"We couldn't wait for a year to write new software," says Rees. "By the end of the production, all the computer guys knew that their own teams had made advances. But we couldn't stop to update. We had to finish on the original system. So they all joked about it, 'Yeah this is the system that is giving us the biggest breakthrough ever on film. It's already a dinosaur!'"

## MEANWHILE...BACK AT ILM

Over at Paramount Pictures, writer/director Nicolas Meyer had finished shooting *Star Trek: The Wrath of Khan*. A scene in the script called for the formation of a new planet out of a dead moon. The footage would be shown on a video monitor viewed by Captain James T. Kirk (William Shatner). ILM was performing the visual effects, but could not get a grasp on the formation of a planet on a video monitor, according to Michael Rubin's book, *Droidmaker: George Lucas and the Digital Revolution* (Triad, 2006).

It was decided to let the Lucasfilm's computer team, led by Alvy Ray Smith, come up with a solution. His team used all the computing power they could muster to make the "Genesis Project" come to fruition, and also sell Lucas on the premise that computer simulation was ready for feature films.

It was now common knowledge within the film industry that *Tron* was being made over at Disney.

"We at Lucasfilm/Pixar had nothing to do with *Tron* of course, but were watching all developments in our business," says Smith. "Ed Catmull and I were always concerned that we would be beat to the draw by our 'loyal opposition' John Whitney Jr. and Gary Demos."

Smith continues.

"We were not worried about *Tron* for some reason. I don't think it ever occurred to us that there was serious competition there. Don't take me wrong. We were thrilled that a major motion picture studio was taking note of the technology. It was great fun being around Lisberger and Bonnie, but the movie was done in many parts by many companies and only a fraction of it was done with computer graphics. But horsepower was king, and we knew our Moore's Law well. We knew when it became possible to 'do' a movie, and the 1980s weren't the time."

## REES AND BIRD PROPOSE SOMETHING RADICAL

George Lucas' former collaborator and producer, Gary Kurtz (*Star Wars*), was interested in a groundbreaking project that Jerry Rees and Brad Bird had been working on at Disney while *Tron* was still being made. As early as December 1981, in their spare time, Rees and Bird had made a trailer for a proposed feature film adaptation of Will Eisner's *The Spirit*. The animators wanted to create the film entirely in a "Computer Oriented Production System" (COPS). Inspired by his experience on *Tron*, Rees had theorized about the future implications of computer usage for character animation, and had drawn up documents to outline such a COPS system.

Freelance writer Steve Leiva had seen the footage from *The Spirit* and acted as a liaison between the animators and Kurtz. Kurtz liked what he saw in the test footage, and once he was guided through their concept documents, he bought into the Rees/Bird plan to use a new computer oriented production method. Kroyer was also consulted on the possibilities of computer animation. Towards the end of Rees' tenure on *Tron*, Kurtz paid him to fly up to Lucasfilm and meet Ed Catmull, Alvy Ray Smith. They were intrigued. Could computers be used to entirely change the approach to traditional character animation?

"If we can reconfigure what the computer does, it can be totally a breakthrough in animation," said Rees. "Not just for an effects live action movie, but how you do animation."

The process Rees and Bird proposed was mind-blowing and completely ahead of its time. First and foremost, the system allowed animators to scan hand drawings into a computer. Inking and painting was no longer needed, as the computer took over the task of line and character coloring.

It allowed an operator to do the job in about 5-minutes. Normally inking and painting took almost an hour-and-a-half per cel to complete. There was no longer any need to lay cels down on an animation stand, because the colorized characters were composited with backgrounds and "filmed" entirely within the digital space.

But that was not all.

Disney always prided itself on its marvelous multiplane camera. However, using the camera was labor intensive and very expensive. The new computerized system could film a multitude of layers and perform camera moves not before possible. COPS would replace the multiplane camera.

The proposal also allowed animators to switch out digitized backgrounds whenever they wanted to, generate layouts, build three-dimensional environments, build a library (sets, vehicles, objects, props, etc.), add computerized objects and let the computer do all of the camerawork. All of those computer files would be stored on video discs.

Wilhite caught wind of what was going on and confronted Rees. He was still employed by Disney, so why was he working on a project with outsiders?

"I can't help having this addiction to innovation," Rees told Wilhite. "Gary is ready to take another innovative step. Look at it this way; there's a whole bunch of other people in the Animation Department who are great people and talented artists. But from my perspective, they're getting paid to sit on their asses and wait for the next thing. I rolled up my sleeves and I'm working with you on *Tron* so we can get this done. That's who I am. I could've been the loyal Disney guy and sat downstairs and gotten my paycheck. I want to keep moving towards something exciting."

Wilhite recognized the spirited attitude that was making *Tron* so special in the first place. He admired Rees' enthusiasm and gave him his blessing to continue on with *The Spirit*.

In early 1982 Gary Kurtz set up a meeting between Rees, Bird, and MAGI's Dr. Mittelman to discuss *The Spirit*, and their plans for the COPS. Mittelman was intrigued by what the young animators were proposing.

"It's not in the distant future," said Mittelman. "This is a good logical next step. Nobody is doing it right now."

A few days later, Mittelman inadvertently spilled the beans about the Rees/Bird COPS plans to folks at Disney, including Lasseter. Already intrigued by what he saw in the Light Cycle footage on *Tron*, Lasseter clearly wanted to jump into the world of computer animation. He would soon began to work on a test with MAGI using a scene from the Maurice Sendak book *Where the Wild Things Are*. Of course Lasseter was not aware that his friends Rees and Bird had been designing much of the computer animation methods that Mittelman was now sharing with his team. Rees and Bird truly regretted the breech of confidence, but held no ill will toward Lasseter or his Disney team.

A good-natured sort, Mittelman apologized to Rees and Bird once he realized the uncomfortable turn of events he had precipitated. But the seeds had already been planted. MAGI and Disney continued to develop what eventually would be dubbed CAPS (Computer Animation Production System). Alvy Ray Smith would eventually negotiate a deal between Pixar and Disney for CAPS.

Making peace with *The Spirit* team, Mittelman rendered test computer animated film frames for Rees and Bird. Richard Taylor was brought aboard to diagram concepts for the film. But funding for the ambitious project did not fully materialize, and Kurtz's company, Kinetographics, was going through some financial difficulties. In addition the Disney/MAGI *Where the Wild Things Are* test began to take the innovation spotlight off of their efforts. Rees and Bird found it necessary to move on to other projects over time.

*The Spirit* was eventually made by an entirely different group with an entirely different story approach in 2008. It used computer generated effects and environments. The film flopped.

# Chapter 13

# CREATING THE ELECTRONIC WORLD: PART TWO

All of the independent computer companies had their hands full with the computerized visual effects. While MAGI worked with Bill Kroyer and Jerry Rees, Triple-I, Robert Abel and Associates and Digital Effects forged ahead with their pieces of the *Tron* puzzle.

## *TRON* TITLE AND FLYNN'S RIDE

Richard Taylor decided that the crew over at Robert Abel and Associates was the best fit to bring not only the opening *Tron* title to life, but to also create Flynn's ride into the "Electronic World." Abel's was infused with a talented group of filmmakers, animators, and computer geniuses. The group included Bill Kovacs, Richard "Doc" Baily, Kenny Mirman, Frank Vitz, Tim McGovern, and Roy Hall. With their collective experience in television commercials and graphics designed to catch the eye, Taylor knew he could rely on them to make their part of the *Tron* puzzle dazzling.

*Tron* was a huge assignment for Abel's, but the small team was ready for anything. Initially, the company was hired to create the trailer for *Tron*. But Taylor realized that they should create the opening title sequence and Flynn's ride.

The director of the title sequence and Flynn's ride was Kenny Mirman. He was a graduate from CalArts. In his late twenties, he went on a personal and spiritual quest to find his life's purpose.

"What I was searching for was the soul of what I was trying to do as an artist," says Mirman. "I found that out in the desert in northern Nevada when I discovered this old Indian sculptor named Rolling Mountain Thunder. I met him and I lived up there in the desert with him for a few months. I decided just a couple of days after he invited me to be a teacher there and to start a school, I was meant to go back to Los Angeles and somehow find my way into the animation world, which is what I did. After a few months, I discovered computer animation. Really, hardly anyone in the world was doing it."

After working on a number of projects at Harry Marks' studio, including the famous poster for the epic television mini-series, *Roots* (1977), Mirman was eventually lured over to Abel's to fill in

Taylor's former position. Taylor had left to work with Terrance Malick's aborted space film project, only to return to Abel's and commission them to work on *Tron*.

The staff at Abel's was eclectic, but incredibly diverse. Mirman was a gifted animator and specialized in bringing spiritualism into his work. Bill Kovacs was a brilliant computer programmer who would eventually co-found Wavefront Technologies. Tim McGovern was an exceptional systems programmer on *Tron*. Richard "Doc" Baily was a gifted artist who would pull all-nighters at Abel's. Frank Vitz came to Abel's in 1980 and was their talented technical director.

In the commercials done at Abel's, the viewing audience was drawn immediately into the commercial's imagery and story. Mirman felt that the audience watching *Tron* had to be thrust into the storyline and theme of the film, thus it was necessary to immediately set up the story from the opening titles. There was a beginning (Tron's formation), middle (the banking of the *Tron* title), and end (the trip through the title into the "Electronic World").

In the late 1970s and early 1980s, most title sequences were fairly simple with credits that faded in and out. With the notable exception of the James Bond films, most credit sequences were routine. *Star Wars* changed all that. It had its logo envelope the screen and fly into the distance of space. A year later, *Superman: The Movie* had its title and credits streak across the screen. *Alien* (1979) had its logo form slowly over the eerie music by Jerry Goldsmith. The logos for some blockbuster films of the era became as famous as the films they were from.

*Tron* would also have its own memorable title opening. After the formation of the character of Tron, which was created by Digital Effects, Inc., a beam of energy flashes on the screen and the *Tron* logo rotates and flies toward the audience. The audience then flies through part of the letter 'o' straight into the "Electronic World."

Syd Mead designed the iconic *Tron* logo, with its slick lines and dynamic colors.

"The initial logo was done by Syd Mead, but it didn't read properly," says Taylor. "So I messed with it and changed the 'r.' It read 'Ron.' So it was a combination of Syd Mead and myself. But Syd had designed the whole typeface for the movie."

As the *Tron* title banks and the audience enters the "Electronic World," many viewers would be given an amusement park ride from the comfort of their theater seat.

"I wanted to get people kind of dizzy," says Mirman. "In a way it was the predecessor to the ride film. You really took people on a ride, and there was a moment in that journey into the computer where things were really topsy-turvy."

Once the camera flies through part of the "o" in the *Tron* title, the audience flies into the "Electronic World." Thousands of lights and grid patterns fill the immense movie screen at this point. As the camera glides into the "Electronic World," it seems as though the audience is flying over a "Real World" cityscape at night. Eventually, the lights dissolve into the opening shot of Flynn's Arcade.

To get the look he wanted, Mirman drove to the top of Mullholland Drive above Los Angeles and would study the city lights.

"I realized it was all dots and glows of lights," says Mirman. "I would go up there for hours at a time. Basically I duplicated the Mullholland view of Los Angeles at night with dots and line segments."

Both the fly-through sequence and Flynn's ride were generated using an Evans & Sutherland Picture System II computer. The vector-graphic computer was state-of-the-art and favored by Abel's. It could play back renders in real time. Normally computer simulation had to be filmed out to see results. Unlike today's sleek and small computers, the Picture System II was fairly large and extremely expensive.

"They had a huge outer-space-looking monitor," recalls McGovern. "They were curved. It sat with a big yoke that would support the monitor. You would have a disc that was maybe twenty inches in diameter. They were about five inches thick, and in the center of them hooked into something that allowed them to spin. We were able to have something like 2mb of disc space. During the production shoot, we had to change the discs five or six times."

Flynn's ride is an exciting sequence in the film. Flynn hacks into the MCP to recover his stolen video game plans. The MCP suddenly beams him into the "Electronic World" to have him fight on the Game Grid. The audience is sucked into the computer with Flynn. The screen erupts into a bright array of light and shapes that mimic a kaleidoscope on digital steroids. The audience's eyes are engulfed in a dazzling array of light.

Even though Abel's prided itself on the use of the latest computer technology, they had to still employ traditional film technology and specially built film recorders to get their sequences completed. They filmed right off of the Evans & Sutherland CRT tube monitor. To get the various mattes and layering necessary for the final shot of Flynn's ride to composite together, the film inside the camera was bi-packed. This meant Abel's used two-to-three different strips of film, layered carefully on top of each other, inside the camera.

During the filming of Flynn's ride, Mirman took every possible precaution to make sure there were no errors that could crop up on film. Fearing that any light leak would ruin hundreds of hours of work, Mirman covered all his bases.

"We had a new camera specifically brought in just to shoot these scenes," says Mirman. "Now we have a camera that I did a test on and we saw a light leak on it. We couldn't trace it down. We didn't have time to replace it. I locked Frank Vitz into this little cubicle of a room, which was our film recorder room, which was about seven feet-by-ten feet. I said you're not coming out while you're shooting. No one opens the door and I was the guard. I duct taped the edges of the door and hung black Duvateen. I draped the door with that and I took every precaution. We actually taped over the camera. So we'd load the film in, then we'd cover the camera in black bags and Duvateen. We were so paranoid."

Mirman figures that Vitz was in that room for five-to-seven straight days in almost pitch black darkness, save for a tiny pen light. To stave off hunger during the endless days and nights, Mirman quickly slid a piece of pizza under the door to Vitz, and closed up the small opening in the door so hardly any light would get in.

"He was in there for days at a time shooting and that's changing filters," recalls Mirman. "He'd have a little pen light. The pen light would go on for a second then he'd turn it off quickly. He'd shoot an element 700 frames in one direction, then you'd have to wind the camera back to zero, which meant all these bi-pack mattes had to go back to zero again. Back and forth thousands of times."

Finally, the filming was done and the footage came back from the lab. It was brilliant and beautiful. Only there was a problem. In Southern California, Santa Ana winds blow through the region from fall to winter. These warm winds, in turn, cause the air to be dry. Electricity permeates the air.

As Flynn rides through the tunnel and banks right, blue electrical flashes appear on-screen. The flashes were not supposed to be there. Vitz had been careful in winding the film in the camera at a very slow pace, frame-by-frame. But film still generates static when it moves through a camera.

"Even though we had a humidifier in the room, the acetate film you used to make the mattes with was touching the emulsion of the regular stock," says McGovern. "Because they were touching each other constantly, and there was a static effect, we ended up with blue flashes in the sequence."

Mirman checked and re-checked the footage. He was contemplating having to redo the sequence.

"I viewed that thing probably thirty times and I said, 'You know what? I think I can live with this. It's actually kind of cool looking. No one's going to know it wasn't done on purpose, except for me and a few of us. And if Richard [Taylor] buys it off on it, then I think I'm going to go with it."

John Hughes, who had created the opening computer-simulated title sequence for *The Black Hole*, was now one of Abel's technical directors. He stood over Mirman's shoulder and watched the footage unfolding on the Moviola. As he stood there, he flipped a quarter in the air. Constantly. He studied the footage.

"Well, it looks like you're going to have to reshoot that scene, Mr. Mirman," said Hughes.

"I don't think so. I think this is a hero. I think I'm going to go with this," answered Mirman.

"I don't think that's acceptable," said Hughes.

"I think it is," Mirman retorted. "I think it's kinda cool looking and you're not the one locked into the closet for seven days."

Hughes grinned and moved along.

"When we showed it to Richard Taylor, we told him about it. When he saw it, he said, 'Eh, it's fine. We're throwing all kinds of other things in your face.'"

Taylor's reasoning was that the blue flashes would probably occur in the "Electronic World" anyway. Besides, the sound department could add a "zap" sound effect and the audience would be none the wiser.

Mirman was also going for a mind blowing theatrical experience for the audience. Flynn's ride, at least for him, was a spiritual journey. Add to that the kaleidoscope images storyboarded by "Doc" Baily, and the audience was in for a dazzling trip into the "Electronic World."

"When people saw these images for the first time in a theatrical setting, the huge screen and the dark room, there was actually a physiological response," recalls Mirman. "Pupils would dilate. It's a moment, as an artist, you can reach into their souls, so to speak. I saw that happening in a potential way on *Tron*."

## THE HIGH LIFE

The visual effects and post-production teams on *Tron* were working insane hours around the clock. There was little time to rest. With the pressure to get its effects finished on *Tron*, many staff members at Abel's resorted to cocaine to stay alert. Cocaine use had climbed to staggering levels by the early 1980s. The drug was considered fashionable to use. Coke allowed people the ability to stay up all night and day if they wanted to.

"I don't know if this is something that we should be proud of, but this was a time period where a lot of us were doing cocaine," recalls Mirman. "It was 1981 and we thought of cocaine as a non-harmful social drug. But the great thing about it is that it could keep you up. We were working such enormous hours that we could use all the help we could get."

Richard "Doc" Baily was one of the more enthusiastic coke users at Abel's. He was known to come in and work all night, producing incredible art while high. But Mirman dispels the belief that artists were only good when they were high. Jimi Hendrix was already an accomplished musician before shredding minds at Woodstock. Baily was already an accomplished artist before he dove into the world of *Tron*.

"I don't know if it was because of the drugs," says Mirman. "There was something about the passion of it all. The cocaine sometimes tripled the passion. We were already very passionate individuals."

Still, getting coke was a weekly happening. One of the employees took orders for coke every Friday. By Monday, each light table had a three-inch line of coke a straw, and razor on top. And each day, one could hear the tapping and sniffing of the drug.

"Fortunately no one died," says Mirman. "We could have lost somebody there. But we did have some addiction problems from some people. I didn't get addicted fortunately. I reached a point where I said, 'You know what? This stuff's evil. I can't do it anymore.' But during *Tron*, we were doing cocaine. It was actually helping us stay up. And it wasn't healthy, but we were young and immortal. Or at least we thought we were."

## THE SOLAR SAILER, LAKE MICKEY MOUSE AND GRID BUGS

The formation of the Solar Sailer is an elegant sequence in the film. Out of thin electronic air, the ship forms into a vessel that is held in place by a beam of energy. The ship uses this beam like a monorail to travel across the Sea of Simulation. The formation, flying sequences and landscape the ship flies over were done by Triple-I.

Moebius designed a version of the ship that was ultimately used in the film's production. He gave it the appearance of a streamlined sailing ship. The sails were translucent. A pipe-like apparatus underneath the ship sends an energy beam through the ship's deck and out an exhaust pipe in the back.

Mead had also taken a stab at the design of the ship, but could not get it the way he wanted, conceding that Moebius's Solar Sailer design fit the film better.

"My Solar Sailer was more organic," says Mead. "I looked at old pictures of old frigates and sailing ships. It had this big sail. The big sail was off to the side with stringers like a sailing ship has to keep the tension on the sail. I thought it was sort of clever. His was symmetrical like a butterfly."

The Solar Sailer flies across the Sea of Simulation with Flynn, Tron and Yori on-board. The scene with live-action footage of the actors talking is intercut with the Triple-I footage. Pursuing them are Recognizers from MAGI. The scene is a clever match of three different elements coming together as one—live-action footage of the actors, Triple-I's footage of the Solar Sailer and MAGI's footage of the Recognizers. The sequence, as cut by Gourson, it is difficult to see any differences between the Triple-I and MAGI's computer simulation. They are seamless except to the most critical eye.

The Sea of Simulation scene offers up some clever gags. The biggest one was the giant lake in the shape of Mickey Mouse's famous head. The lake appears under the Solar Sailer as it sails over and many people did not catch it at first. Durinski came up with the gag and it has audiences clapping with glee.

Still flying over the Sea of Simulation, Yori spots Grid Bugs. Originally, these were planned to be characters throughout the film. Due to time and budget constraints, the animation of the Grid Bugs was very limited. It is a scene that has *Tron* fans abuzz over why it was there in the first place, and why the Grid Bugs did not return in the film.

"You needed a Solar Sailer," says Ellenshaw. "You needed Sark's Carrier. You needed tanks. You needed Light Cycles. These are things you had to have to tell the story. They didn't contribute to advancing the story. But we still wanted to have them because they were cool."

Animator John Norton is solely credited with this piece of animation. He hand animated the Grid Bugs within about a six-month timeframe. The sequence is so well done and playful, it is hard to forget. Out of nowhere, a Grid Bug pops up out of a black square in the middle of the Game Grid. It springs metallic spider-like legs outward and then its body forms. A raspberry colored eye dominates its head. It quickly looks around, readjusts its legs, and scampers on. In the next cut, more Grid Bugs suddenly appear and race across the Game Grid, never to be seen again.

Why did the Grid Bugs appear out of nowhere, then suddenly disappear? There simply was not enough time or manpower to keep them going throughout the film's storyline. With four companies already going full speed on the computer graphics, and with the effects-animation unit working their fingers to the bone, the Grid Bugs were lucky enough to make an appearance thanks to Norton.

## THE BIT AND JEFFREY KLEISER

The Bit became one of the most endearing characters in *Tron*. This is a simple positive and negative bit that only had two words in its vocabulary—yes or no. Flynn flies the broken Recognizer through the "Electronic World" when Bit shows up out of nowhere. Like a curious child, the Bit playfully flies around the interior of the Recognizer, curious to see what Flynn is doing. The scene is one of the more humorous points in the film. Bridges acts with the Bit just as if the digital creature was a child.

The Bit was done with a combination of CGI animation by Jeffrey Kleiser and Judson Rosebush of Digital Effects, Inc, and some traditional cel animation. The cel animation was done to combine the Bit with Jeff Bridges inside the Recognizer. Jeffrey Kleiser was the brother of Randal Kleiser, director of *Grease*.

"Judson Rosebush of Digital Effects and Jeff Kleiser kept calling me and saying, 'There's got to be something we can do in this film. Please!'" says Taylor. "So I came up with two things for them to do. One was the opening when all those elements fall into the Tron character. They did that. And they did the Bit. That way we got them in the credits."

"It had taken quite a while for us to find a company to do the Bit," says Ellenshaw. "It was one of the last things we assigned to a vendor."

Based in New York City, Digital Effects was a small outfit with six or seven employees. They had done commercial work on a computer-graphics display in their offices. The vector line animation was then sent via a 1200-baud modem to a computer in Bethesda, Maryland.

"It would take up a good hour just to make a very crude wireframe of what we were working on," says Kleiser. "It was all remote computing. We didn't have any computing power in New York. Then if you wanted to put something on film, you had to write the images onto a nine-track tape in Bethesda, move that information over to a different machine. That data was written out to another nine-track tape and shipped to L.A."

Both Kleiser and Rosebush realized that incredibly slow rendering times just would not cut it for *Tron*. They hired an engineer who brought the Digital Effects machines up to date with faster chips. Kleiser and Rosebush also bought a new film recorder for their work on *Tron*, but found out that the production in Los Angeles was shooting in VistaVision.

"We had to go find a VistaVision camera somewhere," says Kleiser. "Just out of the blue, we found this guy in New Jersey who had three VistaVision cameras in his garage. I didn't even know what they were. I think we arranged for two of them to be shipped back to Disney because they needed VistaVision cameras desperately."

Creating the Bit was fairly simple for Digital Effects. It consisted of a dodecahedron that could change its shape to "yes" or "no."

There really was no reason for the character to exist. Just like the Grid Bugs, the Bit was simply another character that shows up for a moment because he is cool to watch. Because of the time crunch in post-production, Lisberger, Ellenshaw and Taylor pressed Digital Effects to create The Bit's animation quickly.

"The tricky part was just animating him so that he would be in the right spot," recalls Kleiser. "We didn't have any real way of seeing the background shot that Disney was giving us. Basically we had charts which said the Bit starts here and then by frame 38, it's over here and by frame 60, it's down here. So we would animate it based on this two dimensional guideline we got from Richard Taylor."

The Bit turned out so well that audiences loved the little character. He shows up, chats with Flynn, then flies away. People often wondered why, like the Grid Bugs, the Bit disappears.

"We had a meeting," says Ellenshaw. "How do we kill off the Bit and not make it too noticeable? When the Recognizer crashes, the impact is so great that the Bit disappears! Amazing. The impact of a crash inside the computer can be devastating to bits."

Poor Bit.

## THE MASTER CONTROL PROGRAM (MCP)

The Master Control Program, otherwise known as the MCP, is the supreme ruler of the "Electronic World." Almost nothing can be done without his approval. He rules his universe with ruthless power and will derezz anyone who gets in his way. He is a giant spinning cylinder of evil.

The MCP was one of the earliest characters created for *Tron*. He was also one of the earliest CGI tests done for the film. As mentioned before, Lisberger paid Triple-I to do a simple test to see if the MCP would work, and it did.

Voiced by David Warner and electronically enhanced in post production, the MCP is first seen early in the film. Sark goes into his chamber to give the MCP the latest updates on what is happening in the "Electronic World." From Sark's point-of-view, we see the MCP filling up the screen in a crisscross of vector lines. These lines fill in and create an eerie face of the MCP.

The face of the MCP was none other than Adam Powers from Taylor's Triple-I demonstration reel. Taking the program's basic information, Triple-I stripped Powers' skin off and left him with his skeletal vector lines. His vector face was stretched to fill Sark's chamber screen. To animate his mouth movement in sync with Warner's dubbing, each frame of the footage was blown up and hand animated.

# Chapter 14

# HAMMERTIME! MIGRAINES, EFFECTS, AND ANIMATION

The most famous myth about the making of *Tron* is that the "Electronic World" was entirely made in a computer. In a testament to the visual effects wizards and artists, it only appears that way. *Tron* was a mixture of state-of-the-art computer simulation technology and old-fashioned handmade artistry.

The film's computer-simulated visual effects were already very complicated. The limited computer power of the era was just enough to create many of the elements of the "Electronic World." But there was not enough computer power, people power, or time to render enough backgrounds and animation to insert the actors into the "Electronic World."

It was decided the only practical way of inserting the actors into the "Electronic World" was through handmade visual effects. The trick was to match the human elements of animation, visual effects and backgrounds with the computer simulations being done by Triple-I, MAGI, Abel's and Digital Effects.

## BACKGROUNDS AND EFFECTS ANIMATION

It cannot be overstated how valuable the background artists and effects animators were to *Tron*. Without their paintings, drawings, animation and artistic embellishment, the "Electronic World" of *Tron* would not exist. There was no method in which the live-action footage of the actors could be mixed with computer-simulated environments. Nor was there a way to add computerized visual effects to the live-action footage. If there was an actor running around the "Electronic World" of *Tron*, their virtual world had to be created by hand.

Rarely mentioned in books about Disney animation are the background artists. The character animators at Disney during its "Golden Age" rightly received a lot of credit for their work. But trudging away out of the spotlight were background artists, notably Claude Coats, Al Dempter, and Eyvind Earle.

A background artist paints the backgrounds on which the animated characters move across. These backgrounds can be elaborate, as those seen in *Bambi*, or simple, as those seen in the UPA cartoon shorts of the 1950s.

The "Electronic World" that Bridges, Boxleitner and Morgan inhabit is made of stark black backgrounds, geometric shapes, bright neon lighting, and lines that go on into infinity. For the film, approximately 800 backgrounds were created within a six-month period. This was a staggering amount of work to be done.

It was Jesse Silver who was mainly responsible for bringing the "Electronic World" backgrounds to life. But he is quick to give credit where credit is due.

"Syd Mead really designed the 'Electronic World,'" says Silver. "That's Syd's adventure. He used a lot of digital symbology there. Dots and dashes and lines. He had these oval, egg-like shapes. He was using geometry as a metaphor. When I was starting to be asked to design the show, I kept faith with that idea."

Silver went in the direction of using triangles for the world of *Tron*. His signature designs included the torture room, the computer console on the Solar Sailer, and the control board where Sark disposes of players on the Game Grid.

Silver was one of the new kids in the Animation Building, carefully painting his backgrounds. He preferred that his paintings were smooth to the finish without any specular light shining through that would ruin a shot. Specular light is the shiny light reflecting off a surface. However careful he was, someone else was not and their lack of work ethic caused a number of headaches. Some of the backgrounds were coming back with heavy specular light coming out of them.

"It was about two in the morning, I'm loopy," says Silver. "I'm walking up to the third floor of Animation. It was one wing where all the *Tron* offices were. Harrison's was across the hall from Richard Taylor's. I leave him a note, saying it's two in the morning and I'll probably be in a little bit late. I hope it's not a problem. And I hear voices in Richard Taylor's office. It's more voices yelling. It's Steven Lisberger. He's yelling at Richard Taylor. 'These bimbo spray painters are destroying my picture and I'm going to fire the lot of them!'"

Panic struck Silver. Did Lisberger think he was the one messing up the work? Silver was positive he did his job correctly. He tip-toed out and went home, thinking he could be fired the next morning.

"I didn't meet Steven a lot on this film," recalls Silver. "Frankly, he scared the hell out of me! It was a terribly important film for him. He was very intense about it. Lots of outbursts. This was my first big break. I wanted to be invisible."

Acting like he did not hear a thing, Silver went to Ellenshaw's office the next morning to see if he could help. Ellenshaw showed him one of the paintings. Speculars everywhere. Silver offered a solution.

"I changed the kind of airbrushes we were using," says Silver.

The result was flawless and there were no more speculars. Silver was promoted to Background Painting Supervisor.

# HAMMERTIME

Chris Casady was another CalArts graduate who came to Disney from the outside world. The first major job he had was as an effects animator on *Star Wars*. Rotoscoping explosions and animating lasers were his specialties at $11.00 an hour, which was a considerable wage in the 1970s. Arriving at Disney, he could not believe his good fortune.

"I thought, wait a minute! This is Disney," says Casady. "There's no studio in the world that knows animation better than Disney. I'm going to be surrounded by really good animators. It's only going to be a matter of time before they figure out that I'm an amateur and I'm out."

He was going to work for the legendary Lee Dyer, an effects animation supervisor who did effects animation on *Mary Poppins*, and had worked as an animator on a few children's television shows. Casady was awestruck.

"I'm going to work under the great Lee Dyer," recalls Casady. "I'm going to have a mentor and he's going to teach me how to improve my animation."

Casady animated sparks for a scene in which a tank gets hit. Excited, Casady rushed to Dyer and asked for his opinion. Eager to receive constructive criticism from his mentor, Casady stood next to Dyer as the film ran through the Moviola. He was thinking that Dyer was going to critique how to improve the animated sparks

"Great," said Dyer. "Let's ship it off. Looks good to me."

Dyer left the room. Casady stood there in the room by himself, knowing there must be something wrong with his animation.

"But I didn't get instruction from my department head," says Casady. "After a while, I realized that I'm not such a bad animator. I'm not great, but there's nobody better than me around here. These guys are not Disney people! They came from Filmation. This was a completely green crew."

Peter Gullerud was an up-and-coming animator who had worked at Hanna-Barbera before coming to Disney. He considered himself a peon on the *Tron* production.

"All I did was exeter cutouts, a few animated Frisbee throws and made things flash in the background," he says.

Yet he was keen on the happenings around the effects animation department. Working at Disney was also an eye opener for Gullerud. Dyer had an assistant named Ron Stangl who cracked down on the animators if they were not working hard. He carried around a hammer and patrolled the Animation Building halls, poking his head in the door of the animators with the hammer in hand.

"His big thing, which was humorous, was when break times were over, he would shout out really loud, 'It's hammer time!'" remembers Gullerud. "He was a real character. A little scary sometimes, but fun."

"It was an intense schedule and you were just living there all the time," says Rooney. "You're stuck in a room with eight or ten of us. So we just goof off all the time. I mean working, but we'd tell jokes or do drawings to make each other laugh all day long."

When Stangl marched down the hall for inspection, animators quickly hid their cartoon drawings and replaced them with their real *Tron* work.

"We would behave like the teacher was coming," says Casady. "Better look like we're drawing."

Gullerud recalls there was a rumor around the Animation Building about Dyer and Stangl. On a whim, they took a flight to Oahu. They arrived in Honolulu, went to a hotel bar, had some drinks, got drunk, then flew back to Los Angeles in time for work.

"Oh my god, I thought, these guys must be making some good money to be able to fly all the way to Hawaii then fly back within a few hours," Gullerud says with a laugh.

To relieve some pressure, Gullerud went around and recorded audio interviews of the animators at work. His recordings give us an insight of the atmosphere these artists were working under.

Gullerud asked some of the artists what they thought of *Tron*.

"I think it's fantastic," says assistant effects animator, John Tucker. "If it wasn't for *Tron*, I wouldn't have the most fantastic T-shirt collection right now. It seems like every day I come to work, there's another T-shirt available. An incredibly beautiful orange T-shirt with a big, black light bulb on it, which I'm especially going to wear on Halloween."

Gullerud tape recorded airbrush artist, Bill Arance.

"I think the people at the Disney special effects department are kind of scared by what we can pull off," says Arance. "I don't think they were so sure we were able to do the job we're doing here. They may feel threatened, just as I feel threatened by all the computer animation I've been watching. [Disney's Effects Department] is larger. I'm pretty sure it's larger than the team we have here for *Tron*. But the funny thing is, even though they may be larger, they can't really seem to do as good a job as we can. And if you think I'm blowing my own horn, you're damn right! I'm pretty proud of our small family."

Silver says, "I've just come in, after being here until four in the morning, which is typical. Get the violins going. It would be nice if the people who run the studio would consider the fact that we're trying to do four animated films all synced together. Normally we'd be doing one in two years. We're now doing the equivalent of four in four months. This sometimes presents problems in logistics, especially when animators and background people don't get the information until about four weeks after it's needed. But that's the making of *Tron*."

"What I've seen of *Tron* really amazes me," says Arance. "Everybody talks about the computer animation. I'll have to give it credit. It's really fascinating. The ironic part is that the people aren't going to really notice the stuff that we do. It's been done so well by everybody that it's going to be taken for granted, which I guess is going to make it work. If it was wrong, people are going to notice it. Since they're not going to notice it, it means we did our job right."

The interviewer then records Casady.

"Some of your gut reactions [to *Tron*]," asks Gullerud.

"It's going to be a milestone in films. Some really spectacular effects in the film. It's going to be an extravaganza. It's going to pull this studio back off its feet. I just think there's never been a film like it. I'm really delighted to be a part of it."

## THE LIGHT CYCLE TRANSFORMATION

The "Electronic World" was energized with light. Circuitry glowed, "Identity Discs" (aka "Deadly Discs") swirled in neon, and Light Cycles were charged with electricity. When watching the film, it is difficult not to notice how lighting affects every "Electronic World" person and vehicle.

In the scene when Tron battles other players in a game of "Deadly Disc," the light from the Identity Disc radiates over Tron's face. As he raises the disc above his head after the battle, strong light from it shines on his body as a perfect circle. In the Light Cycle scenes, especially in the sequence aptly named "Illegal Exit," bars of light float over the windshields of the Cycles, giving them the illusion of fast movement.

These lighting effects were not done during production, nor were they done on a computer later on. These were done by human hand. The production had a unit of animators, including Van Vliet, who added the ambient light frame-by-frame.

The effects animators performed stunning work in *Tron*. The transition of Bridges, Boxleitner and Shor into their Light Cycles still fools viewers' eyes today. The trio is transported to the Game Grid, rezzing up into their body shapes, line-by-digital-line. Within seconds, they are formed into their human-like shapes. A bored-looking Sark presses a green button on his console and the players grab a light bar, hunch over and are immediately transformed into their Light Cycles.

Many journalists and audiences assumed that this was all done on the computer. They were wrong. It is true that much of this sequence was done by MAGI. But the formation of the Light Cycles only uses a few frames of the CGI footage.

Van Vliet took the shape of Mead's Light Cycle design and drew, by hand, a wireframe of it. He drew the chassis, the suspension and wheels making it appear as though it was computer generated. He also drew different layers to be animated by Campbell. When these layers were combined in the camera, the animation appeared as though the actors were morphing into their vehicles.

"After the whole show was over, I had no idea that this was going to become one of their signature pieces," says Van Vliet. "I remember suddenly in every computer magazine, there's a picture of that transition going, 'Isn't it amazing what computers can do?' It made me nuts!"

"The rezzing up and the conversion happen within seconds of each other and are all hand drawn," says Campbell. "There's literally not a single computer-generated element there."

"I was flying on a plane one time and I get the little headsets," recalls Van Vliet. "I had been dozing off and I woke up. They were playing something about the miracle of computers. They showed that scene and they're going, 'Look what computers can do now.' I remember sitting up in the plane and not realizing I was yelling, 'NO NO! That's not right!' All these people are looking at me like I have a problem."

It is also notable that Van Vliet animated the grid lines that form the actor's bodies. What appear to be computer-generated grid lines are all hand drawn and painted by Van Vliet.

Once the live-action footage of the actors, the effects animation, and MAGI's Light Cycle footage was cut together, the action appears nearly seamless.

## PAC-MAN AND SARK'S BRAINS

David Warner's Sark was such a good villain, that he was often the center of humorous practical jokes in the film. The centerpiece of Sark's war room is a huge map of the "Electronic World," designed by Richard Taylor. To make the map livelier, the effects animation team added blinking displays. The map is supposed to be as serious as Sark.

"We're passing all this stuff out," says Van Vliet. "I'm going to do this section. You do this section. Everybody's got all their pieces and we're putting it all together. It took forever to shoot the thing. When dailies came up, we're all excited watching this thing. Someone goes, 'Hey! What the hell is that?' We look over and it was Pac-Man! That's got to be Casady. I was, like, we are so screwed. But Lisberger says it's funny, leave it in."

"I didn't tell anybody about it," says Casady. "I just thought it was going to be seen in dailies and they'd laugh and say shoot it without that [being in there]."

Casady animated Pac-Man at a much slower rate than what was seen in the arcade video game. In the arcade game, Pac-Man's mouth moves at an incredibly fast rate, but Casady thought that was too distracting. He animated it much slower, at about eight frames per second, which gives the audience a chance to catch the gag.

One of the favorite scenes for the effects animation department was Sark's demise from Tron's "Deadly Disc."

"That was the first time a Disney character got his brains blown out on screen," recalls Van Vliet. "We were real excited about that."

The top of Sark's head is carved off, causing it to spark, which was proudly animated by Casady. Making the scene more electronically gruesome, Sark's brain is shown after being cleaved. Casady, a fairly quiet guy, went home one night and experimented with Sark's brains.

"I said, you know, if he's going to go forward like that and he's going to hit his head on the floor, there should be something spilled out on the floor," reasoned Casady.

In his kitchen, Casady mixed up pancake batter and Cheerios and poured the mixture down on white paper. With his Nikon camera, he took photographs and had them developed at the Disney photo lab. Liking what he saw in the print, he had the *Tron* camera department film the oozing brains.

Animators did not often see dailies, but Casady knew when they were scheduled. He snuck into the Disney theater to hear everyone's reaction. Sark collapsed to the floor and his brains spilled into a puddle. The reactions were unanimous.

"Oh my God!"

"What was that?"

"It looks like puke!"

"They were right," says Casady. "They axed it. Once I saw it, it did look pretty gross. But then I thought of an alternative."

Casady had a broken clock at home. He smashed it up, took out the parts, and made them spill out of Sark's head. Surprisingly, the scene was left in, despite Disney's penchant for "G" rated movies.

## FLYNN'S DEREZZ

Flynn's derezz by the MCP turned out to be one of the most complicated effects to create. The MCP freezes Flynn in his chair with a shot of a laser beam. The MCP precisely deconstructs Flynn's body, finger-by-finger, limb-by-limb, until he is sucked into the "Electronic World."

The scene was filmed on the extremely limited schedule at Lawrence Livermore. Bridges leaned back in his chair with a frozen expression on his face. That was it. No fancy crane shots. No camera spinning around Bridges to create a sense of chaos. Bridges left the chair. Logan and Lisberger filmed the empty chair. Scene finished and in the can. On to the next location. It was up the effects animators to figure out how to derezz Bridges' body.

"The most hideously complex thing we had was getting Flynn out of the 'Real World' and into the computer," recalls Van Vliet. "Richard Taylor basically says, 'Shoot a bunch of transparencies.' I said what do you want me to do with it? He said, 'Figure it out.' I had the rope around my neck. It can be the most terrifying thing you've ever seen. It's also the most exhilarating thing because you can do anything."

Using his animation skills, he worked with transparencies and an animation camera and optical printer. Van Vliet surgically removed every part of Flynn's body.

"There were a lot of problems we didn't expect," says Van Vliet. "When you're running on an optical printer, you're making mattes because it's a small piece of film. Your expansion and contraction of the film is fairly minimal and it's consistent. All during *Tron*, you see that problem popping in and out, but it's in the 'Electronic World.' You can get away with it. If it was really bad, we put a sound effect on it and say we designed it that way."

Van Vliet continues, "When we were trying to get Flynn out of there, we're trying to treat it like an optical. It was hideous. We had to reshoot a lot of stuff because the film, depending on what time of day it was processed, and sometimes how long it was sitting on the camera, would heat up. The warmer the camera got, everything expands out a little bit so you get all these matte lines."

Once Van Vliet and Campbell worked around the problem of the expanding film, Van Vliet was not happy enough with Flynn's derezz. He wanted to "plus" it up with an additional optical effect. As the MCP's laser zaps Flynn's fingers, there is a lens flare that quickly flashes on the screen. Long before Michael Bay had the ILM visual effects department add anamorphic lens flares to *Armageddon* (1998), Van Vliet and Campbell did it on *Tron*.

"It was fun, but it was a huge pain in the ass," says Campbell. "Disney only had one backlit camera and it had a giant set of fluorescent tubes, so you have nice even lighting. You couldn't get a hot lens flair out of it. I took a dental mirror and drilled a hole through it and then took a light bulb from a flashlight. This is what Disney was great for. I told them what I needed. I designed the basic set-up and they built it for me. In order to get a lens flare, you have to have a light source that points directly into the lens so that it's getting a refraction. We would put the artwork down and I'd put the lens flare device where the artwork was supposed to be."

## THE BUTT GRAD SCANDAL

Other problems cropped up in creating the effects: Tron's butt glowed.

"Steven Lisberger was in dailies one day and noted that because there was so much black circuitry on Bruce Boxleitner's original costume butt, the final shots as finished (to be cut into the film) made Tron's butt glow a lot," recalls Ellenshaw.

Lisberger rightly felt that the glowing behind would be too distractive to the audience.

"All the guys would be running down the hallway and they'd look like blue butt baboons because they have this glowing ass!" exclaims Campbell.

"So we had this thing called the 'butt grad scandal,'" says Van Vliet.

"I still have daily reports that say this shot approved, this shot approved, this shot needs butt grads," says Campbell. "What does that mean? If you didn't know what it was, it meant that a shot has to go back and someone has to go through every frame, by hand, and airbrush a darkening density on a guy's ass so it doesn't glow as much."

"To solve the problem Steven felt that there should be hand-painted/airbrushed grads (frame-by-frame) generated that would be then added to reshooting the offensive shots in order to minimize the glowing butts," says Ellenshaw. "Naturally Richard and I resisted the idea as it meant more re-shoots as well as more work for future shots for the two airbrush artists. But, because we had refined the workflow process by then, we were able to incorporate the grads and make the director's changes possible for the final film."

## THE ENERGY CAVE AND SPECIAL EFFECTS

Escaping from the Game Grid into the nether regions of the "Electronic World," the warriors stumble upon the "Energy Cave." The water glows blue with beams of energy bouncing off its surface. The warriors lie down at the side of the digital pond and take in the liquid.

The "Energy Cave" scene is another one of those scenes that causes an audience to say "Wow!" Sitting in a movie theater on a summer day, it is easy to identify with Flynn, Tron and Ram as they quench their thirst in pools of iridescent water. The water looks so inviting, so pure, and so energizing, even users want a drink.

The effect was one of the more simple ones done on the film. Shot on top of a water tank on a Disney soundstage, Bridges, Boxleitner and Shor pretended they were in an oasis. Effects animators animated water reflections on the walls of the cave, while background artists painted in the interior formations. Getting the water to glow was fairly simple in concept, though still very time consuming.

"The energy water sequence where they're finding the water, that's all moiré patterns," says Campbell.

Carefully lit, the water appears to glow from within. The moiré patterns give the water vibrant life with the addition of carefully placed animation. Ingeniously, the effects department used a number of everyday objects to create some of the film's other effects patterns, as well.

"Part of one of the sequences I like a lot, really proud of, was the 'Energy Cave' with the liquid," says Taylor. "Drinking the liquid was one of my favorites. The design of it. The look of it. Getting the water to interact."

Douglas Eby had come from Robert Abel & Associates with considerable camera and compositing effects experience. He had filmed a number of high-profile commercials, including Duracell batteries and Chevy trucks. Those ads, in the days before CGI, were made with real models and shot for hours on end with a motion-controlled camera. Eby was brought aboard *Tron* to test various effects.

Says Eby, "A test might consist of many dozens of combinations of artwork (often high-contrast film transparencies, such as enlarged frames of actors in *Tron*), artwork overlays such as thin sheets of translucent plastic laid on top of the art, and colored gel filters or scratch' filters in front of the lens: thin squares of clear plastic that was literally scratched with a sharp tool, or sandpaper, to create a flare around bright areas of the artwork."

Eby, Taylor, John Scheele and Campbell's use of filtering tricks lent to the film's striking effects. Clu's horrifying derezz, for example, was done with silk screen, steel mesh and rippled glass found inside a common shower door.

When the Guards patrol the "Electronic World," their staffs are lit with rainbow lighting effects. Taylor had a collection of very fine steel mesh used for silk screening. He placed it over the lens and created one of the more memorable effects in the film.

When Sark is close to being derezzed by the angry MCP, those effects were animated by Casady by scratching moiré patterns onto separate Kodaliths. Once the separate patterns are animated together, the effect of derezzing appears on camera.

## THE LOVE SCENE

The now infamous "Love Scene" in *Tron* was perhaps the first time any sexual intimacy was implied in a live-action film released by Disney. Especially in the 1970s, any suggestion of sex was limited to maybe a glance or small kiss between characters in a Disney film. There had been romantic scenes throughout the history of the studio's features and shorts. Mickey Mouse and Minnie Mouse always had a sweet relationship. Donald Duck was in a bit more assertive cartoon shorts when it came to Daisy Duck. The 1954 Donald Duck short, *Donald's Diary*, is a hilarious riff on the duck falling for Daisy, only to realize it is not all great after the wedding vows. In *Bambi* it is implied that mating is crucial to the circle of life. But mostly, Disney films shied away from any suggestion of sex.

On the run, Yori leads Tron into her apartment. The place is dull until she turns on the lights. Suddenly her apartment is a swanky pad, designed by Syd Mead, which overlooks the "Electronic World" and the I/O Tower. She walks over to a control panel and it transforms her clothes into a sparkling negligee. The front of her body is lit up. Tron casually struts over to her and she lights up his circuitry by tracing her finger downward over his chest and abdomen. The scene cuts before she reaches his crotch.

The morning after, Tron meditates in front of the window.

Lisberger decided that the "Love Scene" had to be cut. He thought it slowed the pacing down. But Ellenshaw says Lisberger took it out for another reason.

"Steven chickened out," says Ellenshaw.

The scene was not overtly sexual. It was not any more explicit than something seen on a soap opera of the day. The film would still have maintained a "PG" rating. And it managed, in such a short amount of screen time, to add some humanity to both Tron and Yori's characters. For the first time in the film, they are relaxed.

"I remember being at that show last year [screening at the Academy of Motion Picture Arts and Sciences in Beverly Hills in 2006] and there were these real young kids sitting beside me," recalls Rooney. "The film was going on and one said, 'This is where the Yori's apartment thing would be! That's the door right there.' I don't even know that and I worked on the film!"

## DILLINGER'S HELICOPTER

Dillinger's helicopter scene has most people stumped on how the glowing effect was achieved. Again, it is assumed that the effect was created on computers. In reality, it was done on a cold night with a small crew, Scotch Light tape, a Super Panavision 70 camera, and two helicopters.

The day before, Taylor applied special reflective Scotch Light tape to strategic areas on the aircraft. The helicopter itself was painted black.

"I was trying to figure out a way to get it to show up at night," recalls Logan. "It just came to me instead of just using a beam splitter, we could do front projection just by holding a Power 64 Globe very close to the lens. The Scotch Light would light up just like front projection material, even though the helicopter was a good 100 feet away."

Flying above Hollywood, Bruce Logan and Richard Taylor followed Dillinger's helicopter and filmed. Logan shot at 100 ASA with a 2.8 lens, and under cranked the camera at twelve frames-per-second to get the light he needed on film. Under cranking also made it easier for the audience to see the helicopter's blades spinning in the glowing light.

At the end of the film, daylight rapidly turns to a nightscape panorama that looks just like the "Electronic World" Flynn left behind. Logan used time-lapse photography to capture the shot. He shot, with a small crew, on top of one of the tallest buildings in downtown Los Angeles.

"We were there for one night," says Logan. "I think it was my idea. You can never tell after that much time. Once again, I used to do a lot of that stuff, so I probably brought that to the party. I shot some stuff two seconds-a-frame, four seconds-a-frame, eight seconds-a-frame. It was kind of nice. It kind of took you back into the 'Electronic World.'"

# Chapter 15

# *ZINGS, ZAPS AND CRESCENDOS: MUSIC AND SOUND EFFECTS*

*Tron* needed a cutting-edge music score and incredible sound effects. But Disney was not fit to do the job by the time Lisberger's film was ready. The studio had a fine pedigree of music in its films over the years, but it was still using a stale formula of outdated film scores. Its sound effects library was the same one used on Disney films since Walt was alive.

The studio relied on its own formulas through the 1970s and early 1980s. One could almost interchange the scores, theme songs, and sound effects on different Disney films and no one would notice the difference.

Although the Walt Disney studio was relatively small, it had employed some of the top composers and song writers in the film business. Oliver Wallace may not have been a household name, but he had an impressive career at Disney. Not only did he compose the music scores for *Dumbo* (1941), *Alice in Wonderland* (1951), *Peter Pan* (1953), and *Old Yeller* (1957), he also composed wonderful music for a number of Disney's short animated films and the theme to the *Disneyland, U.S.A.* television show. Robert and Richard Sherman were young brothers who caught Walt's ear for great songs. They were soon hired to write songs for *Mary Poppins* and the *It's a Small World* attraction.

Once again for Disney, the outside world had changed. By the late 1960s and through the 1970s, film music took a detour. Most of the old-time studio music departments still relied on orchestras for their scores. But the new and young filmmakers breaking into the film business sought change in that venue, too.

## WENDY CARLOS

Pop music had actually been a staple in films since the earliest days of the silent films. Live orchestras no doubt played current melodies or popular songs of the day to accompany films. Pop music was prevalent in the early talkies. So it is rather amusing that old studio executives could not stand hearing the likes of Bill Haley & the Comets (*Blackboard Jungle*—1955), and Elvis Presley (*Jailhouse Rock*—1957).

To modern audiences and some film historians, it was *Easy Rider* (1969) that broke the envelope on film soundtracks. It was not the first film to utilize a rock or pop soundtrack, but it did encourage filmmakers and studios to create scores based on current music made by bands or pop singers. A few years later, George Lucas, with sound designer Walter Murch, stunned Ned Tanen by using only 1950s and early 1960s rock/pop songs to underscore *American Graffiti*.

In the late 1960s, most of the major studios were either bought by independent investors, or by conglomerate companies looking to make money in the film business. Many staff members who had worked at those studios were either close to retirement, or had died. Departments were shut down, including music departments. It was now seen as being old fashioned to have orchestral scores on films. It was seen as easier and cheaper to hire a smaller orchestra or ensemble. Or in the case of *American Graffiti*, it was easier and cheaper to secure the rights to rock songs.

On the fringe of the Hollywood establishment of film scores were independent, yet immensely talented composers who also performed their own music. Wendy Carlos, a Rhode Island native, was a classically trained musician. She specialized in using the Moog electronic synthesizer.

The Moog was a wall-sized unit comprised of separate modules in which various cords could be patched into plugs, creating different sounds. There were a number of pots that a musician could use to change the signature of any sound they wanted. Below was a keyboard that was identical to an organ keyboard. When it was played, it created a haunting and eerie sound like none heard before.

When Dr. Robert Moog invented the Moog electronic synthesizer, many classical musicians and fans derided it. It was seen as taking the humanity out of music by making it electronic, allegedly sterile and cold sounding. Carlos, on the other hand, embraced it as an instrument that could make beautiful music.

"What I was inspired by, and what made me want to write, was probably the use of instrumental colors with each other," says Carlos. "In the beginning with electronics with the Moog synthesizer, you had a pallet from maybe A to J or K, where the orchestra almost could get down to the end of the alphabet. I was giving up a broad range of sound, rather than gaining anything. But some of the sounds were different. For me the best thing would've been if I'd been able to work with a lot more orchestras in which we combined electronic instruments with traditional instruments, because that's the way I think the synthesizer would grow."

One of the more avant-garde recordings of the 1960s was Carlos' *Switched-On Bach*. It shocked some classical music lovers as much as the Moog shocked some musicians. But it found a huge following by becoming one of the most successful selling records of 1968. By melding her own signature and classically trained musical skills with Moog's often haunting yet transcendent synth, Carlos created a groundbreaking masterpiece.

Stanley Kubrick had already firmly established himself as one of the most daring and original directors in the filmmaking. Self-assured and creatively brilliant in what he wanted to bring to the big screen, Kubrick challenged conventional studio filmmaking by using studio money to make his own masterpieces. Some were political satire like *Dr. Strangelove or: How I Learned to Stop Worrying and Love the Bomb* (1964). Others were haunting films like *2001: A Space Odyssey*. By 1971, Kubrick made the controversial *A Clockwork Orange*. That film startled audiences with its portrait of a society of Droogs, sex and violence. Carlos composed the score, utilizing very creatively, Moog versions of music by Beethoven, Purcell, Rossini & Scherzo and her own original compositions. Her music was chaotic and haunting, adding tension to the already intense scenes in Kubrick's strange film.

But Kubrick had become accustomed to using "needle-drop" music (music from already released albums) on *2001: A Space Odyssey*. He decided drop some of Carlos' music cues that she had already composed and recorded. Carlos worked once again with Kubrick on his film version of Stephen King's novel, *The Shining* (1980). The score was moody, actually more eerie than the film itself. But Kubrick did the same thing as he had done on *A Clockwork Orange* and dropped some of Carlos' music from the final film.

"When I lost a few of my music cues in Stanley Kubrick's films, I got pissed at Stanley. It isn't what you do," says Carlos. "But I'm sure that Jerry Goldsmith was pissed when they yanked his *Legend* (1985) score. I think in his case he was right. Stanley, when he took out a number of the cues for *A Clockwork Orange*, I think that he was doing it against his film's best interest. Again, he had the right to do that."

## FREMER THE MUSIC SUPERVISOR

Fremer was not only in charge of the sound for *Tron*, but he was also responsible for the music. He had a few choices for composer. He could go for a John Williams-type score that used an entire orchestra with a classic sounding theme. By the late 1970s, orchestral scores, particularly by John Williams (*Close Encounters of the Third Kind*, *Superman: The Movie*), had returned to the big screen with a huge impact. The rousing marches and pretty crescendos elevated science fiction and fantasy films to a level of respectability. But was *Tron* ripe for a classical sounding score?

Fremer's other alternative was to hire a composer who could do the music electronically. In pop music, especially in the 1970s and early 1980s, it was becoming common for songs to feature synthesizers. Rock bands such as Styx and The Police used the synth with excellent results on "Too Much Time on My Hands" and "Spirits in the Material World."

Electronic music was also being used in television and film. One of the most popular and recognizable scores was John Carpenter's theme to his film *Halloween* (1978). Carmine Coppola's score for *Apocalypse Now* was performed on a Moog and other synthesizers.

"I started thinking what am I going to do?" recalls Fremer. "Who do I want for the music? I want to get Wendy Carlos. *A Clockwork Orange*. Synthesizers. And I'm thinking, if we can do a pure synthesizer score, we can save a lot of money. She's not exactly hot at this point in time. She really wasn't film scoring at that point in time. The film scoring stuff started pouring in from other guys. And I started looking."

Because Fremer was given a limited budget for music, he had to be frugal. Since hiring a person to compose and perform the film's score could be cheaper than hiring an orchestra, he looked at other composers, as well.

"One guy I started talking to was Chris Young (*Spider-Man 3*—2007)," says Fremer. "He had just moved to Hollywood. He was in Santa Monica in this tiny little apartment. He sent me a cassette and it was kind of interesting. I had to get somebody who's new, hungry, and who doesn't want a lot of money. I met with him and he was good. It could've been his first big gig, but I decided I wanted Wendy Carlos."

Carlos had training in both worlds of music. She was aware of the significance of paying tribute to the classical masters. Without grounding in classical music and awareness of other genres, a composer's creation could be limited in its scope.

"I listened to a lot of early 20th century music," says Carlos. "I became very fond of Stravinsky, Bartok and Prokofiev and Respighi, and people who had a fairly sophisticated awareness of how to orchestrate."

She also had a foot firmly planted in the future of music. Though her music was considered by some to be futuristic, it was firmly grounded in all classical forms of music. Fremer realized how Carlos could ultimately transform *Tron* and its electronic landscapes into another realm. Her score could be both futuristic and classic sounding at the same time.

## FREMER THE SOUND SUPERVISOR

Fremer was an audiophile at heart, which is a lofty term given to people who love good-sounding stereo equipment and recordings. He loved music and playing it on his high-end stereo system. His choice of recordings came from vinyl LPs, and he amassed a serious collection of both stereo and monophonic (mono) recordings over the years. He chose the finest turntables, amplifiers, preamplifiers and speakers he could afford to play them on. Not only did he become an expert on excellent audio sound equipment, he also became an expert on how good quality sound could affect the listener.

In the case of *Tron*, Fremer knew he wanted to blow audiences away with a great quality soundtrack.

"I'm thinking this movie has got to have good music and sound effects," recalls Fremer. "Music carries the emotions of the movies anyway. You take it away from the movie, it's amazing how bad it gets. I knew the music had to carry it. Sound had to be really good."

Many of the films released during the 1980s utilized Dolby Stereo soundtracks. Fremer had already used the 35mm Dolby Stereo format on *Animalympics* and was determined to have Dolby used on *Tron*.

Dolby Stereo took the old magnetic stereophonic format that had been used since the 1950s and updated it with Ray Dolby's patented noise-reduction technology. By taking out the hiss common on the old magnetic tracks, and by using updated recording and mixing gear, Dolby soon became the standard for high-quality movie presentation.

One of Dolby's key successes was the introduction of this technology on 70mm film prints. *A Star is Born* (1976) and *Star Wars* put both Dolby Stereo and 70mm Six-Track Dolby Stereo on the map. The 70mm Six-Track Dolby Stereo format used left, center, right and mono surround speakers in its layout, plus "baby boom" for low end bass. Dolby Stereo was very quickly adapted into many movie theaters around the world.

It was a special treat for audiences to experience movies presented in 70mm Six-Track Dolby Stereo. It could lend prestige to an otherwise mediocre film. Audiences had to go to select theaters to experience this high-quality sound presentation. Although it is common today to have 5.1 tracks of audio on anything from feature films to Blu-ray discs, it was a novelty for many years. (The term "5.1" was invented for the home video market.) The term "70mm" told audiences they were seeing something bigger, brighter and more incredible than they normally saw in 35mm.

When Fremer was assembling a team to record sound effects and mix the soundtrack, sound design and mixing were undergoing radical changes due to the effect of *Star Wars*, *Close Encounters of the Third Kind*, and *Apocalypse Now*. Many films made in the 1970s employed stock sound effects like explosions, wind and gunshots. Many of these sound effects were from film libraries and were pulled from the shelf when needed. Walter Murch, Alan Splet, Randy Thom, Richard Beggs and Ben Burtt expanded the envelope by "designing" the soundtrack and inventing new sound effects. They created a fresh approach to the stale use of sound.

As for Disney, it was still using many of the sound effects created by studio veteran, Jimmy McDonald. On some of the studio's films through the 1980s, they were still using the RCA Photophone system, a system that dated back to the 1920s! If one listens to a Disney movie from the late 1960s through the early 1980s, much of the dialogue and sound effects have a distinct sound that is unique to that studio.

"The sound department at Disney were basically guys that were the guys you've seen in *Tron*," Fremer jokes. He is referring to the old programs that are about to be derezzed by the MCP in the final act.

If Disney was going to play with the bigger studios with a film like *Tron*, it had to have a significant soundtrack to accompany its groundbreaking film. Fremer was excited to take on this challenge. But there was a problem.

"I look at the budget," recalls Fremer. "I wished I had kept that piece of paper because everyone's going to deny this, I suspect. But the budget for the whole soundtrack was like $60,000. I swear to God! The looping budget was $5000.00! The sound effects budget was $8000.00 or $10,000. The whole sound effects and the music [budget] was like $80,000 or $90,000. It probably came from Disney. I suspect what they did was take the soundtrack [budget] from *Herbie Goes Bananas*. This budget was ludicrous."

From the beginning of pre-production, Fremer insisted he start building the foundation for the film's sound design.

Fremer continues.

"I walked into Kushner's office. I said, 'I cannot do this. The movie's a fantasy, but this budget's a fantasy. It can't be done. We have to invent sound for everything. You can't use any of the production sound. Any of it. Every sound has to be invented in this movie. The atmosphere has to be invented.'"

At this point in post-production, the virtual set location sound that had been recorded was terrible.

"The first day on the set, I go in to watch them shoot," recalls Fremer. "I'm there for the first take. It may have been an early scene where Jeff Bridges is getting on the Solar Sailer. Bruce Boxleitner picks him up into the ship. So they're walking and it's *eeek, eeek*. So Bruce Boxleitner goes running across this wooden platform that they'd built. Boom! Boom! Boom! Banging. Footsteps. Squeaking. "

During dallies, it became even worse.

"The dailies sounded like a movie from the 1940s, like a Humphrey Bogart movie," says Fremer. "What they were doing was they were compressing the dialogue track in the transfer. Completely. You'd have to compress it for an optical track. It didn't sound like a modern movie. I said, 'Wait a second. Why does it sound like that? We can leave the dialogue in hi-fi with full dynamics and frequency response, then in the mix we can fix that.' The whole movie was going to have to be looped, every last minute of it."

## FRANK SERAFINE

Frank Serafine was a kid from Boulder, Colorado, when he entered the film business in his early twenties. He was a naturally talented musician. Disney liked his talent so much that they hired him and his band for the opening of *Space Mountain* at Disneyland in 1977.

Serafine broke into film business after being hired on *Star Trek: The Motion Picture* to create other-worldly sound effects. He supplemented his income by doing endorsements with different companies. Living in a small apartment in Santa Monica, he packed the place with all sorts of new technological wonders like synthesizers and videotape decks. This was new and hot technology of the day and it was something that appealed to Fremer.

"He showed me a multi-track recorder synced up to time code with a U-matic picture," says Fremer. "First time I'd seen that. He was saying look, you could transfer finished film to video, sync it up with multi-track and lay in all the sound effects. Cutting and pasting without transferring to mag. Then you could mix it. Bring it to the soundstage and sync it up to the dubbers. It would sound better because you wouldn't be losing generations."

U-matic was a videotape format that was popular with television broadcasters.

"I understood the technology," says Serafine. "I met Michael Fremer and we just thought like one brain. So he hired me to do *Tron*."

Fremer was looking into utilizing new recording and mixing technologies such as digital keyboard sound effects and videotape assistance. This would cost some money, but it was not outrageous. He went back to Kushner to upgrade his sound budget.

In his usual calm demeanor, Kushner replied, "Hey, you're the sound producer. That's your job. You gotta make it work within the budget."

"You want me to stay within the budget," said Fremer. "This is a new technology. It's not tried and true. It hasn't been proven. If it works, we can have a fantastic soundtrack within your budget. But if it doesn't work, it's going to cost five times as much."

"Eh, whatever ya gotta do."

## ANTIQUATED DISNEY AND *TRON'S* UNIQUE SOUND

With the picture being edited by Gourson, and many of the completed visual effects still waiting to be cut into the picture, Fremer and Serafine set out to build a sound effects library specifically for *Tron*. They did this from scratch without using anything in the Disney sound library. The question was where to record all the sound effects. Most, if not all, Disney films were recorded on the lot by the studio sound department. It was a tradition, cheaper to do, and the mix could be controlled on the studio lot. But it was not practical for a modern film.

"The equipment was so antiquated at Disney," recalls Serafine.

"I go into the dubbing stage and it's these union guys who are not bright as a bulb," recalls Fremer. "They were basically old timers just kind of sitting around. Let me go see what's going on in the dubbing room. They did not have high speed dubbers. You could not rewind and fast forward fast. It was only real time. For you to go back a minute, it took a minute. If you were to go back ten minutes, it took ten minutes. There was no way we could do this."

"We all lived on the west side," says Serafine. "I lived in Brentwood and Michael lived in Venice. Nobody wanted to drive to Burbank every day. There was a new facility that was going into business on the west side of town, which was a bunch of really young people called Lions Gate Films. We brought the mix there."

He was provided with his own stage area down in the basement at Lions Gate. The building used to be an old airplane hangar for Howard Hughes. It was heaven sent for Serafine.

"It was such a pioneering experience," recalls Serafine. "New equipment was coming out during that time. Back in the day, we were dealing with all this film and the Moviola on *Star Trek*, and I couldn't handle that. For the feat I had to undertake on *Tron*, that old technology just didn't [work]. I couldn't make it work. I ended up bringing in the recording industry technology. Multi-track tape recorders and video and locking them up, and synchronizing them so that I could sit there and work."

"You have to understand at this point in time, SMPTE time code and syncing multi-track audio was not done," says Fremer. "There were a couple companies making these SMPTE time code synchronizers, but it was just a new thing."

Streamlining the process and working from a videotape copy of the edited film sequences, it was much more efficient for Serafine and Fremer to construct and record the various sound effects. No longer were they tied down to hulking magnetic film machines and performing sound work in real time. They could fast forward and rewind with much faster speed. The process was so successful that Wendy Carlos used it for scoring the film in her New York apartment.

The real fun part for Serafine and Fremer was in recording the sound effects. They had the task of creating an "Electronic World" sound palette that had never been heard before. It was smartly decided to use a mixture of real-world sound and electronic effects. The reasoning for this was to give the audience a real-world reference as they heard the various effects. They would not necessarily be aware of how exactly the sound effect was created, but they could tie it into something tangible like a motorcycle.

"The Light Cycle sequence was the biggest challenge for me," recalls Serafine. "There was so much involved in that."

He and Fremer went out to a motocross track called Rock Stone and mounted high-quality microphones on the rider's bikes.

"I would take the samples of those motorcycles and then I'd play them back on the keyboard, but I wouldn't just play one note," says Serafine. "I'd play a cluster of five or six notes. There'd be five motorcycles like a super roar. A lot of those motorcycles, I actually performed those on synthesizers with a pitch wheel shifting the different gears like as if I was actually on the motorcycle."

To throw the Light Cycles into high gear and to give the sound more layering, both Serafine and Fremer used Fremer's Saab Sonnet, a short-lived yet intoxicating little sports car, as the basis for the Light Cycle's growl and gear shifting.

"Frank and I went up to Mulholland Drive," says Fremer. "We took a pair of Scheops mics and stuck them in the engine compartment and drove like maniacs on Mulholland Drive. Rrrrr! Rrrrr! Downshifting. Upshifting."

The recordings were then fed into Serafine's synthesizer. For the other signature effects, they found all sorts of ways to create them. For Sark's Carrier, he and Fremer took a prized ride inside the Goodyear Blimp, using its droning engine sound. For the various video game "bloops" and "blips," they asked the engineers at Apple to create the sound effects. The ambience of Flynn's Arcade was recorded in a real arcade. The zaps audiences heard when guards hit Flynn with their electric staffs, for example, were recordings of the giant electrical machines seen in the old *Frankenstein* films made at Universal Pictures. Those were combined with the sound of a video game.

For the whipping turns of the Light Cycles inside the jet walls, Serafine explains his use of a power saw: "You know how you hit the edge of the wood and it kind of goes WIING? Or you drop it on the ground and it's still kind of going and the saw blade hits the concrete? That's how we created the turns. It was kind of slicey and kind of cool. That was actually Michael Fremer's idea. The jet walls, those were jet motors."

The sound of the Recognizers was created on a Prophet Synthesizer 5, a popular piece of equipment that Serafine bought.

"There was a helicopter-type patch on the Prophet 5 factory patch I modified," says Serafine. "I tried to match everything with what might be in the real world. The Recognizers flew around, so what's the most ominous flying thing? Well, the beating of a helicopter. Kind of eerie, right? So I went with that kind of a sound."

For the tanks, Serafine was challenged by their speed and movement, as well as the fact they occasionally skidded.

"The problem with trying to use real tanks was trying to get the speed proper," says Serafine. "Those tanks were all over the place. I went in and customized them using a synthesizer. When they shot their cannons off, those were sound effects I recorded the fireworks at Disneyland. It was so loud that my headphones flew off my head. I didn't realize it was going to be so loud, man. It scared me to death. It was the loudest thing I ever heard in my life!"

It might be surprising where the voice of the Bit came from.

"The Bit voice was my recorded voice that I sampled and performed by playing a Fairlight synthesizer keyboard, then I processed the pitch through a Eventide harmonizer," says Serafine.

Carlos also got into the technological game that Serafine and Fremer were playing.

Carlos recalls, "I was aware that the little team we assembled here had pioneered using digital sound and music production techniques that were every bit as novel in their own world as the stuff that was being done by Triple-I and MAGI. I had some software I wrote which did the synchronization charts in my little old Hewlett-Packard computer. I was able to lay out all the cue points using digital in a way that had never been done so easily before."

## MICHAEL MINKLER

Michael Minkler was from a family who was involved with film sound since the early days of cinema. Both his grandfather and father were in the business. When he was seventeen years old, Minkler worked at his father's studio after school. There he learned the craft of recording film sound. By the age of twenty-two, he began learning how to mix film sound.

During the 1970s, Minkler worked on a number of high-profile films such as *The Shootist* (1976), *Star Wars*, *Sgt. Pepper's Lonely Hearts Club Band* (1978), *The Electric Horseman* (1979), *Popeye*, and *Wolfen* (1981). Working with a team of sound editors, mixers and sound engineers, Minkler often mixed film soundtracks with incredible richness and depth. When *Tron* was brought to Minkler's attention, he pursued the job and was brought on board.

Minkler's job, along with his team that included James LaRue and uncles Bob and Lee, was to take Fremer and Serafine's sound effects, and Carlos's music score, and build a soundtrack from scratch.

"There was nothing in *Tron* that came out of a library," says Minkler. "Everything was created for that. We wanted to make sure it was unique. And it's the same with *Star Wars*. I mixed *Star Wars* in 1977 and that was George Lucas's edict. 'I will not have a sound that's ever been heard before because we're not in a place we've ever been before. Don't go thinking you're going to get something out of a library.' When it comes to the sound world, *Star Wars* changed it."

The soundtrack for *Tron* was going to be challenging for the entire sound team. The combination of Carlos's music and sound effects by Fremer and Serefine was totally unique. No other film would sound like *Tron*. The problem for the sound team was not just confined with trying to figure out how to make the film sound great. Instead, personalities were going to clash over how the sound was mixed.

## RECORDING AT ABBEY ROAD

When a feature film is scored, a music composer can see most of the action on the screen in the sound recording studio. But on a visual effects film like *Tron*, it was very difficult. An editor can put in a temporary "slug" or pictures from the film's storyboards to give the composer an idea of what is happening in the film. In *Tron*, it was a lot more difficult to gauge what was going on. The live action consisted of Jeff Bridges, Bruce Boxleitner and Cindy Morgan running around a black soundstage on black-and-white film. No backgrounds. Hardly any props. No color. And often times, there were no completed visual effects to see.

The continuing pressure to lock the picture down was frustrating for everybody, including Carlos and the sound department. The original plan for the score was to have Carlos perform the entire score on her Moog synthesizer. But time was running out.

"I suggested what Bernard Herrmann did for *Psycho*," says Carlos. "He had scored a black-and-white movie with string orchestra only. I thought after the big colorful music for the computer world, with this huge orchestra that Douglas Gamley was conducting, and with a big pipe organ and analog and digital synthesizers sounds mixed in, what would be better for the ["Real World"] than sound that's very monochromatic? So I suggested string orchestra. For that there was no time. I was in the middle of the deadline."

It was eventually decided to break up the score into the "Real World," and the "Electronic World" in separate sections. The "Real World" music would be recorded with a string quartet, while the "Electronic World" consists of Carlos' Moog compositions. Fremer reasoned that it was necessary to hire a full symphonic orchestra, then Carlos would overdub her synthesized music. That proved a bit fruitless, so it was decided to go with a combination of both the orchestral score and Carlos' electronic score.

The bulk of the score was recorded in the acoustically brilliant Royal Albert Music Hall with the famed London Philharmonic Orchestra. Fremer, the audiophile, was in heaven. The BBC was to record the soundtrack and it was known for its superb audio recording quality. With the 100-piece orchestra waiting for its cue from the conductor, BBC recording engineer John Mosley and Carlos got into a heated argument over microphone placement.

"Her partner gets into a fight with Mosley about who's going to have a copy of the score," says Fremer. "Both of these people are holding onto this script, pulling at it. And I'm standing in the middle."

The problem was resolved and the score was recorded, though not to Fremer's golden ears.

"There were some real serious problems in the recording, though," recalls Fremer. "If there weren't synthesizer parts being added, it would've been really bad. As it was, there were problems with horns way in the distance in a lot of places. The mix should've been much more closely miked."

"We had an engineer that was really semi incompetent," says Carlos. "He didn't get as much recorded as we wanted. He wasted time. So we didn't finish. There were a lot of things that had to be done. The rest of it I had to either construct with synthesizers, or we had go back to Los Angeles with a pick-up group and then add things on sweetener. Sweeten means you take the thing you record and add parts to it and make it sound like there's more there."

The scoring moved back to Los Angeles where an ad hoc orchestra, dubbed the Los Angeles Orchestra, met for one session and disbanded. It consisted of a small string section and the UCLA Glee Club. The music was quickly recorded and sent back to New York City for Carlos to perform a final rundown.

"I had to do a lot of that work," recalls Carlos. "It made the final job much more difficult to hear. All of the strings, the deadline, the way they didn't give us full orchestra time, the way that it had to be broken apart and do the orchestra first, all those things conspired to make the job much more difficult than it had to be. It was annoying."

# Chapter 16

# *THE RACE TO FINISH TRON*

*Tron* spent almost a year in post-production. The post-production team was scrambling to complete everything from shooting Kodaliths to ensuring the film was ready for release prints. The reason for the scramble was Disney's summer release date, July 9, 1982.

Summer had become a juggernaut for studios to release their big blockbuster films. Before 1975, summer had been regarded as a dumping ground for "B" movies. The release of *Jaws* in 1975 changed the perception of studio executives. They found by releasing big popcorn movies in summer, while kids and families were on vacation, they could earn big box office returns. Especially with the release of *Star Wars*, summer was blockbuster time.

Disney had traditionally rereleased its animated classics during the summer. Since the films were made decades earlier, they had already paid for themselves. Money earned from the rereleases was gravy. For 1982, the studio was set to rerelease *Bambi*. *Tron* was due to come out a few weeks later.

*Tron* was Disney's first major summer release to compete with the bigger so-called event films from other studios. According to Taylor, the reason for the rush was to beat Don Bluth's *The Secret of NIMH* into theaters. This was allegedly due to a grudge that Card Walker had with Bluth. Bluth had left Disney in a much publicized bout over the direction of the studio's animation department. He formed his own studio in Ireland. *The Secret of NIMH* was an animated version of the popular children's book by Robert C. O'Brien. It would be released by MGM/UA.

For Taylor, it was a poor decision by Walker to allegedly rush *Tron* into release. *Tron* needed at least six months more post-production time for reshoots and audience test screenings to finesse the film. According to Taylor, the film was supposed to be released during the Christmas season of 1982.

"All of the sudden we're in production and they say you got to release it six months earlier," says Taylor. "It's like, 'What?' So the only way to do that was to double everything. So twice as many scene coordinators. Another photoroto machine. Another processor. The budget had increased as a result of that. They accepted that. It made it logistically so much more complicated."

Indeed, once the film was finished with production and headed into post-production, everyone had to kick their work into high gear. The film was shot during the spring and summer of 1981, then post-production followed immediately after that. With the tremendous schedule, it was technically feasible that the computer simulations, effects animation and Kodalith work could take over a year to complete and be ready for summer release. At least that is what was planned on. But Taylor tells it differently.

"*The Secret of NIMH* was coming out on that weekend," recalls Taylor. "Card Walker wanted *Tron* to come out on the same weekend to take away from their box office. And that is the reason. No objectivity. Nothing. Pure revenge. No consideration for *Tron* being something really special. It was entirely motivated by revenge. The stupidest thing in the world."

Bluth's film was to be released the weekend before *Tron*, on July 2, in a limited number of theaters. But according to Ellenshaw, *Tron* was *always* intended for the summer 1982 release date. He believes Walker did not mandate that the film be rushed in order to spite Bluth. And according to Miller, the film was always set for summer release, not Christmas.

"Card and I worked well together," says Miller. "We would go over the schedule of all the production and I would tell him when they would be ready. Well in advance, we would sort of pencil that film in for a certain period of the year. He never put any pressure on me to unnecessarily rush a film through."

"For me, there was never a question that the picture was to be released at any time other than summer 1982," recalls Wilhite.

Whether or not the film was scheduled too soon depends on memories and feelings. Certainly, Taylor felt very strongly.

"At the time we were doing *Tron*, it was a totally different administration of the people who are there now," says Taylor. "Card Walker was a fairly old guy. Ron Miller had been a pro football player who married Disney's daughter. Other than Tom Wilhite, there were no other filmmakers out there. The majority of the studio was working on getting EPCOT up. So there were tons of rides that needed animation. I never got one animator, one ink and painter on *Tron* from the Disney studios. Every animator I had to recruit from scratch. John Lasseter wanted to work on the film. There were a bunch of animators who really wanted to work on it and weren't allowed to."

## THE ART OF TRON AND THE NATO TRAILER

In October of 1981, Disney and publisher Simon & Schuster began negotiations on publishing a book about the making of *Tron*. Ellenshaw stepped up to the plate and recommended that Bonifer write the book. Little Simon, a division of Simon & Schuster, was excited about the prospect of a book. Kate Klimo, who was the new editor-in-chief, wrote Ellenshaw back and stated that there was a possibility of a spring 1982 publication.

The book was envisioned as a deluxe coffee table book with approximately ninety-six pages. Bonifer was hired as the author and Ellenshaw was hired as the "art editor." A novelization of the film would also be written by author Brian Daley.

In November of 1981, a *Tron* trailer was rushed out for the National Association of Theater Owners (NATO) convention in Las Vegas. All the major studios had trailers specially made for this convention. A dazzling trailer could entice theater exhibitors to place more prints of certain films in their theaters across the country.

The trailer for *Tron* was rough with temporary sound effects and music, but it was the most exciting looking film to come from Walt Disney Productions in years. But there were two problems. Would exhibitors place *Tron* in a high number of their theaters? And would the film, with its elaborate visual effects, be completed in time?

## OVER BUDGET AND CUCKOO'S NEST (*TRON* EAST)

It has been rumored that *Tron* went well over budget. Some rumors stated that the budget went as high as $28 million. In reality, the film's initial $12,388,000 budget climbed higher due to the necessity to finish the film on time. As the film went further into post-production, the true scope of the project was becoming more apparent.

"We really hadn't done enough of our homework," says Ellenshaw. "Most films 'back into' a budget; the bottom line being that you have to know what will be the maximum number the studio will accept."

Movie budgets then were made up from standard industry-wide forms that listed categories for the filmmakers—everyone from the stars to the writer, the director, the cameraman, the editor to such jobs as prop master, electrician, grip, etc.

"We were in serious denial," continues Ellenshaw. "Our budget forms had no category for computer animation for example, so we just pulled a figure out of the air—total guess. I think it was one million dollars... nice round number, sounded good."

There were also no categories for rotoscopers, scene coordinators or any of the myriad of new job descriptions that had to be invented for the many completely different processes needed to create a very unique film.

"There was no formula," says Ellenshaw. "It wasn't a live-action film. It wasn't an animated film. It was a hybrid and there was no way we could have thought of everything. It was probably just like building the pyramids in Egypt. It took a long time, but back then it was all about slave labor and slave labor was cheap."

It was realized that the Kodaliths being rotoscoped on the Disney studio lot were not going to be done in time. Calculations were made and panic struck. There was an estimate that it would take over a year, quite possibly more, to complete the Kodaliths, the rotoscoping and the subsequent painting of the cels.

"It quickly became clear, or I should say *not* so quickly became clear, that this was a task that could not be accomplished in the period of time required by anything less than a large number of people," says Ellenshaw. "We had already hired the available dozen or so inkers and painters in town."

The post-production side of *Tron* did not have any remaining pool of effects animators to choose from at this point. Disney would not supply any of their animators, either. In the early 1980s, most animation studios were either too small or too specialized to aid Disney. The studio, being proud of its high-end heritage, would have shuddered at the thought of hiring animators from low-cost studios around town. It was a miracle they allowed outside animators from Lisberger Studios to work on *Tron*.

Animation was at a low point, with most of it being done for children's television shows. Hannah-Barbera, Ruby-Spears Productions and Filmation were the largest providers of kid's television programming. But even they were trying to stay alive in a children's market that had grown stale. Kids were not watching as much animation and were starting to gravitate toward cable television shows, particularly those on Nickelodeon.

If Lisberger, Kushner, Ellenshaw and Taylor did decide to raid other animation studios around town, the cost might have been astronomical. Even at the smaller television specialty houses like Hannah-Barbera, animators were still paid well for their work. Eventually it was decided to use some small animation studios around town to complete work on the film.

"The business agent for the animated team had been approached because we couldn't get enough ink and paint services locally to handle all the work," says Silver. "We had gotten his blessing to find another place to do it as long as we were keeping all the people employed locally. Soon as we did that, they started yelling about runaway production. That's a crock of shit."

By January 1982, the *Tron* team eventually found cheaper alternatives overseas. Donald Kushner and Arne Wong took a trip to Asia to find an animation studio that could finish the work on time and under budget. They flew to Korea, Taiwan, and Japan.

Wong recalls, "We chose Taiwan because of two reasons. The first was that the studio was run by someone I trusted and worked for me as my assistant animator, James Wang. The second was that his team of workers was hard working and really enjoyed animation. Korea and Japan seemed too stuffy and the supervisors and workers seemed too separate, and mostly the workforce was not cheerful. I wanted to work with a team of happy campers, who pulled out guitars and sang songs during the breaks, and were able to work around the clock, seven days a week without complaining."

The animation facility was playfully named Cuckoo's Nest, located in Taipei. It was headed by James Wang, who was a former Hannah-Barbera animator. Wong stayed in Taiwan to oversee the Taiwanese painters, many of whom had never painted before. He also had two interpreters available to him, and two main assistants, Lynn Singer and Winnie Chaffee. They covered for him as he slept at his desk after grueling nonstop shifts. The shifts were broken up into day and night shifts to meet the deadline. Approximately 300-400 people were hired, and everytime they came to work, they had to pass though a set of armed guards.

To help the workers understand which circuits or body parts they had to ink and paint, Wong devised a simple color coded/symbol chart. He had drawn small pictures of human eyes, teeth, and face. He went so far as producing a short instructional video to show them how to do it. Once the Kodaliths were printed in the United States, they were flown to Cuckoo's Nest for painting. Despite the language barrier and the lack of formal training, the inkers and painters at Cuckoo's Nest were performing professional looking work.

"We had an incredible amount of work to do in an impossible schedule," says Wong. "We planned out the work, estimating an output of 10,000 mattes a week, cleaned and checked, packaged and shipped out. We had a ten percent error on average, which I believed to be very good considering the pressure and stress we were working under."

The budget went up as a result of farming out the inking and painting, but not as much as the rumors had stated. The initial $12 million budget climbed up to nearly $20 million. Considering how much other major studio film budgets had skyrocketed, *Tron* was a bargain, especially considering how much groundbreaking and handmade work was involved.

Kushner did not worry about the budget or Disney's reaction to farming the work out overseas. It needed to be done, and U.S. companies had been using cheaper labor overseas for years. The kind of wages being paid to the inkers and painters were considered to be very good in a country where wages were low.

"Do you think that when you buy a shirt made in China it's cheaper than made here?" asks Kushner. "These people are getting paid like $50 a month. I don't know what they were being paid at Disney at that time."

In Taiwan the painstaking tracing and painting by hand continued. Each traced and painted cel, which usually took an artist approximately three-five minutes to complete, was then set aside to allow the (black) cel paint to dry. As the next rotoscoped cel was finished, it too was set aside to dry. When dry, these numbered cels (a minimum of forty-eight for each one second of film time) and the accompanying forty-eight Kodaliths (from which each of the cels had been traced) were packed into boxes for shipment back to Burbank. The finished Kodaliths and cels (over three hundred thousand total) would then be filmed through various colored filters, in multiple exposures, on one of thirteen VistaVision animation camera stands. A typical scene would take many hours (and often days) to photograph. The completed footage (eight hundred different scenes) was cut into the final film, giving the illusion that the actors of *Tron* were immersed into a very unique "Electronic World."

Post-production for *Tron* was certainly not cheap; in fact the overruns would turn out be very expensive. By April of 1982, the studio demanded a revised budget. Ellenshaw was tasked with figuring the estimated final cost. He came up with a figure of $6,804,100.00 to complete the film. He included with the breakdown a memo to Miller justifying the added expenses, which placed a lot of the blame back on Disney. With the opening of EPCOT in Florida also taking place later that year, Disney had not fully committed any of their staff personnel to *Tron* as promised. The studio was hugely overextended. In addition, Kushner and Ellenshaw had significantly underestimated how complex and difficult the film would be.

"Eventually we even had to have special custom-made cardboard boxes manufactured for the additional Kodaliths and painted cels," relates Ellenshaw. "Who would have guessed. Certainly not us."

## MEANWHILE...BACK IN BURBANK (*TRON* WEST)

The first shipment of Kodaliths from Taiwan (or affectionately called *Tron* East) with corresponding painted rotoscoped cels arrived back in Burbank (affectionately called *Tron* West). So many boxes started arriving at Disney that it was necessary to rent trailers to store the incoming shipments.

Raulette Woods was a young, witty and very intelligent UCLA graduate who came to work on *Tron*.

"I was working for Harry Marks of Marks & Marks in Hollywood," recalls Woods. "Harry Marks was a pioneer in motion graphics design, broadcast ID (logos) for ABC and NBC. At the time I was working for Harry, Marks & Marks had completed the tag for *Disney's Wonderful World of Color*. Harry asked me to deliver the videotape master to Disney Studios, directly. Upon leaving the office he said to me, 'Someone's going to offer you a job, I know it.' Harry was right."

Riding in an elevator at Disney, she bumped into Bonifer.

"Michael told me he was the publicist working on *Tron* and asked me what I was doing on the lot. I told him I was delivering the finished logo to Disney from Harry Marks. I asked Michael what was going on at Disney. Michael mentioned the associate producer of *Tron* was looking for people to complete post on the film. He described the photographic process they were using and I practically flipped. What he was describing was my heart and soul of photography."

Bonifer suggested that Woods give Ellenshaw a call. After showing him her portfolio with her black-and-white photographs and high-contrast photographic work, he told her about the work they were doing on *Tron*. Her eyes lit up.

"As Harrison was showing me how a sequence of overlapping hi-con Kodaliths were being used with hold-out mattes, and effects animation cels to create the director's look (for inside the computer world), I recall thinking to myself, 'Wow, this is me. This is what I do! I loved it!' I suppose Harrison saw the excitement in my eyes and heard the confidence and ambition in my voice to be a part of the post-production team. I was hitting all the marks in the interview. I understood and spoke the language of photography and enough of cel animation to keep pace with his ideas and his explanation of problems needing to be solved."

Woods was hired as Wong's counterpart in Burbank. One of the first things she recalls was when Ellenshaw and Taylor opened a few boxes with Kodaliths inside for a quick inspection. The smell of vinyl, silver and sesame seed oil permeated the air.

Down in the Camera Department, late at night, a cameraman gingerly took the cels out of the box. He placed them on the animation stand to be shot with the VistaVision camera.

After shooting the one single frame, another set of elements consisting of a Kodalith and corresponding painted cel(s) would be placed under the camera and photographed on the VistaVision animation stand. Usually this process (called "cel-flopping") only took a few seconds per frame of film. But, even so, with multiple number of cels and with so many different exposures (to add color and glow) for each frame, in addition to the fact that it took twenty-four frames just to make up one second of film time (most shots were at least four-five seconds long); a few seconds would turn into many hours (sometimes spanning days) to complete one take for one shot. Many of the shots would take forty-fifty hours to shoot on the animation stands.

Ellenshaw was at the studio working in his office when he got a phone call from the Camera Department.

"They had this very sad voice," recalls Ellenshaw. "It was a camera person who was almost in tears."

"Could you come down here, Harrison? I've got an emergency," said the cameraman.

Ellenshaw rushed downstairs and entered the dark camera room. Standing by the animation stand, with the light reflecting up into his sad face, the cameraman looked distraught. Next to him was the first shipment of Kodaliths in the box.

"Look at this," said the cameraman.

He pulled out a painted cel and slowly peeled it away from another cel. Black paint stretched out like melted pizza cheese. The sound of paint sticking together pierced the night air. The paint, once thought dried, had not. Pieces of the paint ripped off the cels, causing chunks of blank space to appear. The cameraman, worried, had tried covering the missing spaces with black tape just to get the shots completed. To shoot one frame now had taken over an hour.

"He was almost beside himself," says Ellenshaw. "He was so responsible that he had endured a couple hours fixing it. Finally he got to the point he shot so many cels that needed fixing that he was just exhausted from doing this."

The cameraman was worried. Cuckoo's Nest was shipping the cels back to the United States as fast as they finished them. But needing to fix each one at this pace, he would not be able to shoot enough cels to make the deadline. Ellenshaw's face went flush. With the time difference and the way the international calls were handled back then, he had to wait until the morning to call Wong.

"Stop everything!" Ellenshaw shouted into the phone. "We've got a problem."

Wong immediately stopped the production. The fix was fairly simple. In traditional animation, cels were allowed to dry on special mesh shelves for about twelve to twenty-four hours. But with the demand coming from Burbank to ship cels as soon as possible, the extra drying time had been severely shortened. The boxes that had already been shipped and were arriving in Burbank still needed to be checked. Ellenshaw hired a number of assistants to go through the boxes from Taiwan and carefully pry the cels apart. They were fixed and modified to bring them up to specifications.

"Personally, I thought we were doing an outstanding job, with the fact Taiwan has never made a Kodalith matte before, and outputting 10,000 cels a week with a ten percent revision factor," says Wong. "But back at Disney, many grumblings and complaining that we should have 100% corrected elements delivered. Given the schedule, workforce who didn't speak English, never made an effects matte ever, we did great!"

"We all knew we were creating imagery that had never been seen before and we were identifying the 'look' of cyberspace for the silver screen," recalls Woods. "We were changing the way the film industry created animation and live-action films. We were creating a change in how studios would produce films. I took a personal pride in supporting the vision of the director through my work. We all did. We were all pushing the envelope. It's what we strive for as visual effects artists and filmmakers."

"It was a reflection of the difficulty and how labor intensive *Tron* was," says Ellenshaw. "Everybody thinks it was done by computers. They take away the hard labor. *Tron* had both. It had the advantage of computers, but was one of the most labor-intensive films I've ever worked on."

## GOURSON EDITS

As soon as the footage was completed during production, Gourson edited. The editing process was unusual. He was working with traditionally filmed scenes, live-action scenes with the actors on black sets, traditional animation and computer animation. Many times, he edited black-and-white footage with none of the animated backgrounds in place.

"Cutting the virtual world was completely foreign to me," says Gourson. "The sets were all black. No doors, no windows, no ceiling. So when I was editing, sometimes the cuts looked like jump cuts because there was nothing in the background to reference to until the animation was added. I usually had all the story boards photographed, so when there were scenes missing I plugged them with the story boards."

The editing was similar to the way live-action movies with animation were edited. For example, in *Mary Poppins,* Julie Andrews and Dick Van Dyke acted on a black soundstage, pretending they were interacting with penguin waiters. Later in post-production, animators put in backgrounds of the café. They also placed animated penguins into the environment to interact with Andrews and Van Dyke. In the meantime, editor Cotton Warburton worked with either blank pieces of film until the animation was ready, or with filmed versions of the storyboards.

Since the live action for *Tron* was filmed in 65mm, the film elements that Gourson worked with were duplicated down to 35mm. Because his editing was going to be down to the wire, he did not edit a work print for any test screenings.

## ELLENSHAW EARNS HIS STRIPES

As the associate producer on *Tron*, Ellenshaw wore a number of different jackets. Studio liason. Judge. Peacemaker. Negotiator. Office supply order taker.

"Part of his job was just to make things happen at Disney," says Van Vliet. "He sort of had to play both ends. He got called in on a lot on these going, 'Harrison can you go light a fire down here?' The guy just never quit. I think that's why his hair is no longer there."

Ellenshaw often came to the rescue to soothe ruffled feathers and keep the production moving. His training in psychology and experience as a naval officer helped bring a calmness to an otherwise frazzled situation.

"He's one of the most wonderful people I've ever had the privilege of working with," says Silver. "He's great to work for. Never got angry. Never flew off the handle. He'd keep me in stitches because he's a very funny guy. I would've walked through fire for that guy."

There was an instance where even Ellenshaw's calm demeanor came to a point of boiling over. Lisberger was fully immersed in the production and post-production. He rarely left the lot for home, spending nearly every day, including Sundays, working. His personality was such that if he needed something or an answer, he would pick up the phone and call.

Late one night, Lisberger rang Ellenshaw.

"We've got a problem," Lisberger said.

"What's the problem?" asked Ellenshaw.

"The Kodaliths! The emulsions aren't matching!"

"Okay, I'll be right down."

Ellenshaw was exhausted and had not slept much. This was the first night he peacefully slept until the phone rang. He threw on some clothes and drove down to the Disney studio lot.

Lisberger recalls meeting him outside. He was in a mood with the production hanging over his head. Stomping around in the cold outside air, Lisberger looked up and saw Ellenshaw approaching. He was not in a good mood, either. As Lisberger recalls, Ellenshaw marched up to him with his hair frazzled, wearing a bathrobe and house slippers.

"What the hell is so important that you needed to wake my ass up in the middle of the night, Steven?" Ellenshaw pointedly asked.

"The Kodaliths are messed up, Harrison," said Lisberger.

"I'm sure everything's fine and we can fix it in the morning."

"We've got to figure this out now!" exclaimed Lisberger.

"Steven, why don't you take a break and go home for awhile," Ellenshaw said, tension rising in his voice. "We're not going to get this solved tonight."

Lisberger stared right through Ellenshaw, trying to calm himself down. He paused, took a deep breath, and looked down.

"Nice slippers."

"My recollection, and let's never forget, there is no reality, there's only perception," chuckles Ellenshaw. "I was fully dressed. I may have looked like hell, and my hair, what I had then, may have been frazzled. But it was not in my nature, nor is it today, to just wear my bathrobe to go to the studio."

The duo calmed down and tried troubleshooting.

"He would articulate, very clearly, why," recalls Ellenshaw. "He'd seen a shot earlier in the day where there had been an exposure jump. We maybe couldn't quite figure it out. Steven was a great detective. He was very detail oriented."

The exposure jumps made the footage on screen flash from one shot to another.

"At one point Steven discovered that we had not been keeping the same batch of emulsion Kodaliths raw stock. The people making the enlargements would just grab another box," explains Ellenshaw. "Maybe a different emulsion done on a different day. It was somewhat problematic. It wasn't the end of the world. But for Steven, at that time, that was the end of the world."

Lisberger and Ellenshaw simply told the people taking the Kodalith cels out to make sure they did them in order. Problem solved.

"Kodalith film was never designed for motion picture work, so it wasn't that stable from frame-to-frame," says Ellenshaw. "We would do all sorts of kinds of things to cover up some exposure changes. We'd add a little zing to the soundtrack. It didn't detract from the movie at all, maybe even enhanced it."

## TOO LOUD!

The film's soundtrack was mixed by Michael Minkler, Bob Minkler, Lee Minkler, and James LaRue. Between them, they had credits including *Star Wars* and other feature and television film work. With Carlos' score and Fremer and Serafine's sound effects, the mixing team had a high-quality palette from which to choose.

Like the rest of the *Tron* team, the sound mixers had to work with blank pieces of film where the completed visual effects were to be cut in later. Certain departments were delayed in getting their sequences finished, thereby causing the sound team to work nearly 24/7, just like everyone else on the film.

"One thing we had never known anything about was the music," recalls Minkler. "So we had already made a pass through the movie with our dialog and sound effects, shaping it in with the pre-mixes. We got through a pass without the music, then the music arrived. This is where things got wacky because the music was multi-layered with synthesizers. Wendy had incorporated sound effects into her music that I guess came from Fremer and Serafine."

In film, at the most basic level, elements of a soundtrack are essentially divided into sections — dialog, music and sound effects. These are combined in post-production by a sound mixing team consisting of rerecording mixers, sound effects editors, and dialog editors. Putting all of these elements together in post-production can create a pleasing soundtrack. However, if Carlos had allegedly placed sound effects into her music, it would have put up hurdles for Minkler's sound team.

"She didn't show up [to the mixing sessions], but she sent a message, 'You don't need any sound effects. It's all in my music.,'" says Minkler. "We all just went, 'Are you kidding me? We have a 100,000 sound effects we just put into this movie over the last few months, and you're now suggesting we should just turn them off and play your music alone?'"

Lisberger and Fremer sat in during the mixing session at Lion's Gate. As Minkler and his team worked the giant mixing console, the film's various scenes played on the movie screen. The sound team continued to mix the dialog, sound effects and Carlos's score. Fremer was growing agitated.

"We're mixing and to me the only thing that's going to save this movie from being a noisy sterile thing is going to be the music," recalls Fremer. "So I'm pushing for music and Mike Minkler is pushing for sound effects. The sound effects were up way too loud. Way too loud! I'm screaming, 'Too loud!'"

"Fremer was a pain in the ass," says Minkler. "He was more on the music world side. He was siding with Wendy. Not that there should have been sides. She never heard the sound effects. She had no idea what we were trying to accomplish. Michael was on her side. 'We don't need all these things. Let's just take it out.' And we're like, 'Are you kidding me? You're crazy! You're nuts!' Yeah, we had some screaming matches."

"They had these new sounds and they thought they were the cat's meow," says Carlos. "They put them in so loud because they were proud of it. Now they're annoying. They weren't wonderful sounds. They were just a little bit new at that time."

"You couldn't go to the mix," says Franklin. "And the director wasn't doing it. So it was the sound effects team that was really doing the mix. There wasn't anybody there to calm them down."

Minkler felt that the film played better with a more aggressive soundtrack. He felt that the music, though excellent, was too weak compared to the visual effects and story in *Tron*.

"It's not what this movie is," says Minkler. "This movie's going to kick some ass. Why are we doing this mix with this little synthetic music? No, we're going to kick some ass here. And that's why I say Fremer was kind of a pain in the ass. He thought he was just getting it from the music. I'm not saying it was bad. I personally did not think that the movie could sit there and be held by the music alone. There was no way. You play that music and you play that visual and it just weakened the visual. It made it like a cartoon other than an animated movie."

Fremer was frustrated with the sound mix and went to Lisberger to vent.

"This is a disaster," said Fremer. "It's too noisy! All this great music—that's what's going to give humanity to the picture. You've got to tell him."

"You hired him. You tell him!"

"There was Lisberger, Fremer and me kind of figuring out how we were going to deal with this and with all of this music and all of the sound effects," says Minkler. "Lisberger sided with us. We all wanted this thing to be big and Michael had lost that battle. He wanted it to be more musical."

Friction had been developing between Fremer and Lisberger by this point. Everyone working on the film was under immense pressure to get it locked down. According to Fremer, his sound budget was getting the brunt of money issues.

"Things were getting billed to the sound side that didn't belong on the sound side," says Fremer. "I had to fight to get the money taken out of my budget and put where it belongs. I was not a bureaucrat. I was not used to this whole kind of stuff. But I did the best I could."

At a luncheon, Lisberger allegedly called Fremer out and gave him a verbal dressing down.

"He, at this point, had his own problems with the production," recalls Fremer. "He had his own problems with things not showing up. I was given a ridiculous budget to begin with. It was set up at the beginning to fail. And I said it. It wasn't like it was a surprise to me. A lot of what happened to me was because the picture was late. The picture kept getting changed."

Additional sound editors Gordon Ecker and Wylie Stateman were hired to help complete sound mix. Fremer was still supervising the soundtrack, but had to leave the rest of the job to Ecker and his team. For Fremer it was hard to accept blame on the sound side, especially since he had been with the film since the beginning in Venice Beach.

"We should've had this scene in place to begin with," says Fremer. "It didn't have to come down that way. Not in public. It was part of Steve's personality. He had this streak. Everybody who's creative has a nasty streak. People get nasty. But it was unnecessary. I had done a lot of good things for him. I was very bitter about it. Very, very bitter. And I probably still am. I was doubly bitter when everything worked out to the point where it got two Academy Award nominations. It got one for Best Sound."

## JOURNEY

In addition to Carlos' score, there was pressure to include a signature theme song on the soundtrack for *Tron*. It was not unprecedented for Disney to have a theme song on its films that generated album sales. The studio had been doing it since the days of *The Three Little Pigs* and its hit song, "Who's Afraid of the Big Bad Wolf" topped the charts. But Disney really had not ever really used a rock or pop act to sing its songs outside of Annette Funicello. The Beach Boys had recorded the title song for *The Monkey's Uncle*, (1965), but that was about as hard rock as Disney got.

Fremer, being a former disc jockey and music lover, took stock in the bands of the day. Radio and album sales were much simpler then, with rock, Top 40, oldies and some country dominating the charts, so it was easier to pin down an act with a broad and appealing style. By late 1981, the major acts included Van Halen, Styx, REO Speedwagon, J. Geils Band, the Go-Go's, Missing Persons, Foreigner and The Police.

The main band Fremer focused on was The Police. Formed in the 1970s by American drummer Stewart Copeland, the band was fronted by bass player and singer, Sting (born Gordon Sumner), and guitarist Andy Summers. After struggling for a few years, the band began churning out intoxicating songs and albums such as *Outlandos d' Amor* (1977), *Regatta de Blanc* (1979), *Zenyatta Mondata* (1980) and *Ghost in the Machine* in 1981. The hits were built on clever hooks, insightful lyrics, and superb musicianship by each band member. "Roxanne," "Message in a Bottle," "Don't Stand So Close To Me," and "Every Little Thing She Does Is Magic" firmly placed the band on the map. With the band's ability to mix modern rock with reggae and pop, Fremer found his muse for the *Tron* soundtrack.

"We have this character who's like a permanent adolescent, skateboarding type and he lives above a video parlor," says Fremer. "And what I need is The Police. I need jumpy punk rock. If I had any choice at all, it would be The Police. But the soundtrack was coming out on CBS Records, so we couldn't have The Police."

CBS Records was a huge record company that dominated the record landscape with some of the biggest artists of the early 1980s, including Billy Joel, Bruce Springsteen, and Journey. The Police were on A&M Records.

"In fact, the only band that they wanted and they shoved down my throat was Journey," says Fremer. "I did *not* want Journey. Not a Journey fan. You look at the scenes in the video game parlor, it's kind of a skateboard kind of vibe. Jeff Bridges was the young guy. The rebel. I don't want to hear Journey. Steve Perry, great singer, but I don't want to hear these big power ballads. That's not right for the movie. I said okay, if that's who I have to use, I'll use them."

Journey was a San Francisco rock band featuring Neil Schon, Jonathan Cain, Ross Valory, Steve Smith and lead singer Steve Perry in its 1981 line-up. The band had played for a number of years, but hit its stride starting with "Any Way You Want It" off the *Departure* album in 1980. The band was not a giant act on Top 40 radio, but it was huge on rock radio and played sold-out shows.

By 1981, the band released two records, *Captured* in February and *Escape* in August. Off the *Captured* album were hits "Lights" and "Lovin', Touchin', Squeezin.'" It was the *Escape* album that found its way onto turntables across the country. Teenagers could not seem to get enough listening time to "Don't Stop Believin'," and "Who's Cryin' Now." "Open Arms" became a prom and wedding staple for years.

Love 'em or hate 'em, Journey dominated radio air time and concert venues. Fremer knew this was exactly what the soundtrack needed for sales. Plus most people, including Fremer, did not want to raise the ire of powerful CBS Records head, Walter Yetnikoff. After meeting with the band at a Melrose Avenue coffee shop in Hollywood, Fremer agreed that they would record two songs for the film, "1990s Theme," and "Only Solutions."

"If you listen to the song 'Only Solutions,' it's The Police," says Fremer. "It couldn't be more perfect. They did such a great job. I have such respect for them after that. Think about that song. If you literally sat down and listened to The Police and copied the whole thing perfectly. Even the drummer copied Stewart Copeland's drumming. The harmonies are right. This guy from Journey who sings these big power ballads is singing way up in his register. Way out of normal sounding like Sting."

Unfortunately, Carlos was slighted again regarding a score she wrote and performed. Her credit suite, which ends the film, was cut in half to fit in "Only Solutions." Instead of the audience being taken into Carlo's music to the end of the credit crawl, it crescendos into a gigantic goose-pimple-inducing pipe organ note. That fades away when Journey's guitar riff echoes in.

"I was angry," says Carlos. "For me, I'm a team player. I thought it hurt the movie. It was not a matter of ego. In this case, I thought that the Light Cycle music and the end titles music made the film better. If it had been written by anyone else, I would still say the same damn thing. It's not me that I'm talking about. I've never seen any evidence come along since the film was finished that made that argument look like it wasn't so good anymore."

It was not the first time a score had been altered, or completely jettisoned in favor of another score. Kubrick did it to composer Alex North on *2001: A Space Odyssey*, favoring classical music instead. Jerry Goldsmith's score for *Legend* (1985) was ditched in the United States for a more modern score by Tangerine Dream. Carlos' own music for the Light Cycle sequence was gone by the final mix.

"They were working in conjunction with the people who were actually building the sound effects, who were then going to do the final mix," says Carlos. "So they were all excited about their sound effects. To them, the dialogue and the music represented an annoying thing that was getting in the way of being able to hear their sound effects. They sold Lisberger on the bankrupt notion that the Light Cycle sequence was more brutal and realistic if there were no music in it. Well of course it's more brutal. It's much less finesse. It's uglier. It's not as well done. He bought into the argument and they cut out the music."

The decision to include Journey was a mixture of potential album sales and post-production politics. Annmarie Franklin, Carlos' partner and business manager says, "I'm not sure [Lisberger] made the decision [to trim Carlo's music]. I think maybe the mixers made the decision. He left it for the mixers and he was going to see if he didn't like it. He didn't really participate in anything."

"He actually wasn't there every day," says Carlos. "Michael Fremer was, but Michael of course is not the most powerful force there. He didn't have a lot of clout to argue the point with. I feel lucky they didn't mess up the music even further."

Another issue, at least for Carlos, was the longevity of the Journey songs.

"You have to decide when you make a movie, are you doing it just for this year, or are you doing it so when you look back ten years, twenty years, even fifty years, will it still look good?" asks Carlos. "Disney did a few films in the 1940s that used a few pop, boogie-woogie cues. Very dated now. Very dated. Where the stuff they did like *Fantasia*, that stuff is still classy and classic. It still holds up."

She was completely correct on her assessment when it came to "1990s Theme." It was dated with heavy synth and screaming guitar solos. But "Only Solutions" was a solid Journey song, and in retrospect, fit the arcade/skateboarder/man-child atmosphere of *Tron* very well. The opening and memorable guitar riff was as good as anything Journey performed on songs like "Who's Cryin' Now."

"That pop piece by Journey, which I think cheapens the very end of the movie because it was meant to be an emotional, feels like exit music in a restaurant or something," says Carlos.

There was another issue with using Journey's songs in the film. Since the film was almost finally mixed and ready, there was nowhere to put the songs. Ellenshaw, who was in charge of the final credits, was about to film them when Journey was dropped on his lap at the last minute. According to him, it was a time issue getting the songs in.

"I kept saying we can't use it," recalls Ellenshaw. "I was kind of being an obstacle about it because I didn't want to go back and have to remix because we were rushing toward this deadline."

Disney's music division head, Gary Kriesel, thought differently and rushed down to Ellenshaw's office to confront him in front of the staff. He and Ellenshaw got into it.

"It's totally impractical. I can't do it," said Ellenshaw.

"Yes you will!" yelled Kriesel. "We have a contract. We're going to get sued if we don't you don't do this!"

Ellenshaw reluctantly compromised after Lisberger convinced him it was okay to place the music somewhere. Journey was not happy about the "Only Solutions" arcade scene placement, and Carlos was not happy with her end credit music having been cut down. Ellenshaw was simply trying to get film completed for release.

"I was a little bit more stubborn than I needed to be in those days," says Ellenshaw. "I was a pain in the ass a lot of the time."

Nonetheless, Ellenshaw was able to create a cool Journey end credit logo out of the fiasco.

The two Journey songs included on the soundtrack album did surprisingly poorly in sales. The album did not sell well. In fact, the strongest song, "Only Solutions," was hardly, if ever, played on the radio at the time. As popular as the band was, the song did not catch fire. To this day, it is not played on the radio. One can catch "Lights" or "Don't Stop Believin'" almost every day on the radio ad nauseam, but "Only Solutions" has been relegated to the furthest reaches of the record bin.

"The problem was it wasn't what Journey fans were expecting," adds Fremer. "What they should've done was give it a new name. It should've been Journey incognito. They should've called themselves the F.B.I. Agents or whatever."

## LICENSING AND THE *TRON* ARCADE GAME

Disney was strong on licensing its brand-name images such as Mickey Mouse with great success. *Tron*, however, was different from anything done at the studio. How to sell a movie about a guy getting bolted into a computer was not easy. Nor was it easy to market a film featuring the heavy use of computer simulation. The film, in a sense, was trying to cover all the bases at once. It was a technological breakthrough film. It was a film about computers and video games. It was a film that could cater to kids. It was a film that could cater to arcade jockeys. Disney licensed *Tron* in a number of arenas—toys, video games and arcade games.

*Star Wars* showed that inexpensive plastic toy characters and vehicles fired up the imagination of young children. It also proved to be a huge moneymaker for George Lucas. Small plastic action figures were still very popular by the time *Tron* was ready to be released in theaters. Disney licensed a few companies to produce action figures, Light Cycles, Frisbees, mini electronic games based on the arcade game of *Tron*, View Master reels, and yo-yos.

The biggest licensing deals came from Mattel and Bally Midway. Mattel sold the Intellivision game console, a rival video game system to the Atari 2600. Intellivision was considered superior due to its higher quality graphics and better game play. Disney licensed Mattel to produce *Tron Deadly Disc*, *Tron Maze-A-Tron* and *Tron Solar Sailer* video games. *Tron Solar Sailer* was unique in that it talked to players via a voice synthesis module. M Network also produced *The Adventures of Tron* video game for the Atari 2600.

The Bally Midway arcade game was perhaps the most ingenious marketing tool for Disney. Having *Tron* game units in arcades around the country kept the film easily in the eyes of kids and teens. The game featured some of the highest quality graphics produced in the early 1980s. Even though it was not set up like *Space Paranoids*, the 2-D graphics in the *Tron* arcade game were highly impressive.

Tron fights the MCP, tanks, Grid Bugs and races in Light Cycle battles. The game machine itself was something to behold. The blue joystick was clear, the light from the screen illuminating it. The console was covered in graphical mazes and lines designed by Richard Taylor.

Bally Midway was to install thousands of these game units in arcades around North America. Disneyland (California) would feature at least a dozen or more of the units in its Starcade near *Space Mountain*. A year later, Bally Midway would release *Discs of Tron* in arcades.

## *TRON'S* END CREDITS

*Star Wars*, with all its breakthroughs in visual effects and sound, also broke Hollywood convention by not listing its credits in the film's opening minutes. Nearly every Hollywood feature film, due to contracts with various unions and affiliations, were required to list certain key credits in a film's opening. George Lucas bucked the trend and had his name and everybody else's name listed at the tail end of *Star Wars*. For Hollywood's guilds, this was unacceptable. For audiences, it was a treat.

No longer did audiences have to sit through long opening credit sequences. The opening title in *Tron* was one of the rare cases in which no other credits are shown until the end of the film.

Ellenshaw had the enviable task of designing the end credits for *Tron*. Normally end credits were made with fairly standard fonts with white lettering on a black background. Ellenshaw used the film's technology and created stylish lettering. Instead of white lettering, he chose computer screen green to accent the lettering. The font was created specifically for the film, using hard corners that mimicked lettering found on computer screens of the 1980s.

In creating the end credits, Ellenshaw was determined to list everybody who worked on the film. He had worked on some early films in his career without being credited and that had an effect on him. A credit on a film may not mean much to most people in the audience, but for a person who has worked on a film, it means the world.

"I was asked in the early 1970s, after I had done matte paintings for Disney's *The Apple Dumpling Gang*, how I would like my credit to read and I told them," recalls Ellenshaw. "Then later, there was a cast and crew showing. The movie came on the screen and there was no credit for Harrison. I was devastated. Credit is a very personal and important thing. So I decided that I would take responsibility for making sure the credits for *Tron* would be inclusive. When people were hired they would fill out a form that asked them how they would like their credit to read. Nobody had ever done that before."

The crew on *Tron* had pioneered so many new processes in both analog animation and computer simulation, a number of new credit titles had to be created. "Scene Coordinator." "Systems Programmer." "Animation Compositing Camera." "Object Digitizing." "Computer Image Choreographer." "Scene Programmer." "International Cel Coordinator." "Synthavision Technologist."

Ellenshaw also wanted to make sure that the crew of Cuckoo's Nest was credited. He asked James Wang and Arne Wong for a list of the Tawaii crew's names in English. He got the list, then about a week later, received a thank you note on *Tron* stationary from "*Tron* East."

The thank you note read, "To the *Tron* West staff. Thank you for your support and trust in us. We won't let you down. From *Tron* East with love."

On two pages, every name of the Taiwan crew was listed in Chinese characters. The list was divided into inkers and painters. Ellenshaw made sure that every character was carefully placed into the end credits. What did the names mean in English?

"To this day, I have no idea," says Ellenshaw. "It could say, 'Go to hell, you Yankee imperialist dogs,' for all I know!"

# Chapter 17

# SUMMER OF '82

The summer box office returns of 1981 had been strong for nearly every movie studio. *Raiders of the Lost Ark* and *Superman II* battled each other for box office dollars through the season with *Raiders* pulling out ahead for good. *Clash of the Titans*, *Cannonball Run* and *Stripes* brought audiences into theaters looking for escapist entertainment.

But the winter of 1981 turned out to be a major bust for most studios. No one seemed to be able to release a successful film. Most of the features released were turgid, expensive dramas. Not much appealed to younger audiences. The only reasonable successes to be seen were the Paul Newman/Sally Field film, *Absence of Malice*, and the Burt Reynolds action film, *Sharkey's Machine*.

Surprisingly, one of the biggest hits during Christmas time was the rerelease of Walt Disney's *Cinderella*. Though the classic had been re-released just about every seven years to new audiences, they could not seem to get enough of it. For Disney, after releasing *The Fox and the Hound* that summer, it was vindication that perhaps the studio side of the company was finally turning around.

Not helping the studios was a nasty recession that kept the United States in limbo. The winter of 1981, plus the expensive flops of the past few years, were hurting them financially. Perhaps the summer of 1982 might bring audiences back to theaters.

## THE INCREDIBLE SUMMER SCHEDULE AND DISNEY'S DILEMMA

The slate for most of the major studios looked very promising in the summer of 1982.

The Ladd Company, which was founded by Alan Ladd, Jr., released its films through Warner Bros. The Ladd Company was set to release a big budget science fiction adventure called *Blade Runner*, directed by Ridley Scott and starring Harrison Ford.

Warner Bros. had an Australian import called *The Road Warrior*, which was a sequel to the 1979 feature, *Mad Max*. The studio also had the Clint Eastwood anti-Soviet adventure film, *Firefox*.

Paramount had a sequel to *Grease* called *Grease 2*. The sequel was made without most of the original cast from the 1978 blockbuster. The studio also had *Star Trek: The Wrath of Khan*.

MGM/UA had *Rocky III*, Steven Spielberg's *Poltergeist*, and Don Bluth's answer to Disney's animated features, *The Secret of NIMH*.

20ᵗʰ Century Fox had a big budgeted film *Megaforce*, directed by Hal Needham (*Smokey and the Bandit*—1977), a Kenny Rogers comedy called *Six Pack*, and *Young Doctors in Love*.

Universal Pictures had *Conan the Barbarian*, John Carpenter's re-imagining of the 1950s classic horror film, *The Thing*. It also had *The Best Little Whorehouse in Texas*, an adaption of the popular stage musical, and a small movie from Steven Spielberg called *E.T. The Extra-terrestrial*.

Disney was on the outskirts of what was happening in Hollywood. But it did have a trick up its sleeve with *Tron*. There was not another movie quite like it. Considering kids were making arcades their home-away-from-home, it seemed like the perfect idea to want to see a movie about video games. The trick for Disney's publicity department was to market this film not only as an exciting summer flick, but also to make it seem like Disney was suddenly cool.

The other major studios had considerable marketing budgets and marketing teams to get the word out. Advertising on television, on billboards, in magazines, on the radio and in newspapers was second nature for the big studios.

The problem with Disney was that it hardly advertised. In the case of its animated classics being rereleased, it generally relied on title recognition. Nostalgic parents made it their mandate to take their children to see the films they saw in their youth. All Disney had to do was place advertisements in local newspapers, run a few television ads, and audiences showed up. The studio also advertised in its theme parks.

On Disney's newer films, however, there was a serious disconnect. People, especially kids between the ages seven to twelve, Disney's prime demographic, were not watching *The Wonderful World of Disney* as much as they used to. The show, from the very beginning, was a perfect advertising vehicle for Disney products. But without an eager audience to learn about upcoming Disney features, it was difficult to get the word out on its newest films.

Bonifer was not about to let *Tron* suffer the fate of *Herbie Goes Bananas*, or *The Watcher in the Woods*. He set out to make sure that *Tron* was in the public eye and that his publicity brought kids and teens into theaters.

What was the advertising budget for the film?

Bonifer explains, "Whatever was usual for the day. I have no idea. What? Six million dollars? I don't know. It was okay. This was a group of people who had to sheepishly sell *The Unidentified Flying Oddball* (1979), and then go to *Tron*. They're not thinking real hard about the demographics."

"It was a $20 million film. At that time that was pretty expensive," says Taylor. "Disney only put $4 million hard dollars into advertising *Tron*. Now people in Hollywood knew about it. There were rumors about this movie using computer simulation. But out in middle America, all of them didn't know this movie was coming out."

Undeterred, Bonifer found other outlets he used to his advantage. *Starlog* had been a colorful and exciting magazine devoted to science fiction/fantasy movies. He sought out *Cinefex*. Run by Don Shay, the magazine was a high-quality journal on Hollywood visual effects. Its audience was limited, but it was considered to be a trustworthy source. Bonifer also invited *American Cinematographer* to write coverage of the film's numerous film formats it was using. The magazine had been around since the 1920s and was revered amongst cinematographers, filmmakers and film students.

He also got coverage in *Life* magazine, *Omni*, and *Smithsonian*. He even got *Rolling Stone* to print a spectacular cover shot by famed photographer, Annie Lebowitz, featuring Jeff Bridges. Disney's own Magic Kingdom Club magazine, *Disney News*, also wrote a short piece on *Tron*.

## SELLING *TRON* TO THE PUBLIC

The biggest issue for Disney was not just getting the word out. It was the film itself. What was it about? How would it be sold to the public? Was it edgy enough to convince kids and teens to spend their money? Disney could not figure out how to market the film. This upset Lisberger.

"He would just scream about the marketing," recalls Bonifer. "I remember Lisberger would absolutely go apeshit, just apeshit about it—scream."

As cool as the film's effects were, and as cool as the film looked, its story was problematic and a bit confusing. There was the element of Flynn hacking into the MCP. There was the plot involving the love triangle. There was the issue of Bridges and Boxleitner, who with their "Electronic World" helmets on, looked alike. Tron was the hero of the film, but it was really Flynn who saved the day. There was new computer jargon filled with RAMs, ROMs, a master computer program, bits, bytes and so forth. Unless you were versed in computer jargon, a lot of the film's dialogue went over your head. For a summer adventure film, it was not an easy sell.

"They didn't know how to advertise *Tron*," says Bonifer. "There was no story there. They could've advertised it, but they couldn't find the heart of it. That's the trick of it. The heart of it, in a funny way, exists outside of the movie. The heart of it was the production of the movie."

The perception of the Disney corporation was not bad, but it was skewed. Among teens, which were the exact audience the studio was looking for, Disney was not seen as cool. What good was Disney to teenagers? Well, they enjoyed the theme parks and an occasional T-shirt with Mickey Mouse on the front. The biggest problem for the studio, with a few exceptions after the release of *The Black Hole*, was the public's impression that Disney only released films with a "G" rating.

"Let's be very honest," says Miller. "I'll take credit where my credit is due. I'm a big man and I will take responsibility for a lot of bad things that happened. I was frustrated. I was not allowed to make the kind of films I thought the company should be making. At that time, although it's turned around, I think you'll recognize that, any 'G' [rated] film was like poison out there. And of course we were making 'G' [rated] films."

While *Tron* still felt like a Disney movie, it had elements not seen in a Disney movie before. It had some minor cartoonish violence. Game players and Light Cycle riders were derezzed or blown into millions of digital bits after crashing into jet walls. Sark's skull is sliced open by Tron's "Deadly Disc" and his electronic brains fall out. Clu is derezzed with a frightening electronic scream. For Disney, it was heady stuff. And had it remained, the "Love Scene," though very tame, would have given this Walt Disney Production some guts. All of these elements, sans the "Love Scene," earned the film a "PG" rating.

## TIME, NEWSWEEK AND BUENA VISTA

*Time* and *Newsweek* were two major U.S. Magazines and they were highly competitive with one another. The *Tron* publicity team got the film on the covers of both magazines, which was a major coup. Each magazine had sent out journalists to cover the making of the groundbreaking film, and each magazine was publishing multi-page articles on *Tron*. A good story, mixed with being on the cover, could generate positive buzz for Disney. It was free publicity, something that made E. Cardon Walker happy.

"Those two covers on newsstands is the equivalent of about $8-10 million of advertising," says Taylor. "That would've compensated for the lack of money that was put in the advertising."

"*Time* and *Newsweek* each insisted that they would have the *Tron* cover exclusively—we assured them each that they would," recalls Ellenshaw. "We lied and knew that each magazine would be massively pissed off to see the other mag also had a *Tron* cover—but we didn't care. As I recall we, at least, composited two different covers for each. In those days the editors at the mags called it avoiding the '*Time*/*Newsweek* two-step.'"

The film's simultaneous covers were to appear on newsstands just a few days before the film opened in theaters on July 9.

While Bonifer was soliciting stories for the major magazines, Taylor was re-compositing the Kodalith cels to make prints for publication in *Time* and *Newsweek*. There were no full color stills of the "Electronic World" scenes. Hundreds of black-and-white stills were taken during the production, showing the actors in their leotards on the black soundstage. Taylor and his team took Kodaliths and painted them to match the work done at Cuckoo's Nest. A portfolio was made of these and they were sent to various publications and outlets.

Another issue for Disney was its distribution channel. Buena Vista was an extremely successful division of Walt Disney Productions for years. By the 1970s and 1980s, however, Disney had lost some clout with theaters. The studio was not putting out a healthy amount of films to keep theater exhibitors happy. And again, Disney mostly relied on its animated and live-action films to fill the theater marquee.

"An important point that should be made is that Disney had NO distribution leverage, unlike the major movies who (in spite of "no blind bidding" allowed) could leverage their movies into important venues/theaters by promising to give the theaters their 'major' releases if they also played the lesser movies," says Ellenshaw.

By the time *Tron* was ready for release, Disney films were mostly shown in second-rate theater complexes. These were cheaply built theaters with minimal seating capacity, small screens and awful sound. These multiplexes were mainly popular in malls. Occasionally, Disney showed *Sleeping Beauty* in big theaters in 70mm, but that was an exception. A film with the scope of *Tron* required bigger theaters with big screens to show off its dazzling visuals.

"Card Walker had a running feud with two or three of the major cinema distributors," says Taylor. "What happens each year is that you have a NATO [National Association of Theater

Owners] [convention] and you go show films that you've got. You show them ten minutes of them. People bid and figure out what films will be in theaters. Disney would just show up with the same old films or maybe a new *Herbie* film or something. When Card Walker would go negotiate with people, he had nothing to negotiate with. So they were kind of shitting on him. He'd say, 'Well, you're not going to get *Cinderella* this year.' They'd say, 'Fine. We'll take *Firefox.*'"

"I don't believe there was a conscious effort by anybody at the studio, including the very top management levels, to favor one project over another," says Ellenshaw. "That would be insanity. It doesn't do any good to be CEO of a company and have a movie come out and fail. CEOs don't get a free pass."

## COMPUTERS ARE PEOPLE TOO! TRONKITE AND *THE ART OF TRON*

*Tron* was getting a lot of exposure in the media, despite its fairly low advertising budget. To add to the growing publicity, Bonifer had written the book, *The Art of Tron*. Rather than writing about the behind-the-scenes action, he focused on the exquisite artwork associated with the film. The result was a beautifully illustrated book, which is still valued by collectors, and it is the only *Tron* book that shined a light on the work of Syd Mead, Moebius and Peter Lloyd.

Meanwhile, Disney spent money on a radio campaign. Back in the early 1980s, it was not uncommon to hear ads for upcoming movies on the radio. A *Tron* ad was produced, featuring an ominous narrator's voiceover, snippets from the soundtrack and Wendy Carlos' score.

With a $300,000 budget, Bonifer produced a television special called *Computers Are People, Too!* The show focused on early computer graphics by John Whitney Sr. and Taylor's Triple-I demo with Adam Powers. Bonifer was a co-writer on the show.

"It's the best collection of computer graphic imagery from that era. It's worth it for that," says Bonifer. "The rest of the show kind of sucks."

The program was fairly typical fare from the early 1980s. Actress Elaine Joyce is all dolled up in 1980s clothes and hair. She talks to a computer (voiced by actor Joseph Campanella) who convinces her that computers are our friends and not something to be afraid of. The program is a bit slow in its pacing. But it does offer viewers of today a glimpse of how computers were being used back in 1982.

"We never pulled off the host," says Bonifer. "It was Elaine Joyce, who was famous for hosting *The Dating Game* at the time. It was the most inappropriate casting ever. She was a blonde and a babe. That was just an example of the opportunity that was there. You were allowed to make mistakes."

Bonifer went a step further and got venerable newsman, Walter Cronkite, to do a segment for his new series, *Universe*, on *Tron*.

To Americans living in the 1950s and 1960s, Cronkite was considered the most reliable and trusted newsman alive. He gave television viewers a closer view of the world's most challenging events like the assassination of John F. Kennedy, the Vietnam War, and mankind's walk on the moon.

Cronkite was known to have an interest in new technologies and *Universe* focused on them. For the *Tron* crew, it was exciting to have the legendary newsman show interest in their groundbreaking film. Bonifer's meeting with Cronkite was an eye opener.

"I worked with Walter Cronkite's producer and fed him information that he would turn into the script for Walter Cronkite," recalls Bonifer. "I walked into the dressing room to meet with them before the shoot, and Walter Cronkite's in his underwear and he's wearing garters for his socks. Outside of a *New Yorker* cartoon or a Rock Hudson movie, I'd never seen sock garters in real life."

On a Disney soundstage, Ellenshaw and Taylor directed Cronkite in a short segment to demonstrate the magic of computer graphics. They shot the segment in 65mm black-and-white film, just as *Tron* had been filmed. Dressed in a white tuxedo with a top hat and cane, Cronkite was encouraged by Ellenshaw to do whatever he wanted. Cronkite tap danced for the camera crew.

"Walter just kind of surprised everybody how he caught the spirit of it," says Bonifer. "We were all just thrilled. It was just a sign of how important it was. Walter was getting interested in it. He was genuinely interested in it. He got it. He understood it. That's why that piece worked so well. He believed like Walt Disney believed in Mickey Mouse. Richard and Harrison would explain to him what was going to happen. So whatever you see in that piece, he's selling it."

After Cronkite finished his segment, the 65mm footage went through the process of Kodaliths, effects animation, and sound effects. As endearing as Cronkite's performance was, and how incredible his speech about computer effects was, there was not a single minute of CGI in this segment. But it did not matter, especially by the time the show finally aired. The concept of computer simulation was almost completely new to the public. Seeing Cronkite dance in a "computerized" world still looked cool, and viewers believed he was really tap dancing in the "Electronic World."

Meanwhile, Bonifer had completed his first draft of *The Art of Tron*. The book was to be a real showcase of the beautiful and ingenious artwork of *Tron*. However, the editor-in-chief at publishing house Little Simon, Kate Klimo, wrote Ellenshaw a letter requesting that the book be cut down to a mere sixty-four pages.

"Dear Harrison, We are having cost difficulties on *The Art of Tron*," Klimo wrote.

Ellenshaw fired back a letter pleading for more pages.

"We are hopeful that *The Art of Tron* can be longer than sixty-four pages," Ellenshaw wrote. "With that in mind I have enclosed enough art that should cover a book of almost any length. If you must go with a shorter book, my preference is that we use as much Syd Mead and Moebius as possible (B/W) and use all the 4"x5" color EKTACHROMES."

Both Bonifer and Ellenshaw were putting together an extraordinary book filled with behind-the-scenes stories, artwork, and photographs. It was going to be a visionary tribute to the artists and artistry of *Tron*.

## STAR TREK: THE WRATH OF KHAN—THE GENESIS DEMO

On the periphery, *Tron* had competition in the computer simulation arena.

*Star Trek: The Wrath of Khan* was perhaps one of the earliest films under Jeffrey Katzenberg to be made fast and cheap. *Star Trek: The Motion Picture* was so heavily weighed down by its high budget that Michael Eisner and Katzenberg mandated that any sequel made had to be under $15 million. Paramount made money on the first film, but it wanted to make sure it made more on the sequel.

One of the highlights of *Star Trek: The Wrath of Khan* was the "Genesis Demo" (seen in the film as "Project Genesis"), directed by Alvy Ray Smith at ILM. The sequence was short, yet it was breathtaking. The villain, Khan (Ricardo Montalban), relentlessly pursues the "Genesis" device, which can create a living planet out of a dead moon. Whoever gets their hands on this device could cause havoc in the universe. Captain Kirk (William Shatner) learns about this and calls up a video presentation of it on the Enterprise computer.

The sequence is shown on the ship's computer monitor. We fly through space to a dead moon as actress Bibi Besch narrates. A rocket fires and flies to the moon. It hits and causes a fireball to envelope it. The virtual computer camera flies in and over the moon's surface. Right before our eyes, the moon develops landscapes and oceans. The camera flies away from the moon and we now see it as a new living planet.

With limited computing power, Smith's team took this sequence to a whole new level. The virtual computer camera, for instance, was not jerky in its movement. The camerawork was incredibly smooth. The creation of the planet gave the scene plausibility. The mountains and oceans were surreal, haunting and beautiful at the same time. This was a milestone in computer simulation.

"Many people are surprised when I tell them that *Trek* beat *Tron* to the big screen," says Smith. "The 'Genesis Demo' in *Star Trek II*, our big break, hit the screen a month before *Tron*. And it was a financial success. I still have the storyboards I used to land the 'Genesis Demo' project. I drew them in an all-night frenzy realizing that this was it. Hardly ever does one get a chance to design a shot in a major motion picture!"

Smith's sequence was important because it combined all the elements of early computer animation into one sequence. There is the moon, the star field, the virtual camera movement, and the creation of life on the moon. Each of those elements was very time consuming to render. This was not a vector drawing of Ed Catmull's *Hand*. This was not a computer rendering of Peter Fonda's or Susan Dey's face. This was a fully animated, full-motion sequence in color.

Adds Smith, "The reason 'Genesis Demo' worked was because it was a video (that is, at video resolution) inside a movie. Nobody could compute full-res movie footage yet. Too expensive, although we were worried about Whitney/Demos on that front."

*Star Trek: The Wrath of Khan* was released on June 4, 1982, beating *Tron* into theaters by little over a month. The film, at that point in time, had the biggest opening weekend ever.

## *TRON*: BREAKTHROUGH

Although *Star Trek: The Wrath of Khan* beat *Tron* into theaters by little over a month, *Tron* was already going to be monumentally groundbreaking.

- *Tron* was the first feature film to use computer simulation to fill its entire film frame (i.e. film negative) with computerized characters, vehicles, and environments. This was significant. Previous films that filled the entire film frame with computer simulation either used it strictly for titles, such as *Getting Straight* (1970) and *Superman* (1978), or for short visual effects sequences. *Westworld* (1973) used pixilated computer simulation (optically combined with live action footage) to simulate Yul Brynner's "android vision." *The Black Hole* (1979) used vector graphics for its opening title sequence. In the case of *Star Trek: The Wrath of Khan*, its CGI sequence utilized the middle of the movie screen. Aside from the films mentioned above, all feature films using CGI before *Tron* presented their computerized footage on computer monitors, or were projected on a screen within a scene.

- *Tron* blew open the amount of time computer simulation was played out on-screen. With Jeff Gourson's editing, the total amount of CGI footage was approximately sixteen minutes in length. In comparison, both the "Genesis Demo" in *Star Trek: The Wrath of Khan* (counting the computerized DNA footage), and the opening title sequence in *The Black Hole* were over a minute in length.

- *Tron* broke free from the limitations of the virtual computer camera on a large scale. In previous features, the virtual computer camera would film an object with limited or no movement. In *Tron*, the virtual computer camera in the film flew, banked, turned, and went anywhere its human operators told it to go.

- *Tron* used computer simulation to help tell its story. Much of the film takes place inside of a computer world. Each and every sequence of computer simulation is in service to the plot. Tanks, Recognizers, Light Cycles, Sark's Carrier, the Solar Sailer, and the "Electronic World" are all part of a fictional environment. With the notable exception of the computer effects in *Westworld* and *Star Trek: The Wrath of Khan* being used as plot devices, no other film used computer simulation as *Tron* did to advance its story.

- *Tron* introduced fully animated CGI characters into a feature film. The electronic version of Tron, the Bit and the MCP qualify as CGI characters. They were not characters who simply appeared on a computer monitor, but had movement and interacted with their environment.

The real test was to see if this groundbreaking computer simulation in *Tron* would translate into box office dollars.

## ROB HUMMEL AND THE MYSTERIOUS TECHNICOLOR BUBBLES

Since *Tron* was filmed mostly in 65mm and VistaVision, it was necessary to have 70mm prints to maintain the picture quality. In the 1980s there were two ways feature films were shown in theaters. The traditional method was on 35mm film prints. These prints had been used for decades and were reliable and universal. But the print quality could vary significantly from good to bad. The upgraded method was to go with 70mm prints. These prints could offer superior screen brightness, sharpness, and overall impressive picture quality. An added bonus was the ability to have up to six tracks of stereophonic sound.

Rob Hummel was hired to oversee the prints being done by Technicolor. Hummel was a St. Louis newscaster who saw *Star Wars* and decided that his destiny was in the film business. He packed his bags and moved out to Hollywood. His first job was at Technicolor, which had a long-standing relationship with Walt Disney Productions ever since the studio made *Flowers and Trees*. He worked as an assistant for Skip Nicholson and eventually supported cinematographers when they came to Technicolor.

Hummel then moved to Douglas Trumbull's Entertainment Effects Group. The effects company was creating visual effects for Trumbull's film, *Brainstorm*. Actress Natalie Wood, unfortunately, drowned during production and EEG was shut down for awhile.

Hummel was out of work when he got a call to be a liaison between Technicolor and the production of *Tron*. Personable and technically proficient, Hummel knew his way around the labs at Technicolor. The company was printing footage for *Tron* and the results were not good. The bright neon look of the film was being printed in dull, lifeless color.

"The best lab for handling 70mm was Metro at that time. We had used Technicolor, and sometimes called it 'Dreknicolor,'" recalls Silver.

Ellenshaw was not pleased with the results that Technicolor was printing out.

"They were having troubles with Technicolor," recalls Hummel. "I came over as a post supervisor of sorts since they were doing so many of the opticals through Technicolor in the Technirama format. It was February of 1982. They were in a total pickle as far as getting good elements out of Technicolor."

Technicolor was responsible for striking the film prints, both in 35mm and 70mm, that were to be shipped to theaters. They ran the edited film negative through a special chemical bath. This chemical bath sealed any scratches on the negative. Unfortunately, when the test prints were shown on a movie screen, huge bubbles appeared.

"Technicolor hadn't been doing anamorphic for a couple decades at that point," says Hummel. "They'd lost the expertise. The bubbles would turn out as big white spots. Not small, but big circular spots and they were just bubbles in the wetgate solution."

Ideally, running the negative through the wetgate solution provided for nice high quality film prints, especially in the premium 70mm format. Hummel sought out an old-time lab technician named Joe Schmidt who had been with the company for over forty years. Both he and Hummel figured out the right chemical to use and the bubble problem went away.

More issues arose by using Technicolor, though. Once it was time to get the important and costly 70mm prints made, nearly everyone on the *Tron* team was away on press junkets. The responsibility of quality control fell on Hummel's lap. He needed someone with authority to sign off on the 70mm prints. In the days before cell phones, it was not that easy to track down Lisberger,

Ellenshaw or Taylor for a quick answer. Hummel managed to get a hold of Ellenshaw in New York City. Ellenshaw said he trusted Hummel's judgment.

To be sure he had his bases covered, Hummel decided to get an answer straight from the top with Miller.

"I call him into the scoring stage," recalls Hummel. "It was the only theater in all of Disney that had a 70mm projector. He wouldn't come over to Technicolor. He was too big and important person to do that. No other studio would have a problem with that. Everybody goes to the lab. But this guy says, 'No I'm not going to do it.' So what am I supposed to do? I need somebody to sign off on it."

Reluctantly, Miller walked from his office down to the scoring stage.

"He looked at like thirty seconds of it and goes, 'Looks fine to me. Go ahead.'"

Technicolor printed a number of 70mm prints. The quality was good, but not as good as the original VistaVision footage.

"The VistaVision dailies of the Light Cycle race, all that stuff looked spectacular," says Hummel. "Then when we did the blow up to 65mm, and what we didn't notice in all of our tests, we realized the optics that Technicolor had were desaturating the colors. As vivid and vibrant as everybody thought *Tron* was when it came out, it wasn't as vivid and vibrant as Steven, Harrison and Richard originally wanted it to be."

## THE ATTACK OF *E.T.*

Before *E.T. The Extra-terrestrial* was released, *Time* ran a multi-page article on director Steven Spielberg. Only in his early thirties, Spielberg was considered a *wunkerkind*, a genius filmmaker who not only excited and moved audiences emotionally, but he also seemed to mint money at the box office. *1941* was a rare misstep for him. *Raiders of the Lost Ark* put him back on the map and he was once again invincible. He had two projects due to be released in the summer of 1982. *Poltergeist*, directed by Tobe Hooper (*Texas Chainsaw Massacre*—1974), was the first film to be released. Spielberg's other summer release was a low-budget film called *E.T. The Extra-terrestrial*.

*Poltergeist* was Spielberg's modern take on the old haunted house story. Instead of placing his victims inside an old haunted house, he placed them in a modern suburban home. He had co-written the screenplay and produced the film. But in looking at the completed film, it clearly has his signature directing style.

*E.T. The Extra-terrestrial* was a much smaller and more personal film for Spielberg. It, like *Poltergeist*, went into Spielberg's childlike curiosity. Instead of being afraid of aliens from outer space, young Elliot (Henry Thomas) befriends the little E.T. Both are alone. Both need each other. It was the complete opposite of *Poltergeist*, relying on our need for friendship and devotion, whereas the other film thrived on effective frights.

Early that June, *Time's* article by Richard Corliss was published and it fawned over Spielberg. Though the director was relatively famous at that point, he was still a mystery to the public. This article placed Spielberg on a pedestal from which he has never come down.

Corliss' portrait of Spielberg was painted with careful strokes, making Spielberg out to be the new Walt Disney. Was the article carefully planned to coincide with the upcoming releases of *Poltergeist* and *E.T. The Extra-terrestrial*? No doubt. But it was not any more outrageous than writers who praised Walt Disney when he was alive.

Universal released *E.T. The Extra-terrestrial* on June 11 and knew they had a hit on their hands. Word-of-mouth spread and the reviews were astounding. The film made you laugh yourself silly, then gave you a huge lump in your throat. The film hit audiences directly in the heart. Lines formed around theaters like the Cinerama Dome in Hollywood. People waited for hours just for a chance to see a little space alien run around the screen for two hours.

*E.T. The Extra-terrestrial* had what people were looking for: an old-fashioned story. Many critics said that the film was something that Walt Disney Productions should have made.

## ALEXANDER HAIG CRUSHES HOPE FOR *TRON*

The *Tron* covers for *Time* and *Newsweek* were ready to go. The *Time* cover featured Boxleitner in his costume with the "Electronic World" behind him and Sark's Carrier flying above him. The title read, "Hollywood's Hot Summer." Below it is a subtitle that reads, "In Computerland with TRON." The *Newsweek* cover featured Boxleitner in his costume, as well, standing with his hands on his hips. The title read, "Creative Computers: They're Making Movies, Painting Pictures, Writing Music." Below that reads, "'Tron' Disney's Video-Game Movie."

The weekend before the *Time* and *Newsweek* articles were to hit newsstands on July 5, President Ronald Reagan's Secretary of State, Alexander Haig, resigned. His resignation hit the media hard and was all over television and newspapers the following day. Just as *Tron* was set to make history by appearing on both magazine covers simultaneously, the cover stories were killed over the weekend. In *Tron's* place, pictures of Haig and incoming Secretary of State, George Schultz, were published. The disappearance of the simultaneous covers was a huge blow to the marketing of *Tron*.

"Most kids or anybody, they don't read *Time* magazine or *Newsweek*," says Taylor. "They saw it on the front, 'oh man!' That was a major, major kill."

"Richard was making the *Time* covers," recalls Bonifer. "They actually composed the art because nobody at *Time* or *Newsweek* could do it. They hired a Lear jet to fly the comps back to meet the magazine's deadline, then all of this blew up."

The elaborate stories about *Tron* still appeared in *Time* and *Newsweek*, but readers were engrossed in the Haig/Schultz scandal. Oddly enough, most people forgot about the Haig/Schultz scandal over the years, while *Tron* still remained in people's minds.

## FIRST SCREENINGS

Disney had invited members of the press and stock analysts to preview screenings in New York City and Los Angeles on Tuesday, July 6. Critics were invited to review the new blockbuster, while analysts were invited because of interest in Disney's merchandising of *Tron*. It was estimated that

*Tron* merchandise could bring in as much as $400 million to the studio. One of those invited was a thirty-nine year-old stock analyst named Ted James.

Disney's stock had been doing well, trading at about $58.00 by July. It was thought that the stock was doing well based on the anticipation that *Tron* would be a huge summer hit. Other analysts felt the stock was high based on the upcoming opening of EPCOT.

The Los Angeles screening was held at the Academy's Samuel Goldwyn Theatre in Beverly Hills. It was filled with industry people, critics, and some analysts. James sat there in the Samuel Goldwyn Theater with his large-framed glasses, staring at the film unfolding on-screen. After the film ended and applause from the audience subsided, James walked out and started spreading the news.

James saw it, hated it, and recommended to his Wall Street peers to dump their Disney stock. His "review" appeared in newspapers around the country, including the respected *Wall Street Journal*, and eventually appeared in a scathing *Time* sidebar a few weeks later. Disney's stock was hit hard, dropping from a high of $58.88 to $55.00.

He had seen a thirty-minute clip of the film a few months before and spread the news that *Tron* was not very good. After seeing the entire feature, his review was more acidic. *The Wall Street Journal* covered James' reaction and the reaction from the stock market in their July 8 issue.

"It was a seriously flawed, disjointed story," James was quoted. "The acting is wooden, the dialogue is inane and the special effects were distracting."

Disney's Senior Vice President of Finance, Mike Bagnell, was furious.

"Ridiculous!" he exclaimed. "One analyst decides he doesn't like the picture, puts out the word, and the stock just drops. That's crazy. Nobody knows what's going to happen until *Tron* opens. And even if it doesn't do well, it isn't a big deal one way or the other for the company as a whole."

The article mentioned that there was speculation that if the film did not perform at the box office, top Disney management could be affected.

Another analyst who saw the film disagreed with James. Lee Usgur of Paine Weber Mitchell Hutchins, Inc., felt the film was good.

"I liked the movie a lot," he told the *Wall Street Journal*. "The dialogue has a lot of video-game puns that the analysts probably didn't understand, but which I think will win over the kids. The ones I talked to at the screening like it—the film—a lot."

On July 8, Disney held another premiere on the Disney studio lot to benefit CalArts. Various Disney committee members and CalArts supporters were invited, including Ron Miller, Diane Disney Miller, Card Walker, Michael and Jane Eisner, Roy E. Disney, Bobbie and Peter Ellenshaw, Sharon Lund, Dr. Phil Mittelman and Lew Wasserman.

For Harrison Ellenshaw, it was a relief that the film was finally finished. But it was also the realization that the visual effects torch had been passed to him.

"By that time, having worked on *Star Wars* and *The Empire Strikes Back*, I think had certainly gained a certain amount of respect and admiration from my father, which was very meaningful to me," says Harrison. "He was interested that I was working on *Tron*."

Harrison had seen the film hundreds of times already, so he excused himself from the theater and got a drink. His parents, Bobbie and Peter, watched *Tron* unfold on the screen. No Luddite, the elder Ellenshaw clearly admired the use of computer simulation used in the film. But the film, with its storyline and loud soundtrack, was not his cup of tea.

After the screening, the audience, much of which were over the age of fifty, emptied out into the cocktail reception. Waiters and waitresses, wearing *Tron* costumes, served hors d'oeuvres and wine. Much of the crowd was not sure what they had just experienced. Bobbie, Peter, Lynda and Harrison Ellenshaw joined each other in a makeshift arcade Disney had built on the studio lot.

"I remember he [Peter] was very polite in that he stayed through the whole thing," recalls Harrison. "He came out and he didn't really say much. So I knew it wasn't his kind of film. He was not necessarily in love with the score, which a number of people, especially people of the older generation, found a little bit strident."

Disney was also sponsoring "*Tron* Prom" for everyone who worked on the film. The screening was to be held at the Academy of Motion Picture Arts Sciences' Samuel Goldwyn Theatre the next night.

Almost two years of endless nights and days of frustrating mishaps, *Tron* was finally ready for its public debut. Lisberger had completed his first feature film as a writer and director. Kushner had produced his first feature film without seemingly ever breaking a sweat. Ellenshaw had tackled the responsibilities of not only producing a feature film, but of co-supervising some of the most elaborate visual effects ever committed to film. Taylor had broken the barrier of computer simulation by co-supervising the amazing computer effects.

*Tron* was something to be proud of. It was going to make history. It was going to open up the frontier of computer visual effects. It was going to change how films were made. It was a film that had never been made before and would not be made again.

# Chapter 18

# *RECKONING*

On July 9, 1982, *Tron* opened in over 1000 theaters across the United States and Canada.

Since Disney had trouble getting its films booked into better theaters, it was a coup that it booked the film into the famous Mann's Chinese Theater in Hollywood. Mainly Paramount, Warner Bros. and 20th Century Fox ran their big pictures there. Getting booked at the Chinese Theater was a huge deal, for many of the biggest box office hits of all time opened there, including *Star Wars*. The last major Disney releases at the Chinese were *Mary Poppins* and *The Black Hole*.

The Chinese Theatre was considered to one of the best movie theatres in the world. Part of the allure of the theater was its presentation quality. But because of the loudness of the soundtrack, *Tron* ended up destroying the Chinese Theatre's speaker system.

"It was so powerful, that we blew *all* the channels of speakers at the Chinese, first day," recalls Minkler. "We sent it [film print] in there for a check-run the day before and we made some recommendations. Two days later, I went to the 8 [p.m.] o'clock show. All the speakers were blown. The only one that was playing was right center—the bass part of it. There wasn't even a high frequency! Eighty percent of the soundtrack was completely missing, and they were running it to a full house! I think we had to shut them down and bring in a whole new set of speakers and amplifiers. Their stuff was old and beat up and couldn't handle it."

There was another problem in Disney's unveiling of *Tron*. Much of the market, especially for prized 70mm prints, was booked with the summer's early hits like *Rocky III* and *Star Trek: The Wrath of Khan*. In fact, *Star Trek: The Wrath of Khan* had one of the biggest 70mm print runs ever at that point in time. Many of the big theaters that could handle the large print were booked. This meant for Disney to get 70mm prints into decent theaters, it had to scramble for any remaining available big screens.

Taylor and Lloyd produced an impressive poster for the film, showing Tron communicating with his user, bathed underneath heavenly light. Yori crouches down by his side. Mead's eye-catching logo adorns the poster. *The Los Angeles Times* ran a large ad that Friday, featuring a unique "Presented in 70mm" logo specially made for the film.

Disney also planned to book a 70mm print into the high-end Mann Village theater located in Westwood near UCLA. Instead, Disney had struck 35mm prints for the Mann Westwood complex nearby. It ran a 70mm print at the Village later in its theatrical release.

"Disney ended up running it at one of the dumpy Westwood multiplex theatres, but on ALL the screens," recalls Ellenshaw. "The ad in the *LA Times* said 'See *TRON*! A new showing starts every twenty minutes.' I was never quite sure how that would translate to getting 'bottoms on seats.'"

From its humble beginnings in Steven Lisberger's mind, to the film's hectic post- production, *Tron* was finally finished. Prints were struck. The advertising campaign was in full swing. Without the *Time* and *Newsweek* covers, the film still had a chance to light the box office on fire.

There were no other major films opening that weekend. Disney had the weekend to itself. Better yet, it was a week after the Fourth of July holiday, so the studio was guaranteed to get a huge audience of kids. Since it seemed that almost everybody had seen *E.T. The Extra-terrestrial* at least a few times, it stood to reason that people were looking for something more exciting and cutting edge. *Tron* was assured to be a big hit.

## REVIEWS POUR IN

When the film was released on July 9, reviews for *Tron* were generally quite positive. Both Gene Siskel and Roger Ebert of *At the Movies* gave the film two enthusiastic "Thumbs Up."

Ebert wrote in his *Chicago Sun-Times* review:

"Using computers as their tools, the Disney filmmakers literally have been able to imagine any fictional landscape, and then have it, through an animated computer program. And they integrate their human actors and the wholly imaginary worlds of *Tron* so cleverly that I never, ever, got the sensation that I was watching some actor standing in front of, or in the middle of, special effects. The characters inhabit this world."

Ebert continued.

"Here's a technological sound-and-light show that is sensational and brainy, stylish, and fun."

*Variety* marveled at the film's visuals, but found it lacking in the human story department.

"*Tron* is loaded with visual delights but falls way short of the mark in story and viewer involvement," wrote *Variety*. "Screenwriter-director Steven Lisberger has adequately marshaled a huge force of technicians to deliver the dazzle, but even kids (and specifically computer game freaks) will have a difficult time getting hooked on the situations."

Janet Maslin of *The New York Times*, an influential film critic, seemed to praise the film and deride it at the same time.

"It is beautiful—spectacularly so at times—but dumb," she wrote. "It is a hard film to follow, because Mr. Lisberger's script is an odd blend of technical terminology and childish slang. The characters sound more goofy than bold when they're forced to say things like, 'I knew you'd escape—they haven't built a circuit that could hold you!'"

Judy Stone of the *San Francisco Chronicle* admitted she was reluctant to use computers. She preferred using a trusty typewriter when she wrote her film reviews. But fear of new technology did not stop her from loving *Tron*.

"I have averted my eyes from the sight of kiddies feeding quarters into the insatiable maw of *Pac-Man*," she wrote. "I have even refused, at risk of starvation, from sticking plastic credit cards into the Versateller machine. It seemed obscene to take cash from a helpless hole in the wall under cover of darkness.

She continued, "However, I am duty-bound to report that *Tron* (opening today at Bay Area theaters) has changed my life. It blew my mind right into the digital decade. *Tron* is not only an eye-opener in every sense of the word, but a film that does that rare thing: opens the imagination and mind to the future."

Pat H. Broeske of *The Register*, located in Santa Ana, California, enjoyed the film immensely.

"*Tron* gets an 'A' for ingenuity," Broeske wrote. "The summer's most unconventional film, it is also a milestone for Walt Disney Productions. At long last, the giant has awakened to traverse the decades. Coonskin caps were yesterday's heritage; the computer is today's."

Local Los Angeles television critic, Gary Franklin of KNXT-TV raved, "A 10! If the scale went to 11, it would get that."

Other reviewers seemed to like the look and technology of the film, but did not care for the supposed lack of humanity.

Sheila Benson of the *Los Angeles Times* wrote, "Where was it written that to accommodate an outburst of new effects, no matter how revolutionary, we agreed to give up character, subtlety, a well-told story, clearly understood action and even—heaven help us—humor. Where?"

She admitted, "*Tron* (citywide) fairly bristles with its intricate technology and certainly it is milestone stuff."

If there was a critic in the bunch who hated the film as much as Ted James, it was Rex Reed. Among critics and readers, Reed was considered a stick-in-the-mud and seemed to hate everything he saw.

"Now I have seen a lot of boring, expensive wastes of time and talent in my life (especially in the last few years, as movies have begun to come apart at the seam and stop making sense), but *Tron* is the biggest waste of everything known to man that I have ever encountered," he wrote.

Reed must have forgotten that there were great movies released in the last few years—*Raiders of the Lost Ark*, *All That Jazz*, *The Empire Strikes Back*, *Apocalypse Now*, *Alien*, *Annie Hall*...

Reed concluded his review with a nasty jab.

"As far as I'm concerned, computerized movies are a total disaster. Can they really be planning future movies made by robots in which computers will replace both conventional animation and live action? Walt Disney must be turning over in his grave."

## STUNNED SILENCE

Nearly two years of non-stop work left Ellenshaw exhausted. He and his family took a much needed vacation in Hawaii. Basking in that Hawaiian sunshine with the waves hitting the crystal sand, Ellenshaw's vacation signaled the end of a long and yet incredible production. He knew that *Tron* was going to be a blockbuster and a game changer.

He took a break from the sun and waves. Relaxed, he casually walked back to his hotel room and put in a call to Dick Cook, head of publicity at Buena Vista Distribution. Ellenshaw felt in his heart that *Tron* opened big over that July 9 weekend. But how big?

"So how much did we gross?" asked Ellenshaw, his face beaming with a smile. "Fifteen million? Sixteen million?"

Cook paused for what seemed to be an eternity.

"Four-point-seven," answered Cook.

"That's for Los Angeles, right?" asked Ellenshaw.

"That's all domestic," said Cook.

"You're kidding me."

"I'm afraid not, Harrison," replied Cook.

Ellenshaw was stunned and his face went flush. The hot Hawaiian sun suddenly felt cold.

"Four-point-seven was nothing," recalls Ellenshaw. "It was dead-on-arrival if you looked at it from the entire country. So much was riding on helping maintain the change of direction of Disney. We had a big article in *Life* magazine. We had just barely missed getting the cover of *Time* and *Newsweek*. There were feature articles in *Time* and *Newsweek*. There was *Rolling Stone*. There was a huge media presence about this film."

What happened? The movie had everything going for it. It was groundbreaking. It had incredible visual effects. It had computer animation! The movie, as kids in 1982 were saying, was "bitchin.'" Video arcade teens were supposed to eat it up, just like Pac-Man ate glowing dots. But they were not. Instead, kids and young adults were going to see *E.T. The Extra-terrestrial* for the second, third or fourth time.

The weekend *Tron* opened at $4,761,785 on 1,091 screens, it was ranked #2 in box office revenues. For Disney, this was a major accomplishment. The rerelease of *Cinderella* in 1981 earned $1,300,000 opening weekend. Yet the other major studios maintained their box office successes going through the weekend *Tron* opened. *E.T. The Extra-terrestrial* showed an impressive *increase* in ticket sales over any other movie in release. The little alien movie grossed almost $13 million dollars that weekend. Compared to other weekend openings that summer, *Tron* was indeed disappointing. *Star Trek: Wrath of Khan* broke opening weekend records with over $14 million in ticket sales. *Rocky III* cleared over $12 million during its opening weekend. As *Tron* raced to gain an audience during its opening weekend, *Firefox* and *Annie* nipped at its heels. Only Don Bluth's much anticipated *The Secret of NIMH* was also dead-on-arrival.

There was still a lot of awareness for *Tron*. Audiences who saw the film opening week enjoyed it for its groundbreaking computer effects and its bright and beautiful "candy apple neon" glow. Everybody seemed to enjoy the character of Flynn. Some even enjoyed the disjointed story. Lisberger said at one point, "Those who got it, got it." Nearly every arcade in America had a *Tron* video game. Teenagers swarmed the game machines and eagerly dumped their quarters into the coin slot. There was no way of escaping *Tron*.

"The campaign itself was good; the company just didn't spend enough on media," recalls Wilhite. "They spent the same amount that was spent on [other films] like *Cat From Outer Space*. This was early in the evolution of mass-marketing an opening weekend. Disney's marketing and distribution was a little behind the curve at that time. It was frustrating, of course."

The vibe going around Hollywood was that *Tron* failed. *Disney had again failed to connect with the audience. Disney still did not get it. Its management was poorly run.* People began writing off not only *Tron* that first weekend, but they wrote off Disney as a film studio, as well.

"As soon as that happens in Hollywood, everybody has to search for a reason why," says Ellenshaw. "Nobody will ever know for sure. I can come up with reasons. Somebody else can come up with reasons. The critics, who were mixed can come up with reasons. We will never ever know. It's a mystery. It's insoluble. It cannot be solved. It's kind of an enigma about motion pictures that causes all sorts of conjecture. It wasn't anybody's fault. And I get really tired of this continual need to assign blame. It's called entertainment. It's not curing disease. Lives are not involved. This is not life and death. Some people will try to make a name for themselves saying they know what makes a movie great. Well, if you know what makes a movie great, why aren't you Pixar? You're not. Which looking back on it, I find hugely entertaining and a little bit sad."

"It would've been better if we tested it," says Kushner. "I was disappointed. There was really no video market then. There was no DVD. I know the video game was a big hit at the time."

For Lisberger and Taylor, the negative box office reaction to the film was hard to take.

"We wanted to be the movie made by the underground cool guys who were into computer graphics and backlit animation," says Lisberger. "Card Walker held a press conference two weeks before the movie came out, and actually said, this is a quote, '*Tron* is going to out merchandise *Star Wars.*' So with that one statement, he destroyed the whole truth of the movie. We went from being the cool guys in the black shirts, the underdogs, the cutting edge guys, the rock and rollers, to being the establishment."

"The worst part about that is we never got to show it in front of a test audience. Ever," says Taylor. "It went from getting done to the theaters. All I knew that if we had another four weeks, five weeks, six weeks to work on the film, to show it for some test audiences, we would've re-cut it. We would've made the first reel understandable. We would've gotten rid of some stupid lines. Looped in some different lines. Shortened the film some. And it would've been a better film. A better dramatic film."

Boxleitner recalls, "When *Tron* came out, it was so luke warm. I remember seeing the first screening and there didn't seem to be a lot of excitement about it. I was very excited about it. I thought it was going to be really big. It was going to launch me into movies. So I went right back to where I was safe. I went back to TV."

Still, not everyone was down on the box office performance of *Tron*.

"There's always a little bit of disappointment," says Bridges. "You make a movie and usually I'm onto something else where I'm putting my energy in. You feel a little disappointed. Most often it doesn't break my heart. I usually got all my attention that I'm doing at the moment. The movie is not the main thing. For me, the experience is what I take away from it. The movie is sort of like the skin that the snake leaves behind."

"I thought it played well," says Miller. "I thought it was a good film. It had a lot of unique looks to it. I just felt it would do better than what it did."

## TRON'S GOT LEGS…MAYBE

Maybe its circuits were a little fried, but *Tron* continued to plug along in theaters. The sluggish opening weekend could not keep it down. Disney expanded the release by adding twenty-one more screens by week two. The film stayed among the top five box office earners and was still making money. Maybe it was not a dud after all.

*Time* ran an article on the summer's box office hits in its July 19 issue. The article covered the fact that the film industry, despite there being a recession across the nation, was doing extremely well. At the tail end of the article was a sidebar on *Tron* titled "Tremors on Dopey Drive." Anyone who was a stock holder, studio or company employee, or fan of Disney looked at this sidebar and said, "Oh no."

The sidebar, highlighted in green, featured Ted James. His early "review" had already appeared in newspapers around the country just two weeks earlier. The sidebar explained, in further gruesome detail, what the analyst thought about *Tron*. He spoke of the early morning Academy screening he attended on July 6.

"Thirty-five minutes into the film, the coughing started, and halfway through, people began to talk," said James. "This was a sympathetic audience that had turned apathetic. Walt Disney used to tell his people, 'Start with a story, then make the movie.' This time they got it backward."

James dug in deeper.

"*Tron* could be one of the five or six biggest films of the summer, grossing $30 million to $50 million. But that matters less than that it won't be the blockbuster they counted on. The expectations of the investment community just weren't in line with the reality of the film."

Just as *Tron* was picking up steam, and word-of-mouth was getting out that the movie was cool, James' remarks in *Time* did an unexpected thing; his opinion of the film did far worse damage to Disney and *Tron* than any film critic did. The perception was that Disney truly laid an egg.

Mike Bagnell was incensed with James' critique. He dug in and struck back. The idea of inviting a securities analyst to a screening was now considered a no-no.

"We never did it before, and we may never do it again," Bagnell told *The New York Times*. "What does a securities analyst know?"

What did James see that other audience members did not? The storyline and dialogue certainly were not the film's strongest points, but some of the lines did get laughs in the right spots. The visuals were the strongest element of the film, and if anything, kept eyes glued to the big screen. The film moved along at a fairly fast clip and was entertaining. But was the movie really that bad?

Ebert took issue with James during an interview with Wilhite on July 18. The film critic slammed the stock market analyst. The audience he saw the film with in Manhattan, on the same day as James, enjoyed the film. Ebert was concerned. Whereas James claimed people were restless at the screening he attended, Ebert countered that the audience he was with was totally into the film.

Ebert asked Wilhite if he would invite a guy like James to a future screening.

"Probably not, to be quite honest," said Wilhite. "Not because we'd be afraid for one of our movies, but because people like to make a name for themselves in any profession, and there's no better way to attract attention to yourself than through controversy. He has a right to his opinion, but I'm sorry the movie opened surrounded by that controversy. Since *Tron* has opened, all of the reviews have noted its innovative nature. If people aren't fond of the picture, they criticize its story, but nobody has said they don't like the visual design. And the visuals are really what we're excited about with *Tron*."

Ebert further championed the film, stating that it still opened well despite the impression of being a bomb. He went on to say that the film was doing very well in certain theaters like the popular McClurg Court in Chicago.

The influential film critic fired back at James.

"It is not ordinarily the film critic's job to comment on the stock-market performance of a movie studio, but, then again, it's not usually a financial analyst's job to review a movie before the critics do. Thanks a lot, Ted. I just wanted to ask you, one movie critic to another, what you thought about that scene where Master Control is zapped by the electronic Frisbee?"

## Chapter 19

# AFTERMATH AND THE REVOLUTION CREATED BY TRON

As fast as the euphoria of *Tron* happened, it faded out slowly. The film continued to play in a small number of theaters across the country long after summer ended. In Los Angeles, 70mm prints were shown in additional engagements around the city.

The film, considered a disappointment by Disney and the film industry, managed to pull in approximately $33 million in the United States and Canada. Based on a budget of nearly $20 million, plus an approximately $4 million advertising campaign, the film lost money. But the amount Disney lost on the film's theatrical release was not as catastrophic as it may seem. Audiences, however small they were, were still discovering the film. At the Cinerama theater in San Diego, California, for instance, the film was successful enough to have a 70mm engagement by May of 1983.

In reality, *Tron* was not a total bomb for Disney. The studio took two major write-offs prior to *Tron*. For the fiscal year of 1981, Disney wrote off approximately $3 million for the reissue of *The Watcher in the Woods*. Early in 1982, the studio took an even bigger write-off for *Night Crossing*, a well-meaning drama about a family's attempt to escape from East Germany in a hot air balloon. The studio lost over $10 million on the film.

Disney released *Tron* on videocassette in December of 1982. The home video craze, which included the VHS, Beta, Laser Videodisc, and RCA SelectaVision formats, was still in its infant stage. But home video was making inroads into homes across the country. Home video was a huge market that was waiting to be exploited. By putting *Tron* on videocassette, Disney could off set some of the losses it incurred.

Disney released *Tron* in a plastic "clamshell" case. This was Disney's signature videocassette container for years.

The video version of the film was a far cry from how it was seen in theaters. Since the film was shot in Super Panavision 70, there was no letterboxing format widely available in 1982. The 2.21:1 aspect ratio was cropped down to fit a normal television screen's 1.33:1 aspect ratio, thereby necessitating the use of the dreaded "pan-and-scan" format.

Pan-and-scan created new pans and compositions not found in the original film. It attempted, badly, to show the audience what a telecine operator wanted them to see. It did not matter if the panning made no sense or impeded on the director and cinematographer's intent. What mattered was to get the wide-gauge film frame to fit on a television screen. One example of the brutal re-composing of *Tron* takes place with the *Pac-Man* gag. All the television audience sees is Sark yelling at the map. *Pac-Man* is nowhere to be seen.

*Tron* became a surprise best seller and became a perennial part of the Disney video library. Disney had already had success selling a select group of titles on tape. *Dumbo, Mary Poppins, The Love Bug*, and *The Black Hole* were perennial best sellers on videocassette.

By Christmas Day, the video release of *Tron* was number twenty on Billboard's video rental chart, and number twenty-two on the sales chart. By January 15, 1983, the film jumped to number two on the rental chart. Sales of the video earned *Tron* an International Tape/Disc Association (ITA) Gold Cassette Winner award. This was awarded to studios and companies with sales of 75,000 videos or $3 million in sales on select titles. The video release earned the studio $1.7 million in sales. Rentals may have accounted for more revenues.

Michael Bonifer's *The Art of Tron* was finally published in December 1982, well after the film was released in theaters. The book was an incredible tribute to the artists and work on the film. But as a result of the cost cutting, the book was not how Bonifer and Ellenshaw envisioned it. It went from being originally conceived as a deluxe coffee table book to a short paperback marketed for children. Little Simon took the stills Ellenshaw carefully culled from the film and re-produced them with dreary colors. Unfortunately, the book did not sell well.

## THE BAKE-OFF

In early 1983, the Academy of Motion Picture Arts & Sciences sent out ballots for films that were eligible to be nominated from 1982. The Visual Effects Award Committee was small, consisting of approximately thirty to forty members. By 1983, members from other branches of the Academy were now allowed to vote for Best Visual Effects and technical awards. Thus actors, directors, cinematographers and producers were able to nominate and vote for their choices for Best Visual Effects.

Academy members showed up at the prestigious Samuel Goldwyn Theatre to view sequences of the films they wanted to nominate. They also had an opportunity to ask the visual effects supervisors questions about how the effects were achieved. That year, the top visual effects films were *Tron, Star Trek: Wrath of Khan, Blade Runner, The Dark Crystal, Poltergeist, E.T. The Extra-terrestrial, Das Boot*, and *Firefox*. Out of those films, only three or fewer would be eligible for an Oscar nomination.

The "Bake-Off" was held on February 1, 1983. *Tron* was threaded up on the Academy's state-of-the-art projection system. It was second to the last of the films shown that day. Both Richard Edlund and Doug Trumbull had already finished their presentations for *Poltergeist* and *Blade Runner*, respectively. The clips from *Tron* were shown with its dazzling visuals and groundbreaking computer animation. Taylor represented the *Tron* team.

The theater lights faded up and Taylor went up on stage. He explained how they were the first filmmakers to break the computer simulation barrier by producing a significant amount of CGI footage. He described how they used raster graphics and super advanced computers at four different companies to create the computer world of *Tron*. He pointed out how both computers and humans made this groundbreaking film, and how computers would change the way visual effects were made. He finished his speech.

"Well that's how we made *Tron*. Any questions?"

Looking out into the vast Samuel Goldwyn Theatre, he saw that no one was raising their hand. The visual effects professionals were dead silent—for almost two minutes.

"There's got to be someone with a question," said Taylor.

A brave, lonely soul meekly raised his hand.

"What kind of camera did you use?" he asked.

Taylor explained that they shot the film in Super Panavision 70, but had used a variety of different camera formats and Kodaliths to get the look of *Tron*. He explained that in using computers, they effectively used a virtual camera to shoot the computer scenes, but that footage was recorded out to film. The audience sat there in silence. As advanced as they were in cameras, technology, and "gee-whiz" effects, what Taylor was describing went over their heads.

"Okay. Any other questions?" Taylor asked, searching for any signs of life.

Pure silence.

"There must be another question of some kind."

Another person raised his hand.

"Um, did you make any models?"

Taylor explained that, yes, they made some models but only for study of the Solar Sailer. Standing there, he scanned the audience for any other questions. There were no more and he felt that the audience was hostile without saying a word. He ran into Edlund.

"God, that was really weird," said Taylor, sweat perspiring on his forehead. "It's like everybody was mad at me or something. What do you think is going on? How come nobody would ask any questions?"

"I think they think you cheated," said Edlund.

"What do you mean by that?

"I think they think the computer does it all," said Edlund.

"What do you mean?" asked Taylor. "Do you mean they think that we type in what we want and the computer just does it?"

"Yeah," said Edlund.

"Everybody was really scared of computer simulation," recalls Taylor. "They didn't understand it. They believed it would take over. And it has."

"Most of the industry was happy to see *Tron* fail," says Ellenshaw. "When *Tron's* box office demise happened, there was some glee from others. The effects were done by movie outsiders. Lisberger and Taylor only had experience in commercials. How dare they try to join the club?"

## OSCAR MISSES AN OPPORTUNITY

The Oscar nominations were announced on February 17, 1983. For the first time since *The Black Hole*, the Disney studio had Oscar nominations on a film it released. The field was crowded over the year in the technical categories, many for which *Tron* was eligible. The film could be eligible for almost any award from the Academy. It was highly unlikely it would be nominated for Best Picture or Best Actor. It could, however, be eligible for editing, art direction, costume design, sound, sound effects editing, and visual effects.

When the nominations were announced for Best Visual Effects, *Blade Runner*, *E.T. The Extra-terrestrial* and *Poltergeist* were acknowledged. *Tron* was shut out for Best Visual Effects.

Everyone who worked on the visual effects, from the background painters to the computer animators, was stunned. How could the most innovative and groundbreaking film since *Star Wars* have been shut out for Best Visual Effects?

The Academy was normally fair in choosing nominees for Best Visual Effects. It was also usually good in choosing a winner. There were very few years in which the visual effects winners were weak. *Star Wars* was a groundbreaker. *Superman* was stunning for its ability to make a man fly. *Alien* was an odd choice, as the visual effects in *Star Trek: The Motion Picture* and *The Black Hole* were superior. *Raiders of the Lost Ark* was a great choice. But in not nominating *Tron*, the Academy missed the boat on a film that would ultimately transform the visual effects industry.

Ellenshaw was quick to point out that just because *Tron* was incredibly innovative, there was no guarantee that it would be nominated for an Oscar. As early as October, 1982, he wrote a memo highlighting the obstacles the *Tron* team faced in getting nominated. Many Academy members voting for Best Visual Effects had personal stakes in many of the films that year. There was the sheer number of potential visual effects nominees to sift through. There were Academy members who were not knowledgeable in visual effects who were now eligible to vote. Plus, there was the factor of ILM and its dominance over the majority of the visual effects field, not to mention Douglas Trumbull's Entertainment Effects Group (EEG) was a strong contender with its effects in *Blade Runner*.

"I can assure you that in this category and the others the competition will be extremely stiff," wrote Ellenshaw.

He had predicted in that October, 1982 memo that *Poltergeist, E.T. The Extra-terrestrial* and *Blade Runner* would possibly be the nominees.

Out of the group of nominees, *Blade Runner* had the most stunning and well-crafted effects. The effects in *Poltergeist* were very good. *E.T. The Extra-terrestrial* was not the strongest visual effects film that year. Though very good, the effects were not in the same high-caliber work for which ILM was known. The famous sequence of Elliot and E.T. flying past the moon still bothers Taylor.

"I'll put it this way," says Taylor. "*E.T.*—people loved the movie. They don't say, 'Did you see those matte lines?' They don't care because they loved the movie. It was an emotional vote. It was not a technical vote. The special effects in *E.T* quite frankly were not that extraordinary. Likewise, you could go to a movie that has phenomenal special effects, done perfectly and you don't care at all. The bottom line is it's got to be a good story and you got to do it well."

What really bothered Taylor was the exclusion of a Scientific/Technical Award from the Academy. That award was given to what were considered to be significant achievements in science and technology in film. Film stock, camera systems and sound advancements are just some of the award winning achievements honored. Those awards were, and still are, treated as an afterthought during the Oscar broadcasts. But to the winners, they are highly prized.

"I don't know the inside story why we were never nominated for a Scientific or Technical," says Taylor. "How could it not be? I mean it was the first film to use computer simulation full screen negative."

## OSCAR NOMINATIONS AND OSCAR NIGHT

*Tron* was nominated for two Oscars in the Best Sound and Best Costume Design categories.

The nomination for sound was hurtful to Fremer. He had been on the *Tron* team since its inception. He had put the department together from scratch and hired Wendy Carlos for the score. It stung to see his and Serafine's names not on the nomination list. However, nominations were done differently in 1983 when the Oscar nomination ballots were mailed out.

Sound Designer Randy Thom (*Ratatouille*—2007) clarifies, "Each branch (craft) in the Academy makes its own rules. In 1983, only sound mixers were eligible for the Best Sound Award. Neither Fremer nor Serafine were considered to be mixers. Since that time the rules have been changed so that Supervising Sound editors, and in some cases people with the title Sound Designer, are eligible to be nominated for a Sound Oscar."

*Tron* was competing against *Das Boot*, *E.T. The Extra-terrestrial*, *Gandhi*, and *Tootsie* for Best Sound. Other contenders that missed an Oscar nomination were *The Thing* and *The Road Warrior*. Perhaps the most glaring omission for Best Sound was *Blade Runner*.

For Costume Design, *Tron* was competing against *La Traviata*, *Sophie's Choice*, *Gandhi*, and *Victor/Victoria*. Rossana Norton was shocked she was nominated on a film from which she had been fired. She was doubly shocked that Eloise Jensen was nominated.

"The woman who replaced me, because the union required that I be replaced, was very powerful and old and in the union," says Norton. "I think she was very important in getting that nomination."

On Oscar night *E.T. The Extra-terrestrial* took home Oscar for Best Sound. In 1980s, most films that took home Oscar for Best Sound were usually films with incredibly layered and often loud soundtracks. Many were also shown theatrically in 70mm Six-Track Dolby Stereo. This often led to the perception that louder soundtracks sounded better and more dynamic. Most often they did sound better, especially compared to dialogue driven films like *Toostie*.

The sound for *E.T. The Extra-terrestrial* was very good, but in reality, most of the film's power came from John Williams' score being pumped up throughout the film. If any of films from 1982 had serious competition with *Tron*, it was with *Das Boot*.

Watching the Oscars, Norton was dumbfounded with the winners that night.

"*Gandhi* won. Don't you just love that?" says Norton. "In the Academy Awards, they never want to nominate science fiction, except for historical stuff."

In reality, John Mollo won an Oscar for Costume Design for *Star Wars*.

"I finally get nominated and then *Gandhi* wins!" exclaims Norton. "I'm sitting there thinking, that's what they wear. They wear that in India. They go to India and they see people wearing clothes that they wear. *Tron*, that's not what anybody wears. What are you talking about here? *Gandhi* was a *terrible* movie. That movie's a soap opera. I hate that movie. Let me just tell you, it was torture."

## WILHITE CONTINUES TO BRING DISNEY INTO THE MAINSTREAM

Life continued on at Walt Disney Productions after *Tron*. Undeterred by the lack of box office returns for the film, Wilhite continued to work on his upcoming slate of new films. He also nurtured talent he had working at the studio.

In the pipeline were some intriguing projects. *Something Wicked This Way Comes,* based on Ray Bradbury's book, was going to be Disney's attempt to correct their misstep on *The Watcher in the Woods. Never Cry Wolf* was a film directed by Carroll Ballard about a scientist living with wolves in the wild. Wilhite pushed ahead *Return to Oz,* a gigantic production by first-time director, Walter Murch. *The Black Cauldron* continued in production. Wilhite also picked up a script for a little romantic fantasy movie called *Splash.*

Though the modest returns on *Tron* seemed to spell the end for further development in CGI, there was still a ray of light shining on the future of filmmaking and visual effects. John Lasseter had been so struck by the abilities and possibilities of computer simulation, he and animator Glen Keane embarked on testing computer graphics in traditional animation. Wilhite commissioned a test for Lasseter and Keane to develop a short reel to see the feasibility of CGI. The animators chose Maurice Sendak's *Where the Wild Things Are* as their foundation.

In the short test, Max, dressed in a costume, scribbles on his bedroom wall. His dog playfully pounces into the room chasing a rubber ball. The boy chases the dog under the bed and then down the staircase.

The animation is infused with Lasseter and Keane's style and fluidity that they developed as Disney animators. Working with MAGI, the team created a delightful short test film. The boy's room is computer generated, while the boy and his dog were painted by computer. The animators proved that traditional-style animation and computer generated animation could work in harmony, while still maintaining the need for good storytelling and great characters. It is remarkable how advanced the CGI footage became so soon after *Tron.*

Another one of the talents Wilhite kept under wraps was Tim Burton. This odd, skinny kid was one of the most talented animators on the Disney payroll. When he was not working on the studio's main features, he was working on secret projects on the side, funded by the studio. Apparently, the studio was not aware of this.

"Tim Burton had a girlfriend who worked for Tom, Julie Hickson," says Bonifer. "She got a charge number opened for Tim. Before they knew what was going on in production, he had run up a million dollar tab on *Frankenweenie*. Nobody even knew what was being billed to this number or why! He was having sets built on the soundstages and the head of production, Ted Shills, would just go apoplectic when he would find this stuff out. There was nobody to stop it. Wilhite funded money for Lasseter to do his first experimentation with Glen Keane on *Where the Wild Things Are*. The older guys at the studio are just looking at each other going, 'How did this shit get done? How did they get away with this?'"

Burton also directed the whimsically Gothic, *Vincent*, featuring the voice of his favorite actor, Vincent Price. After leaving Disney, he went onto direct *Pee Wee's Big Adventure* (1985), *Batman* (1989) and the feature-length version of *Frankenweenie* (2012), just to name a few.

## DISNEY'S LUCASFILM CONNECTION: A BLOWN OPPORTUNITY

*Tron* was a true breakthrough in proving that, with the use of computer technology, eventually the workflow of making animation and visual effects could become streamlined. Computer technology allowed filmmakers to do just about anything they could imagine. Indeed, *Tron* did not perform as well as anticipated. But it did show Disney and the rest of the film industry that by using computers for simulation, bits and bytes would transform filmmaking forever.

In February of 1983, Ellenshaw and a small group from Disney flew up to Lucasfilm. The group included John Lasseter. Lucas' company had developed four technologies that could help filmmakers work more efficiently. Ellenshaw felt that investing in Lucasfilm's technology would enable Disney to finally compete with the bigger studios and effects houses.

Lucasfilm's small computer division had technology that could help animators work more efficiently. The technologies were broken down into four areas: Graphics Tool Kit, main graphics, video/audio digital editing and service bureau.

For commercial products, Lucasfilm had what was then called a Graphics Tool Kit. This enabled animators and artists to paint and create animation on a Sun Systems workstation with a graphics tablet. The animators worked on a 1000-line high-resolution monitor. The station could save, restore, rotate, change size, matte, paste and sketch pictures in 2-D. A future version of this workstation would eventually enable animators and artists to scan pictures, "tween" (auto in-betweening in animation) and move images in real time. This system cost around $100,000.00.

Main graphics was called "Pixar." This processing and synthesis software could utilize 3-D image processing, blue screen, digital color correction, format changes, and image synthesis. A laser scanner recorded out images to 35mm film and eliminated the need to film off of a CRT screen as *Tron* did. There was a plan to use "Pixar" on the upcoming *Star Trek III: The Search for Spock* (1984), but it was not used. The system was being upgraded over the course of time and would eventually surpass the speed of the hot Cray Computer. The "Pixar" system would also be cheaper to operate than the Cray.

The video/audio digital editing systems were going to revolutionize film and video editing, and bring audio into the realm of feature films and television. The video editing system eventually became EditDroid, Lucasfilm's LaserDisc-based editing system. For the first time in film history, it was now possible to edit a feature film without cutting or touching actual film.

The audio digital editing system was at least two years away when Ellenshaw and crew visited Lucasfilm. But the concept was intriguing for the time. It allowed for better flexibility in editing and recording audio for film.

The service bureau involved utilizing computer simulation, and Ellenshaw felt that this could be a worthy alternative to using MAGI.

Perhaps the most suitable developments here for Disney were the Graphics Tool Kit, the "Pixar" system and service bureau.

Both the Graphics Tool Kit and "Pixar" would have effectively enabled Disney's animation department and visual effects department to streamline their work. Disney's animation unit had been using essentially the same technology for decades. Animation cels and animation camera stands had been used since the earliest days of the art form. But *Tron* showed what could be done with computer simulation. The Lucasfilm tools eliminated the need for the camera stand. The cels were placed onto a scanner, scanned directly into a computer, and then animators could go to work.

The Disney visual effects department could have used the "Pixar" system for any number of tasks, including image processing, blue screen work and digital color correction. The studio had been developing *Who Censored Roger Rabbit* (later titled *Who Framed Roger Rabbit*), and *Basil of Baker Street* (later titled *The Great Mouse Detective)*.

A week after the Lucasfilm visit, Ellenshaw sent out a memo to Wilhite showing his enthusiasm for the new technologies.

He wrote, "My extreme enthusiasm for their facility and product remains undiminished. It is not too difficult to see that their application of high technology to post-production film making will truly revolutionize the industry. The possibilities are very exciting. Not only are the applications to the studio's film production possible, but with the extended special effects capability there is no reason that Walt Disney Productions cannot do special effects for many additional films (such as *2010*). ILM does not have to be the only game in town (I should say, 'out of town')."

The sequel to *2001: A Space Odyssey*, *2010: The Year We Make Contact* (1984) featured visual effects by Richard Edlund and his new company, BOSS Films. One of the film's signature shots used a Cray Supercomputer to collapse the planet Jupiter into itself.

There were some problems for Disney and its Animation Department regarding any investment in the "Pixar" system, though. Already, *The Black Cauldron* was costing the studio a small fortune at $25 million and featured a small bit of computer-generated animation during its climax. The film was rumored to have a holographic sequence, but it did not come to fruition in the final film. [The "Pixar" technology could make the simple CGI sequence in that film seem like child's play.]

However, the studio, it seemed, was losing interest in animation. It became Roy E. Disney's biggest complaint before he left in 1977. Besides Ellenshaw and Lasseter's excitement about what they saw at Lucasfilm, there was little support at Disney for the technologies. But Doug Le Blanc of W.E.D. (Walt Elias Disney's Imagineering unit) clearly saw the potential.

"It is my opinion that, provided a satisfactory working arrangement can be agreed upon, a collaborative effort with LFL [Lucasfilm, Ltd.] on the development of a sophisticated computer graphics facility is our best option for bringing this technology to Disney," LeBlanc wrote in a memo. "I believe it is an exciting opportunity that should be vigorously pursued."

But apparently, Disney's upper management did not see the potential in the "Pixar" technology. They passed on any investment in the system. Eventually Lucas sold Pixar to Steve Jobs for $10 million in 1986.

It can be reasonably debated whether or not Disney was committed to its animation department. *Tron* proved that, with the help of incredibly talented outside animators, the studio could make animation in both computers and by hand. *The Fox and the Hound* performed well at the box office. *The Black Cauldron* was purposely designed to make a statement that Disney Animation was attempting to do something extraordinary and different. It seemed that the studio was still committed to the very process that built it. But it can also be debated that the studio committed a major blunder by not taking opportunities that were sitting right there in front of it.

"It was amazing that Disney even picked up *Tron*," says Kroyer. "They only did it because there was a young guy there named Tom Wilhite. He was the young genius at Disney who was going to get movies going. Wilhite should get the credit for being the champion. He was a young guy who wanted to try something different and new."

The studio also had, within its grasp, some of the world's most talented animators working on its lot. Tim Burton, John Lasseter, Bill Kroyer, Jerry Rees, John Van Vliet, and Richard Taylor were, technically speaking, under the Disney umbrella and could have been given very handsome offers to stay.

By pursing a collaboration with Lucasfilm, Ellenshaw, Lasseter and Le Blanc were trying to bring Disney up to modern standards in a number of ways. Had Disney invested in the "Pixar" technology, and Lucasfilm's editing and sound systems, the studio could have been at the forefront of film production and post-production technology.

Instead of breaking through on these levels, the studio missed an opportunity to become a quality artistic haven for imagination and technology. Ironically when Walt Disney was alive, his studio had been a leader in technological breakthroughs since the earliest days of its existence. Walt Disney had always looked to the future to use technology to further enhance his staff's ability to tell stories. Technology was not there just to do neat things. Technology helped him and his staff tell stories. He was a leader in breaking barriers. By the 1980s, the company lost a fleeting opportunity to ride the wave of the future in film.

"Pixar" technology eventually transformed the way people saw animated shorts, commercials, and features. Disney had an opportunity to buy the company for little or no money, as Alvy Ray Smith mentioned. It took Disney many management changes and many years to appreciate the potential of creative CGI. But a company not listening to the good advice in 1983 eventually cost them dearly: $7 billion.

## LASSETER AND THE FORMATION OF PIXAR

In just a year after the release of *Tron*, computer simulation started to work its way into film and television in a gradual wave.

In May of 1983, George Lucas' *Return of the Jedi* opened in theaters around the country. The highly anticipated third chapter in the *Star Wars* series was hit-and-miss. There were some great visual effects and interesting story developments, but Ewoks nearly killed the movie for many viewers. Despite the missteps taken in the film, it still became one of the biggest box office hits of all time.

The film naturally had state-of-the-art visual effects from the famed ILM team. Most were spectacular, including the much celebrated Speeder Bike chase. The film featured a computer-generated effect involving a three-dimensional hologram of the Moon of Endor and the Death Star. The effect was impressive with its three-dimensionality and smooth motion. The effect was created by Lucas' Computer Division.

Around this time, Lasseter was preparing to direct his first feature at Disney, *The Brave Little Toaster*. It was going to include a mixture of traditional and computer animation. Just after Lasseter had finished his presentation to the head of the studio, he was fired. Rejected by the company he dreamed of working for, he met Ed Catmull in a chance meeting aboard the Queen Mary in Long Beach, California. Catmull immediately hired him to work for Lucasfilm's computer division as an "Interface Designer." The company needed an animator and Lasseter needed a job. Lasseter never looked back.

Lasseter had found a home in Lucasfilm's Computer Division. He debuted his computer animation skills *The Adventures of André & Wally B.* (1984), directed by Alvy Ray Smith. The film was used to show how computer characters could act just as they did in traditional cartoons. One of the fears of traditional animators was that computers could not render believable or likable characters. Smith and Lasseter proved that characters could be cute, warm, funny and do the same movements that hand-drawn characters did.

Lasseter and Bill Reeves took their combined talents and created the "Stained Glass Knight" for the 1985 film, *Young Sherlock Holmes*. In what is perhaps the first combination of live-action footage and a computer generated character, Lasseter and Reeves created a frightening image of the "Stained Glass Knight" who flies out of a window and scares a priest to death.

The effect was groundbreaking, as the CGI character is not only lit with perfection, but the camera pans with him as we see his flat body walk on by it. We then see the reverse angle of his body in the same shot.

Lucas loved what the computer team was doing. They were creating new ways to do animation and effects on computers. Their goal was to eventually make an animated feature film solely on computers, just as they had at NYIT. But Lucas figured it would be too costly. Catmull and Smith asked for his blessing to spin off the division.

"I don't know how many times I've read (even in the *New York Times*) that Steve Jobs and John Lasseter founded Pixar and Steve named it," says Smith. "All wrong of course. In a nutshell, Ed and

I cofounded it, I named it, John Lasseter was one of forty founding employees, Steve was our venture capitalist. (On the naming, there were actually three of us who named a machine the Pixar, and it was I who suggested that we use the machine's name for the new company's name—It was reluctantly accepted, believe it or not.)"

As one of the founding employees of Pixar, Lasseter continued to refine his computer-animation techniques. He directed short films, including *Luxo, Jr.* (1986), in which the little character became the icon for the company. It was also a showcase, in only a few short minutes, of Lasseter's playful animation and grasp of what computer animation could do. As *Tron* broke the barriers of limited computer animation and effects, Lasseter and Pixar refined them just as Disney had refined animation.

Through the late 1980s and early 1990s, Lasseter had directed a few television commercials for Lifesavers, Listerine and Tropicana orange juice. These commercials featured squishy and squashy Lifesavers, Listerine bottles with personalities, and Tropicana cartons which were full of life. By 1995, Lasseter and his talented team convinced Disney and the world that fully computerized animation was possible in a feature film. The result was *Toy Story*.

## *THE LAST STARFIGHTER* VERSUS *TRON*

CGI had advanced since *Tron*. Gary Demos and John Whitney Jr. went to Universal and took charge of the visual effects for *The Last Starfighter*. The film was about a young video game player who is taken into space to fight real aliens. The duo formed Digital Productions and led a team to perform the visual effects.

Digital Productions built a computerized star field, which had been very difficult to do just a few years before. Their most impressive achievement was the creation and movement of the Gunstar spaceships. The Gunstars, based on concept drawings by legendary artist, Ron Cobb, were rendered in the expensive Cray X-MP supercomputer.

It was quite an achievement to make the Gunstar ship fly, bank, turn, spin, and shoot lasers, all based on using computer animation. The computer simulation in the film was very impressive. But the biggest difference was the lack of realism compared to *Tron*. As simple as the vehicles and the "Electronic World" of *Tron* looked, nearly everything looked realistic within that environment. The drawback for the vehicles in *The Last Starfighter* was their "video sheen." They appeared computer generated as opposed to appearing realistic. Cutting from the cockpit of the Gunstar with live actors to the exterior of the Gunstar was somewhat jarring. That said, the effects in *The Last Starfighter* were impressive enough to earn Demos and Whitney, Jr. a Scientific/Technical Award from the Academy.

The film, released in the summer of 1984, was a good-spirited adventure whose star attractions were actors Lance Guest and Robert Preston. In a way, it was not too difficult to compare some of the elements this film and *Tron*. The central character is a video game jockey who plays a three-dimensional video game. Both films feature computer simulation and both used or had dealt with computer artists who worked on *Tron*. *The Last Starfighter* went a step further than *Tron* by using all computer-simulated effects.

The Gunstar ships were digital offspring from the X-wing fighters in *Star Wars*. How? In 1977, Triple-I commissioned its own CGI photo of Lucas' X-wing fighters flying in space. Durinski went to a model shop and bought a plastic model kit of an X-wing fighter and digitized it into a computer—roughly 16,000 polygons worth. The digital model was very detailed and looked just like the X-wing fighters seen in the film.

"At one point George Lucas was actually in town, and John Jr. got George to drop in at Triple-I," says Durinski. "We had this kind of quick meeting where one-by-one we showed George these transparencies and he looked through a loupe. George didn't react at all. We must've had about ten (transparencies) that we showed him. Finally he said, 'Well, these don't look like my ships.' We were all flabbergasted because we thought he was going to say, 'This is it! This is the future!' He told us that his ships had been in wars. They've been in fights. They were banged up, scratched up and had oil stains on it. They were dirty, and the photos of the X-wing we were showing George were perfect. And he was absolutely right. We all learned from that comment."

A year later, the team at Triple-I rendered a short test of real footage of the X-wing fighters in CGI. This time, Lucasfilm paid a small fee to see what the company could render. The test was successful. The X-wing fighters looked nearly identical to the models used in *Star Wars*.

"It caught his eye," recalls Durinski. "But I think what happened was the next movie was done, George was thinking of actually incorporating digital ships, but I think they couldn't work out the kinks. They would've had us as subcontractors. But in a way, George was being a very good businessman. I think what he was thinking was, yeah, there's potential here, but right now it's too costly."

Lucas, ever the businessman, knew that computer animation and graphics were possible, but he was smart in biding his time. He encouraged his ILM wizards to try certain sequences or creatures in CGI over the next few years.

## FROM STEVEN SPIELBERG'S *AMAZING STORIES* TO *JURASSIC PARK*

In the summer of 1985, the rock band Dire Straits released their studio album, *Brothers in Arms*. The single, "Money for Nothing," was one of the album's most popular songs. The music video was one of MTV's most played in the channel's short history. Directed by Steve Barron, the video featured crude but effective computer animation.

Later that year, Steven Spielberg returned to network television by presenting *Amazing Stories* on NBC. He directed two episodes for the first season. This was a highly ambitious series, presenting an anthology of different stories by high-profile directors and writers. The idea of the show was not innovative. *Twilight Zone* was an early example of making a series based on anthologies instead of being episodes. What was innovative was *Amazing Stories* use of CGI for the opening title sequence. *Young Sherlock Holmes* was released during the Christmas season that same year.

Computer-generated imagery (CGI) continued to be used in more films and television shows as the 1980s progressed. In *Labryinth* (1986), ILM created a CGI owl. In *Howard the Duck*, the effects team used an early form of digital wire removal. Later that year, ILM produced the effects for *Star Trek IV: The Voyage Home*. In the time travel sequence, the audience flies through a dream-like world where the statuesque heads of the Enterprise crew bob and weave in the clouds. Those heads were created with CGI. *Star Trek: The Next Generation* (1987) used computer-generated visual effects, as well.

Director Ron Howard teamed up with Lucas on *Willow* (1988). It featured the use of "morphing" technology whereby a human or animal was transformed, in one continuous shot, into something else. The technology was refined and used to great effect in James Cameron's *The Abyss* (1989) with the water pod. ILM took the morphing technology to new heights in *Terminator 2: Judgment Day* (1991).

It was Steven Spielberg's adaption of Michael Crichton's *Jurassic Park* (1993) that showed that visual effects done on computer had advanced quite a ways since *Tron*.

"I thought it was going to be a lot longer to get to *Jurassic Park* where you're seeing foliage, creatures and believable monsters," says Taylor. "We can do photo-real people now. We can do photo-real faces. But it took a lot less time than I thought it was going to take to get where we are. It's taken half of the time. To get to *Jurassic Park* I thought would take twenty years to get to doing the organic creatures, plants and water. Computer simulation is the most powerful visual tool mankind has ever created."

# Chapter 20

# *DISNEY CHANGES FOREVER*

On February 24, 1983, Ron Miller was elected CEO of Walt Disney Productions. Card Walker stepped down to retire after being with the company since 1938. Upcoming film and theme park projects for 1983 looked very promising.

The studio was about to release another "PG" rated film called *Trenchcoat*. The film bombed. The next film to be released was Ray Bradbury's *Something Wicked This Way Comes*. The famous writer, who was friends with Walt Disney and consulted on EPCOT, wrote the screenplay. A large set had been built on the Disney studio lot. The story dealt with a mysterious carnival coming to a New England town, led by Mr. Dark (Jonathan Pryce).

The film was supposed to be eerie and filled with a number of visual effects, including a planned CGI scene in which Mr. Dark's carnival transforms out of a train.

"The changes will take place in the moonlight," Taylor told *Box Office* writer David Linck. "Steam from the locomotive will turn into a sort of ectoplasm that develops into tents and cages housing extraordinarily strange creatures. It is turning out to be a real challenge for our staff."

The scene was eventually scrapped because the technology was not yet ready. Taylor, Ellenshaw, Dyer, Silver, John Norton and a number of ex-*Tron* effects artists also worked on the film shortly after finishing *Tron*.

The film struggled at the box office, though it did find an audience on video. The film had an eerie premise, great production design, and stirring performances by Jason Robards and Pryce. The problem was it was not scary by any stretch of the imagination. It had too much of an old-fashioned sense of atmosphere to scare even a child. But the magnificent set remained on the studio lot for years.

The month of April was busy for the studio. The Disney Channel, the brainchild of company executive Jim Jimirro, went live on April 18, 1983. At the cost of $28.8 million, the channel was a huge gamble for the Disney, as cable television was still a fledgling industry.

Tokyo Disneyland opened that same month and was a colossal success. Disney clearly had done its homework building and catering the theme park to the Japanese. The park was very Americanized and Japanese guests could not seem to get enough. Disney did not own the park but managed it. The company made money on admissions and merchandise sales, but most of the theme park's income went to the owners of the Oriental Land Co.

In May, the New Fantasyland was unveiled at Disneyland in Anaheim. Walt had run out of money when the park was built in 1955 and the themed land featured bland facades for many of its attractions. W.E.D. Imagineers went back to the drawing board and designed a more faithful and old-world European-influenced Fantasyland. Many of the rides now featured state-of-the-art optical effects and sound. The refurbishment was extremely successful with park guests.

However, critics and stockholders of Disney began to question the direction of the company again. The costs of starting Disney Channel were seen as outrageous, especially since cable was only in a relatively small number of homes across the United States. Some critics called the reimagining of Walt Disney's EPCOT a watered-down world's fair. In rebuttal, the company tried to convince shareholders and the press that the expenses for EPCOT were justified. The theme park, it was felt, would pay off in the long run.

In June Richard Berger, who had been the head of production at 20th Century Fox, was hired by Miller to run the new Walt Disney Pictures subsidiary. Miller was trying to invigorate the Disney brand by further making its family films more relevant to the era's audiences without shortchanging its corporate values and heritage.

Fortunes for the studio started to turn around by fall of 1983. The long-awaited *Never Cry Wolf*, directed by Carroll Ballard, bowed in a limited number of theaters. Critics were ecstatic. Released under the new Walt Disney Pictures label, the film attempted and succeeded in breaking the barriers normally associated with a Disney film. The tone of the film was starker than most Disney films and it was reminiscent of the *True-Life Adventure* series. Actor Charles Martin Smith was excellent in the role of a scientist who studied caribou. Audiences flocked to the film. *Never Cry Wolf* became one of Disney's biggest hits and continued to play in theaters for months.

Walt Disney Productions, despite its successes in operating theme parks and operating an immensely successful merchandising division, was still struggling with its image as a film studio. As a whole, Walt Disney Productions was a large company with approximately 27,000 employees. In addition, with its Florida property, Disney was a huge real estate owner. But shareholders and investors in the 1980s were looking for companies that appeared to be weak enough to exploit their assets. Disney looked weak because its studio could not compete with the other big studios anymore.

The weak box office performance of *Tron* from the year before, despite it succeeding on home video, was deemed the culprit for Disney's woes. It was seen as the reason for the studio's flagging reputation. The film actually ranked high in the studio's highest grossing films in recent years. In terms of initial theatrical film releases in the fifteen years prior to *Tron*, only *The Jungle Book* in 1967, *The Love Bug* in 1969, *Herbie Rides Again* in 1974 and *The Black Hole* in 1979 had surpassed its grosses.

Critics seemed to forget that Disney's merchandising, including the home video game of *Tron: Deadly Discs* and the Bally arcade video game, were highly successful moneymakers based on licensing alone. According to Walt Disney Productions' 1983 Annual Report, "Revenues were up fifteen percent over the prior year due to royalties from 'TRON' and from the overwhelming popularity of the Disney character merchandise sold at Tokyo Disneyland."

*Tron* had turned out to be a moneymaker.

It did not seem to matter. *Tron* was seen as a flop. It was seen as a reason for Disney to get out of the movie business. Critics and shareholders who wanted the company to do better also forgot that Disney had taken a huge risk in financing *Tron*. There had clearly been a desire to shake things up. The regime of Miller and Wilhite showed it was serious about turning the studio around. Risks needed to be taken and they were poised to turn Disney around. Unfortunately, *Tron* tainted the Disney image, whether it was warranted or not.

Predatory "investors" began to buy Disney stock, and by early 1984, circled like sharks. Their plans were to buy the studio and sell its valuable animation and live-action library, while keeping the profitable theme parks. For Disney purists, it was a nightmarish scenario. Disney was the only major studio to remain independent in the film business. If taken over, Disney would become a shell of its former self.

## *SPLASH* AND MILLER'S EXIT—1984

Since 1979, Disney had been releasing a series of "PG" rated films. Miller had been bothered that the studio's clean family image was hurting its chances at the box office. The co-ventures in financing and distribution of *Popeye* and *Dragonslayer* in 1980 and 1981 were noble attempts by Disney to branch out. But the company was not reaping the financial rewards. Miller went back to Walt's comments about *To Kill a Mockingbird*. He figured it was time to branch out and start a new studio division at Disney called Touchstone Films. On February 24, 1984, ads in *Variety* and *The Hollywood Reporter* announced the formation of Touchstone Films.

"When I became CEO, I knew that for the motion picture end of the business, we had to make some very serious, dramatic changes," says Miller. "And that's why I came up with Touchstone. I was trying to signal to the people out there, the moviegoers, Touchstone was something outside of the Disney-type of production."

In founding Touchstone Films, Miller showed that Disney was finally committed to making more adult-themed movies and that the studio wanted to gain a bigger share of the box office. One of the first scripts suggested to him was *Splash*.

Miller recalls, "When I got this script I read it and I went to Berger and Richard said, 'Ron I've got to be honest, I turned this down at Fox.' I said, 'Richard maybe you better read it again, because I think it's really what we're looking for with Touchstone.' He read it and said, 'You know, I'm with you.' But it was Tom [Wilhite] again who brought it to my attention."

Touchstone Films continued to be Miller's battle cry. Through Touchstone, Disney would release films made for older children and adult audiences. They would still be quality films without the need to go overboard on anything gratuitous. Miller believed he would be able to lure successful actors, directors and producers to the studio. Touchstone would release the films under Buena Vista Distribution. Audiences, except for those who paid attention to such things, would not know that a Touchstone "PG" or "R" rated film was from the same studio that released *The Apple Dumpling Gang.*

But not everyone was so certain that the new strategy would pay off. One day, Walker called Miller.

"Ron, can I see *Splash*?"

"Sure! Hell, I'll set it up, you can look at it."

Walker saw the film and laughed in all the right parts. After the lights faded up, he went into Miller's office with a smile on his face.

"That's a damn fine film, Ron. It's really a good film."

Miller smiled. "Well, good, I'm glad you like it, Card."

"Just one thing," Walker said as his smile turned into a frown. "If you were to eliminate about five or six things in that film, we could release it as a Disney film."

Miller shook his head. Walker just did not get what he was trying to accomplish. Walker wanted to take the "PG" rated Touchstone film and water it down to make a family and "safe" Disney film.

"I think he also felt a very strong commitment to Walt," says Miller. "Would Walt make a film like this? But you can't ask that question because times change. Walt would've changed. He changed a lot. He kept growing and pursuing other things."

Walker might have been unfairly cast as the villain for Disney's woes. To his credit, he was trying to keep Walt and Roy O. Disney's philosophies and desire for high quality alive. Walker believed in his heart that the name brand of Disney meant family entertainment at its best. He did not believe that raising Disneyland's gate admission, as an example, was fair to guests. They could get a full day's worth of entertainment, and Disney still made more than enough money to build big attractions.

Though Walker played the safe and steady lead for many years until Miller stepped into the spotlight, he always tried to maintain Walt's vision. Even under his leadership and watchful eye, the company eventually began to struggle. Miller realized that times and people had changed and it was possible to maintain Walt's philosophy without selling it out. This was not lost on Wilhite.

"Card always treated me respectfully," recalls Wilhite. "But Ron told me that Card once said, 'I don't think Tom Wilhite understands what Disney is all about.' I felt it was easier to understand the essence of Disney having come from the outside and growing up on entertainment actually produced by Walt Disney, rather than having worked there my entire life, as Card had. I would have loved meeting Walt Disney, but I bet he cast an immensely intimidating shadow for anyone who knew him and had to follow in his footsteps."

In March of 1984, Touchstone released *Splash* to tremendous box office success. Critics fell in love with it and audiences adored it. Tom Hanks, who had not yet attained superstar status, charmed audiences with his performance. The Ron Howard-directed film was the biggest box office success Disney ever had until that point. Miller finally had his breakout hit. But the day it opened, Roy E. Disney resigned from the board and launched a fight to take back the company from Miller.

Miller stood his ground and made speeches to various shareholders and the press that the company was on the right track. Disney Channel and EPCOT were expensive projects to launch, but they would prove to be high income earners for the company. EPCOT had been open since October 1982, and despite some critics deriding the theme park, crowds showed up in droves. Touchstone Films just released the company's biggest hit ever and demonstrated that the studio could be profitable in the long run. And WED had a number of projects being planned for the theme parks, including a theme park in Europe.

But the corporate sharks were circling. After an attack on the company's stock, the board elected to pay corporate raider Saul Steinberg $32 million in what was termed "greenmail" to call him off. The company then made a purchase of Arvida, a land development company in Florida. It also tried to buy Gibson Greeting Cards to make the company take on debt it had not had for years. Debt would make the company less desirable to takeover. Fed up with what he perceived as Miller's lack of leadership and vision, Roy E. Disney and his financial partner, Stanley P. Gold, put together a team to take over Walt Disney Productions. They wanted Michael Eisner and Frank Wells, from Paramount and Warner Bros. respectively, to run the company. Just two years earlier, Miller had pursued Eisner to run the studio.

In September of 1984, Miller resigned from his position as CEO. During a tense boardroom confrontation, Miller made an impassioned speech to save his job. The company, under his leadership, was turning around. From starting out as a gopher shuttling plans from Burbank to Disneyland, to a film producer, then as leader of the company, he was a true Disney employee. But shareholders and outside corporate raiders did not see it that way. The board unanimously asked for his resignation. After spending most of his adult life for the company of his father-in-law, Ron Miller was no longer working for Walt Disney Productions.

## WILHITE MOVES ON

Tom Wilhite's tenure at Disney also came to a close in 1984.

Earlier in 1983, Richard Berger had been promoted to run Walt Disney Pictures. In an article written by Ray Loynd in *Variety*, dated November 7, 1983, Wilhite was quoted, "Richard Berger and I didn't see things the same way. We disagreed on the viability of *Splash*, which he'd turned down at Fox. He never fulfilled his promise to bring staff salaries and titles up to industry standards. Everyone who came from the outside got good salaries, but not those already here. I think my exit has been inevitable, one way or the other, for some time. The film company is big enough for only one head of production."

Wilhite pointed out that *Tron* would "break into profit once it has been exploited on pay-TV and all the merchandising receipts are in." According to the article, the film's merchandising earned $6 million.

Wilhite stayed on board in various executive capacities through 1984. But it had been as Vice President in Charge of Production that he accomplished so much in so little time. *Tron* was his biggest gamble.

"For many years I thought the title of the movie should be 'TRON-comma-a-disappointment,' which seemed to always be how it was described," says Wilhite. "I always felt, however, that it would be revisited as an important, ground-breaking film."

He was grateful to his bosses, Walker and Miller, for giving him a chance to take risks.

"I thoroughly enjoyed working with Ron," says Wilhite. "He had good instincts. He had a tough job. There were a lot of second-guessers within the top management and board at Disney. Many of them were great at criticism but weak on being proactive. I felt Ron was on my side and the side of the people who were making films for us."

Wilhite formed an independent animation studio called Hyperion Pictures. The studio's name was a nod to the first studio Walt Disney had located on Hyperion Avenue. Joining him were Jerry Rees and Joe Ranft. Ranft was an extremely talented writer and animator at Disney. Their first collaboration was *The Brave Little Toaster* (1987), the abandoned CGI film that Lasseter was working on at Disney. Both Wilhite and Kushner produced. James Wang, who headed Cuckoo's Nest, was the associate producer. Darrell Rooney and John Scheele also worked on the film.

*The Brave Little Toaster* was traditionally animated and was a sweet treat. The film was a huge success on home video and was a popular staple on the Disney Channel for many years. Many people who watched it thought it had been produced by Disney.

## THE NEW BOSSES MOVE IN

When Michael Eisner, Frank Wells and Jeffrey Katzenberg team came onto the Disney studio lot, there was fear that many jobs would be lost, and that the "Disney Way" would be changed. The team assured employees that they wanted to keep the company values alive. They wanted to keep Walt Disney's philosophies as part of their daily regime. Eisner and his team cleaned house almost immediately. A number of employees who had been on the studio payroll for years were let go.

"There were certain people, who shall remain nameless, who were working in departments and literally not lifting a finger just having been on the payroll grandfathered in," says Campbell. "Eisner and Katzenberg came in and said why is this man drawing breath much less a salary? Why is he still on payroll when he literally does nothing?"

Katzenberg ripped into the animation team working on *The Black Cauldron* and started editing the film. The animation directors were furious and told him he could not just cut an animated film. He did it anyway and the film barely made back its production costs in the summer of 1985. The film was too intense for young children, too tame for teenagers, and had little of the Disney magic audiences had been desiring. That Disney magic would not come to fruition until *The Little Mermaid* was released in 1989.

The Animation Building was cleared of animation. The staff was moved to a dreary industrial park in nearby Glendale. The Animation Building became a control center for screenwriters. Katzenberg became known as the "make it fast, make it cheap, make it profitable" studio executive. He hired out-of-work actors such as Bette Midler, Richard Dreyfuss and Robin Williams. He cut their normal salaries. Their movies, at first, were big financial successes for Disney.

Eisner, Wells and Katzenberg raided the Disney animation vaults and found treasure. Much to the horror of Disney fans, the first move was to release *Pinocchio* on videocassette. It was decided to release the cassette for a limited time and return the film to theaters a short time later. But it turned out that releasing the classics on tape was a huge moneymaker, bringing in more money than theatrical rereleases.

Shortly after Miller's departure, Touchstone released the critically acclaimed *Country* with Jessica Lange and Sam Sheppard in late 1984. Lange was nominated for an Oscar for Best Actress, but the film did not do much business. *Return to Oz* and *My Science Project* failed to ignite the box office in 1985.

By early 1986, the first films under the Eisner/Wells/Katzenberg regimes began to be released under the Touchstone label. The first feature released was the raunchy "R" rated comedy, *Down and Out in Beverly Hills*. It was a smash hit. That was followed by *Ruthless People*, another raunchy comedy that did excellent business.

The Disney theme parks received upgrades. *Captain EO* was an extraordinary short film directed by Francis Ford Coppola and executive produced by George Lucas. Starring Michael Jackson, who was truly at the peak of his success, the 70mm 3-D science fiction adventure was the hippest attraction ever done by Disney. Harrison Ellenshaw supervised the visual effects. The attraction went well over budget and is considered one of the most expensive films ever made. Yet when it opened, guests at Disneyland and Walt Disney World's Magic Kingdom crowded the parks just to see it.

*Star Tours* opened in 1987 at Disneyland in Anaheim. Disney teamed up with George Lucas on the ride simulator.

Ironically, the Peoplemover ride passed by the *Star Tours* building, shuttling guests into the *Tron Speed Tunnel* above the old *Carousel of Progress/America Sings* attraction. The *Tron Speed Tunnel* featured the MCP threatening guests as they entered the Game Grid. He warned them to watch out. Footage from the "Electronic World" scenes was shown on huge curved screens that surrounded the Peoplemover cars. The attraction lasted from 1982-1995.

In very little time, the new management team at Disney was seen as brilliant. There is no doubt that in those early years of Eisner's leadership, Wells' business smarts, and Katzenberg's eye for picking hits, Walt Disney Productions was resurrected. It was a fairy tale come true.

Eisner's leadership was strong, but it did not take a Wall Street broker to figure out that by releasing more of Disney's animated classics on video, huge rewards would be forthcoming. It did not take a land developer's savvy to figure out that by developing Walt Disney World's vast property, the company could bring in more tourists to Central Florida. Much of what Eisner and his team exploited had been done by the previous regime, just at a more gingerly pace.

The fairy tale of Eisner's reign over the Disney empire began to show signs of discontent. After a new "Golden Age" of animation that began with *The Little Mermaid* and ended with *The Lion King* (1994), Disney relinquished its animation crown to upstarts such as Pixar and DreamWorks Animation. Disney eventually became a technically proficient animation studio through the use of CAPS and computer animation (i.e. *Tangled*—2010), but it was only after years of struggling to reinvent itself as the premiere animation studio. Disney Animation had not fully recovered, though *Tangled* did well at the box office. Pixar and DreamWorks continued to lead the animation industry into the 21st century.

Michael Eisner left Disney in 2005 after a successful, yet ultimately tenuous ride as CEO. The first ten years of his leadership won the hearts of stockholders and Disney fans alike. The company expanded greatly. Yet his style of management and princely leadership eventually rubbed many of his subordinates the wrong way. It has been said that after the tragic death of Frank Wells in a helicopter accident in 1994, Eisner and Disney were never the same again.

Katzenberg left and co-founded DreamWorks with Steven Spielberg and David Geffen. The studio became a powerhouse and main competitor to Disney, especially in the field of animation. Roy E. Disney and Stanley P. Gold, fed up with Eisner's corporate stumbles during the late 1990s, led a stockholder and public revolt against the very person they championed in 1984. Eisner stepped down after twenty-one years of heading Disney and Robert Iger took his place. Roy E. Disney passed away in 2009.

It was *Tron*, for better or worse, that facilitated much needed change for the studio. The perception of its failure, supposed out-of-control budget, and the lack of Disney being able to hit a home run sealed the studio's fate. If it were not for the risk taken by Miller and Wilhite to put the film into production, the studio might have been shut down.

If it were not for a rag tag band of outside animators, a Disney veteran, an inexperienced first-time film director, a computer-simulation genius, and hundreds of creative people, *Tron* would not have changed visual effects and Disney forever. If anything, the poor reaction to *Tron* reenergized the will to make Disney great again. This was exactly what Lisberger, Kushner, Ellenshaw, Taylor and everyone on the crew of *Tron* intended to do in the first place.

# Epilogue

# *LEGACY*

*Tron* started a revolution of computer simulation and imagery in film. Computer generated imagery may have taken another dozen years for computer technology to fully ramp up and to become a viable tool for visual effects artists and animators, but once the technology matured, it became a staple for movies, television, gaming and all other visual storytelling in the digital age. Computer software has evolved with such precision that consumers can buy it off the shelf and create their own personal version of *Tron* or *Star Wars* or *Toy Story*. Whatever can be imagined can be created. What used to be visual effects magic is now all too common.

"Part of the problem, part of what's evolved, is that special effects aren't special anymore," laments Taylor, "and they haven't been in quite some time. Children from this era have been surrounded by media of incredible complexity all the time. Not only in film, but in print. On television. Everywhere. Inundated by incredibly complex visual imagery. When I was growing up, you knew it was a special effect and you'd say, 'How did they do that? Look at the rocket ship. Boy that's amazing!' Even watching *Buzz Corbet*, those old movies with rockets on strings and smoke rising, there's none of that anymore. There's no *wow* factor as far as that goes."

Richard Taylor's "wow factor" about old time (now considered "quaint" by some) special effects may be a thing of the past, but there must always be some "wow factor" in any successful entertainment. Good storytelling is the real magic; it is the impact of the story and the characters, not the technology, that is the key.

Computerized animated characters are now commonplace. Adam Powers and the Bit evolved into Shrek and Lightning McQueen. Pixar, whose humble beginnings began at Lucasfilm Computer Group, grew into an animation powerhouse. John Lasseter and his team of animators have created some of the most endearing characters of the modern era. Woody, Buzz Lightyear, Flick, Nemo, Mater, Sulley all came from the minds at Pixar. While Disney has stumbled with its Animation Department in recent years, Pixar continually made excellent films with memorable characters. Ironically, Pixar released its films through Disney, the same company that passed on its computer simulation technology years before.

The combination of computer simulation and animation used in *Tron* has spawned multi-billion dollar industries outside the film industry. The film kickstarted the concept of arcade and video game movie tie-ins. Just based on that fact alone makes *Tron* a tremendous success. That success inspired an entire generation of people to enter the entertainment business, creating jobs and opportunities not even conceivable when *Tron* was being made.

"So many young artists and designers, who were 11-13 years old when the film came out, tell me it was the greatest thing," says Bonifer. "And the video game is underrated for its impact. People saw it all tied together. So it was kind of this bugle call for people. The same reaction that John Lasseter had to it, a whole generation of young artists grasped that movie. Everybody who's working with computers today to create art can somehow look at *Tron*. It had a huge influence on them."

For years, Lisberger carried the burden of having created one of the most influential films of all time.

"*Tron* was Steven's life; his passion," recalls Ellenshaw. "There is such tremendous pressure on a director to hit the ball out of the park every time. I can remember a studio executive telling me once, 'All I want is singles and doubles.' What total bullshit. You better make the next *Avatar* or *Inception*, otherwise you go to what they call 'director's jail.' And then once there you have to do time, sometimes it's a long time. And sometimes you never get out, they just take you down death row and kill you. It is a brutal and very unforgiving business."

Lisberger stepped away from the director's chair after his next two feature films, *Hot Pursuit* (1987) and *Slipstream* (1989).

"After that, there was no reason for me to direct live-action movies if I didn't have a passion and appeal for the material," says Lisberger. "I really sort of pulled back. I just worked on writing."

He sold scripts to some of the major studios. But *Tron* would not leave his mind. He struggled to convince Disney that the film was ready for a reboot, but no one saw value in a potential franchise. After years of pitches, Lisberger was saved from death row and was finally released from director's jail. Ultimately called *Tron: Legacy*, the 2010 film was made by the generation of young people who grew up admiring the original film. It was made at Disney which had become a powerhouse in the entertainment industry.

One of the producers of the film was Steven Lisberger. Executive produced by Donald Kushner and directed by newcomer, thirty-five year old Joseph Kosinski, the film starred Jeff Bridges, Bruce Boxleitner, Garrett Hedlund, Olivia Wilde and Michael Sheen. Though earning over $400 million worldwide, *Tron: Legacy* garnered only mixed reviews. The visual effects were praised by the critics, as was the score by Daft Punk, so in many ways the reaction was very similar to the reaction to *Tron* back in 1982.

"The next generation was given the challenge of having to integrate all this new technology into their lives, make it more than just a far out dream," says Lisberger. "*Tron: Legacy* reflects that generational change. Some of the idealism has been lost, but that's okay—it's time to get real, make it safe for families and corruption free. Like any civilization it has to grow up—no more excuses."

In a sense, Lisberger is Kevin Flynn and found himself beamed back into the "Electronic World" after all these years. The world of cyberspace, something he created on film in 1982, has transformed into a completely different place. It is more technically advanced and more streamlined.

The Cray Supercomputer has evolved into the iPad 2. Video games have become a bigger business than the film business. And as Lisberger points out, we have all become users.

"The story of *Tron* came true," says Lisberger. "Space wars didn't happen, aliens didn't hide out in suburbia, time travel didn't happen and neither did the Apocalypse, thank heaven. We don't have to deal with flying cars or replicants or giant robots. But when we laser scanned Jeff Bridges for *Tron: Legacy* and watched his digital alter ego come up on the Game Grid, what was pure fantasy 28 years ago became routine."

Unlike the sequel it spawned, *Tron* was a hybrid film. Part analog, part digital, part paint, part circuitry, *Tron* was truly unique. There was something magical in the fact that it had a human touch to it. People, not computers, made it come alive.

"I have so much respect for everybody who worked on the original film," says Bonifer. "It's really a wonderful little fraternity of people that have this singular experience early in their professional careers. I think all of us use it as a yard stick for what our experiences are like. It had that kind of vibe to it. You just always remember. We were serious at play. The experience of *Tron* was such a great improvisation."

The spirit of the artists on *Tron* was contagious. Everyone who worked on the film knew they were making something special, and something incredible. There was not a single person from *Tron* who came away thinking that it was just a normal job. Everyone, through the good, the bad and the messy, is proud to have *Tron* on their résumé.

"Many people look back at *Tron* as a cult classic; as ground breaking," says Ellenshaw. "But it is so very much more.... after all, film critic Kenneth Turan of the *Los Angeles Times* did name *Tron* as 'one of the most influential films in the last century.' It certainly deserves that, it was influential on so many levels, it changed the course of filmmaking and a studio forever. There will never be anything like it again."

"What kept me going," says Lisberger, "was not just the radical imagery but the fact that I had found a way to align big themes and iconic characters with the inert but powerful world of digital technology. I always felt the story was true. Now I am pleased to see that on many levels it came true."

Epilogue written by William Kallay and Harrison Ellenshaw

# APPENDIX

## The Cast and Crew of *Tron*

# *WHERE ARE THEY NOW?*

### STEVEN LISBERGER

Writer-Director Steven Lisberger made his first project of note while a graduate student at the School of the Boston Museum of Fine Arts. It was an animated short called *Cosmic Cartoon,* which earned a Student Academy Award nomination in 1973 and led to the formation of Lisberger Studios. Lisberger and his fellow Boston artists and filmmakers went on to produce and direct numerous award-winning commercials, documentaries, and many hours of Saturday morning animation for ABC network. He then received an AFI grant to create an animated parody for the 1980 Olympic Games. This short eventually became a one-hour animated musical special for the Summer Games and a half hour special on the Winter Games. Entitled *Animalympics,* it was voiced by Gilda Radner and Billy Crystal and ran on NBC. The songs were created by Graham Gouldman and the band, 10cc.

While still independent, and with an animation studio on both coasts, Lisberger wrote the screenplay and developed *Tron,* staring Jeff Bridges, which was then financed and released by Walt Disney Productions. *Tron* pioneered the use of computer graphics, virtual sets, and backlit effects. Its unique blend of live action and animation sparked the careers of dozens of artists, directors, programmers, and game designers when it introduced the world to cyberspace for the first time. The digital language spoken by the users and avatars in the film, so strange and shocking in 1982, is now understood by children around the world.

Lisberger next wrote and directed *Hot Pursuit* (1987). It was filmed on the Pacific off Mexico for Paramount starring John Cusak. Gary Kurtz, producer of *Star Wars*, then called him to helm his indie airborne-adventure, *Slipstream* (1989), which was filmed in the skies over Britain and starred Bill Paxton. No computer graphics were used in either film.

Lisberger's focus and passion remains fantasy and original screenplays. As one of the producers of the long anticipated *Tron: Legacy* sequel (2010), he welcomes the chance to help redefine the world of *Tron* with Disney Studio's next generation of talented and cutting edge filmmakers.

## BONNIE MACBIRD

Bonnie MacBird went on to write and sell a number of screenplays. She became a well-respected teacher at UCLA by teaching the fine craft of screenwriting with the class, "Screenwriting on the Write Side of the Brain." Her husband, Alan Kay, received accolades for his pioneering work in computers.

"In 2003-4 he collected the Draper Prize, the Kyoto Prize, and the Turing Award for his work in inventing the personal computer," MacBird proudly states. "The Turing is the highest award the ACM gives, the Draper (shared with some PARC cohorts) is for Engineering Achievements that benefit humanity, and the Kyoto is likened to the Nobel.

"What was going on back then at PARC with Alan and his colleagues was very important stuff."

## DONALD KUSHNER

After *Tron*, Kushner produced a several films including *The Brave Little Toaster (1987), Andre* (1994), *Whole Wide World* (1996) starring Renee Zellweger, *The Adventures of Pinocchio* (1996) starring Martin Landau and Jim Henson's puppets, and *Freeway II: Confessions of a Trickbaby (1999).*

He produced *Monster* (2003), for which Charlize Theron won the Academy Award for Best Actress, and he was the executive producer on *Tron: Legacy*. He also produced several action films starring Wesley Snipes, Jean Claude Van Damme and Steven Segal.

His TV credits include several movies and mini series including *Sweet Bird of Youth* with Elizabeth Taylor (1989), and *1st & 10* (1984-1990), a long running series on HBO.

In 2011, he and producer Elie Samaha purchased the world famous Grauman's Chinese Theatre in Hollywood, California.

## RON MILLER

Ron and Diane (Disney) Miller bought a ranch in the Napa Valley in 1976, then purchased the Silverado Vineyard in 1978. They helped turn Silverado Vineyards into the one of the most respected wine makers in the Napa Valley. Perhaps their proudest achievement was the opening of the Walt Disney Family Museum in the Presidio, located in San Francisco. The museum was the family's loving dedication to Walt and his tremendous accomplishments. In recent years Miller has been regarded as an intelligent and effective leader of Disney during his tenure.

Miller is still proud of the risk taken in bringing *Tron* to Walt Disney Productions.

"I think [Walt Disney] would've undertaken something like *Tron* if the technology was available to him at that time," says Miller. "He was always sort of a futuristic guy. He looked at horizons of what was about to emerge. He just loved challenges. He was a very curious man and always wanted to know how things worked. That's what excited me. The challenge of it all."

## HARRISON ELLENSHAW

Harrison Ellenshaw continued to supervise visual effects after *Tron*. His impressive film credits included *Something Wicked This Way Comes* (1983), *Captain EO* (1986), *Superman IV: The Quest for Peace* (1987), *Dick Tracy* (1990), *Ghost* (1990), and the last two seasons of the television series *Xena: Warrior Princess* (1999-2001). In 1989 he directed a comedy feature film, *Dead Silence*.

From 1990 to 1996, Ellenshaw headed Buena Vista Visual Effects (BVVE) and Buena Vista Imaging (BVi). BVVE credits included work on such films as *Honey I Blew Up the Kid* (1992), *Dave* (1993), *The Santa Clause* (1994), *Congo* (1995), *Escape From L.A.* (1996) and *The Phantom* (1996) as well as over forty other films. In 1993 Ellenshaw supervised the first all digital restoration of a feature-length film, Disney's classic *Snow White and the Seven Dwarfs*. But in spite of a growing reputation and remarkable profitability, BVVE was suddenly shuttered in 1996 by its parent company (Disney). However, it is still regarded as one of the best effects facilities of the time.

Then in 2001 after supervising visual effects on the two very popular television series, *Hercules: The Legendary Journeys* and *Xena: Warrior Princess*, Ellenshaw turned his attention to a fine art career. His well regarded paintings are now coveted by collectors worldwide, his artwork being featured in galleries in Japan, the U.S. and Europe. In 2011, he was commissioned to create "Disney View" paintings for the Blu-ray release of *Fantasia*. Harrison's art can be viewed at www.harrisonellenshaw.com and www.ellenshaw.com.

## BRUCE LOGAN, ASC

Bruce Logan, ASC continued his career as a cinematographer and visual effects producer. His credits include *Firefox* (1982), *George Carlin: Playin' with Your Head* (1986), *Batman Forever* (1995), *Fear and Loathing in Las Vegas* (1998), *Kelly Live: The Light It Up Tour* (2007), and *Drones, Clones and Pheromones* (2011).

## JEFF GOURSON

Jeff Gourson edited *FM* (1978), *Somewhere in Time* (1980), *The Incredible Shrinking Woman* (1981) prior to *Tron*. He later edited CBS television show episodes for *Magnum, P.I.* (1982-1983), and *Airwolf* (1984). In 1986, he edited *Flight of the Navigator*.

Gourson was a co-producer on the television series, *Quantum Leap* (1989-1991) and he produced (and directed an episode) the series, *Tequila and Bonetti* (1992).

He was Adam Sandler's favorite editor on a number of the comedian's films including *Happy Gilmore* (1996), *Big Daddy* (1999), *Anger Management* (2003), *50 First Dates* (2004), *The Longest Yard* (2005), and *I Know Pronounce You Chuck & Larry* (2007).

## JEFF BRIDGES

Jeff Bridges continued his illustrious acting career. He starred in *Starman* (1984) and was nominated for a Best Actor Oscar. He acted in the box office hits *Against All Odds* (1984), and *Jagged Edge* (1985). In 1988, he played automaker Preston Tucker in the underrated *Tucker: A Man and His Dream*. He acted with his brother, Beau, in *The Fabulous Baker Boys* (1989). In 1998, he acted as "The Dude" in the Coen Brother's *The Big Lebowski*, creating yet another cult classic character. He won an Oscar for his role in *Crazy Heart* (2009). In 2010, he stepped back into the "Electronic World" of *Tron* in *Tron: Legacy*. He reprised his role as Kevin Flynn and Clu in the film. That same year, he acted in the Coen Brothers' critically acclaimed remake of *True Grit*.

In 2011 Bridges recorded a self-titled album with acclaimed producer T-Bone Burnett.

## BRUCE BOXLEITNER

Bruce Boxleitner acted mainly in television, adding a significant amount of credits to his resume. He co-starred with Kate Jackson in *The Scarecrow and Mrs. King* (1983), and starred in *Babylon 5* (1994), *Tron 2.0* (2003), and *Chuck* (2008). He reprised his role as Alan Bradley/Tron in *Tron: Legacy* and returned to his role as Tron for the Disney XD animated program, *Tron: Uprising* (2012).

Boxleitner is amazed by the groundbreaking aspects of *Tron*.

"This is an actual film that predicts that we can see," says Boxleitner. "It has predicted, somewhat, a fantasy future that we're living, the age of information. Who knew the computer then? More importantly, it shows the trajectory of video games and importance of video games in pop culture. They were arcade games then, just a generation past pinball games. So we've gone from *Pong* to *Donkey Kong* to *Grand Theft Auto*. We're making movies based on video games now. They're making them so realistic now, so cinematic."

## CINDY MORGAN

Cindy Morgan went from *Tron* to *Bring 'Em Back Alive* (1982) on CBS. The show was a riff on *Raiders of the Lost Ark* and starred none other than Bruce Boxleitner as adventurer Frank Buck. The show lasted only eighteen episodes, but both Morgan and Boxleitner had a blast working on it. She then had a number of roles in various television series including *Falcon Crest*, *Matlock*, *Hunter*, and *The Larry Sanders Show*.

Morgan has grown into a fan favorite at science fiction and fantasy around the United States. As both Lacey Underall and Lora/Yori, she was the belle of the convention circuit.

"You go to these autograph shows. These are people who come up to you and tell you twenty-five years ago, 'I got into computers because I saw this movie,'" says Morgan. "Or I've got the guys who come up to me and say, 'Before I go out with a woman, I rent *Caddyshack* and if she thinks it's funny, I'll continue to date.' It's also put me into a lot of different kinds of work. It's very much getting re-rezzed."

Part of the popularity of *Tron* over the years is not lost on Morgan.

"Most folks are so darned kind and have so cool things to say. But the person who determines what becomes pop culture is the people themselves. They determine what becomes popular culture and they determine also what becomes a part of history. People ultimately make the decision and I think that's the coolest thing of all."

Morgan came back to the world of *Tron* in the videogame *Tron 2.0: Killer App* as Maзa and appeared in a publicity campaign for *Tron: Legacy* (2010).

## DAN SHOR

Dan Shor continued acting in major feature films and television, including *Cagney & Lacey* (1985), *Bill & Ted's Excellent Adventure* (1989), and *Star Trek: Voyager* (1996). He eventually decided to get out of the film business.

"My story was that I ran away from the world," says Shor. "I left Hollywood. I ran away to a tropical island called Saipan. I was brought there to teach filmmaking at the community college. It's an American commonwealth, so I was brought there to teach filmmaking to the indigenous people of the islands. I was there for six weeks which turned into one year, which turned into becoming the director of the visitors channels, Saipan, Tinian, Guam, which turned into meeting my wife and falling in love."

Shor currently owns a video production company called ShodaVision. He was featured with Bruce Boxleitner on the *Tron: Legacy* Blu-ray (released in 2011).

## WENDY CARLOS

Wendy Carlos released more albums of her music including *Digital Moonscapes* (1984), *Beauty and the Beast* (1986), *Peter & the Wolf* (1988, with "Weird" Al Yankovic), and *Switched on Bach 2000* (1992).

In 1995, Disney released *Tron* on LaserDisc and to the delight of fans and Carlos, her score for the "Light Cycle" battle and end credits was restored. In 2002, Disney released the film on DVD with her missing score, as well. That same year, Disney released for the first time ever, the soundtrack on CD.

## SYD MEAD

Syd Mead's reputation as a futurist and designer lept into the public's eye with *Blade Runner* and *Tron* during the summer of 1982. His incredible designs can be found in *2010: The Year We Make Contact* (1984), *Aliens* (1986), and *Elysium* (2013).

Mead was featured in director Joaquin Montalvan's film, *Visual Futurist* (2007). He continues to draw huge crowds of fans to his shows and guest speaker appearances. He is the author of two books, *Sentury* and *Sentury II*, which showcase his work.

## MICHAEL FREMER

Michael Fremer decided to get out of the film business to concentrate on his passion, high-end audio. He has been into vinyl records and good audio since he was a child, and after hearing his first compact disc in the early 1980s, he found the sound so unpleasant, he decided to dedicate himself to the quixotic goal of saving the LP. He eventually became a senior contributing editor at *Stereophile* magazine and a contributing editor at *Home Theater* magazine. He has reviewed thousands of pieces of stereo and home theater equipment, some in the six-figure range. Decades of touting vinyl seems to be paying off. Records are making a comeback, particularly among young people, and CDs are fading. Fremer is regarded as one of the top authorities on vinyl records.

He gives turntable set-up seminars around the world and has produced two acclaimed vinyl-related DVDs: *21st Century Vinyl: Michael Fremer's Practical Guide to Turntable Set-Up* (2006) and *It's a Vinyl World After All* (2008) and owns and edits the music review website www.musicangle.com.

## ROSSANA NORTON

Rosanna Norton continued to be one of the most sought after costume designers in the film business. Her high-profile credits included *Airplane II: The Sequel* (1982), *Explorers* (1985), *Innerspace* (1987), *The Flintstones* (1994), *The Brady Bunch Movie* (1995), and *The Pool Boys* (2010).

## FRANK SERAFINE

Frank Serafine continued recording amazing sound effects for numerous films, commercials and special venue attractions (i.e. theme park attractions) including *Brainstorm* (1983), *Manhunter* (1986), *The Addams Family* (1991), *The Lawnmower Man* (1992), *Orgazmo* (1997) and *Hoodwinked Too! Hood VS Evil* (2011). Serafine is also an accomplished musician, having worked with Peter Gabriel, Thomas Dolby and Andy Summers on various projects.

## MICHAEL MINKLER

Michael Minkler continues his career today as one of world's elite rerecording mixers. Since *Tron*, he has mixed over one hundred and seventy-five films. His credits include *The Cotton Club* (1984), *A Chorus Line* (1985), *Born on the Fourth of July* (1989), *The Doors* (1991), *JFK* (1991), *Cliffhanger* (1993), *True Lies* (1994), *Kill Bill Vols. I and II* (2003-2004), *Inglourious Basterds* (2009). He earned Oscars for *Blackhawk Down* (2001), *Chicago* (2002), and *Dreamgirls* (2006). He is currently the Lead Mixer at the world renowned Todd-AO Studios in Hollywood.

## TOM WILHITE

Tom Wilhite co-founded Hyperion Pictures, a successful independent company specializing in live-action features and animation. Credits include *Rover Dangerfield* (1991), *Bébé's Kids* (1992), *The*

*Brave Little Toaster Goes to Mars* (1998), *The Proud Family* (2001), and *Marigold* (2007). Wilhite was a producer and executive producer on a number of Hyperion's productions including *The Brave Little Toaster* (1987), *Playing by Heart* (1998) and *The Need* (2006).

Although Wilhite is not the type of person who is very nostalgic, he is still fond of *Tron*.

"I loved it," says Wilhite. "Having had an association with *Tron* is one of my proudest career experiences."

## RICHARD WINN TAYLOR II

"After *Tron,* Triple-I and MAGI, I decided to take a break from the CG business for awhile," says Taylor.

He went back to directing television commercials and created some more indelible classics such as the Duracell Battery campaign of the late 1980s, which featured mechanical dolls demonstrating the power of Duracell versus other batteries. He also directed the popular 7-Up *Spot* campaign.

Ironically, twenty-five years later Taylor became the Cinematic Director for Electronics Arts (EA Games), and helped to create video games like *Lord of the Rings, Command and Conquer 3, and Red Alert 3.*

When working on *Tron*, did he see himself creating the very type of games that Kevin Flynn might have created? "No, way," says Taylor.

Taylor is currently Creative Director of XLNT FX, his own company.

## BILL KROYER

Bill Kroyer was an early advocate of computer animation in the 1980s.

"When I finished *Tron,* I wanted to stay in this new world of CG," says Kroyer. "Every day you had the potential of going to work and doing something no one had ever done before! It was like Christmas morning every day. Disney wasn't going to do it. They were going to do *The Black Cauldron.* So I quit Disney the second time and looked for any job I could find in CG—and there weren't many! I freelanced for Triple I, then MAGI, and then got a full-time gig for John Whitney Jr. and Gary Demos at their new company, Digital Productions. I was just hungry for anything in computer animation."

By the mid-1980s, however, Robert Abel and Associates, Digital Productions, MAGI and Triple-I were out of business.

In 1987, Kroyer and his wife Sue started their own company, Kroyer Films, Inc. After an Oscar nomination (with Brian Jennings) for his short animated film, *Technological Threat*, Kroyer went on to make many projects combining hand-drawn and computer animation, like the opening titles to *Honey, I Shrunk the Kids* and *Christmas Vacation* (both 1989).

Kroyer then directed *FernGully: The Last Rainforest* (1992), a cautionary tale on mankind's infraction upon the environment. The film featured the voice talents of Robin Williams and Tim Curry. After a stint at Warner Bros., he became Senior Animation Director at Rhythm & Hues Studios and supervised computer animation on the feature film versions of *Cats and Dogs* (2000) *Scooby-Doo* (2002) and *Garfield* (2004).

## JERRY REES

Jerry Rees went on to direct the animated cult classic, *The Brave Little Toaster* (1987) and the live-action feature *The Marrying Man* (1991), followed by many mixed-media theme park attractions for Disney including *Cranium Command* at EPCOT. One of his most popular was *Extra-Terrorestrial Alien Encounter* at Walt Disney World's Magic Kingdom. This scary attraction made audiences believe that a hungry alien from space was let loose inside the theater. His film *Back to Neverland* (1990) played at Disney MGM Studios and starred Robin Williams and Walter Cronkite, which led directly to Robin being cast as the genie in *Aladdin* (1992).

Rees' specialty venue reach-out-and-touch-you film *Cinemagique* for Walt Disney Studios Paris won the 2003 THEA award for best attraction. He is currently putting the finishing touches on his fifteenth attraction *Animation Magic* which will play aboard Disney's two new cruise liners, Disney Dream and Disney Fantasy. This attraction at sea blends analog and next generation technologies, allowing seven hundred people at a time to add original creations directly into his movie. His current obsession is to redefine the use of avatars and virtual reality for the masses. Rees has also had the pleasure of directing such diverse talents as Steve Martin, Aerosmith, Juli Delpi, Tcheky Karyo, Martin Short and Michael Eisner.

## CHRIS LANE

Chris Lane went on to work for many film companies such as Universal, Paramount, MGM Studios and Disney and became a main concept designer for such features as Bakshi Productions' *Lord of the Rings* (1978), and *Meteor* (1979). He worked on TV movies like Sony's *Journey to the Center of the Earth* and TV series *Battlestar Galactica* (1978), *Man from Atlantis* (1978) and *Captain Power and the Soldiers of the Future* (1987).

He then ventured into the theme park world and designed for Landmark Entertainment and Universal's theme parks in Japan before moving into the online computer game industry and worked for respected game companies such as Origin, Electronic Arts, Acclaim Entertainment, Retro Studios, Digital Anvil and Funcom Studios on such top online games as *Conan Online*, *Anarchy Online*, *The Secret World*, *Ultima Trilogy Online* and the well-received Retro Studio-Nintendo computer game, *Metroid*.

## LYNDA ELLENSHAW (THOMPSON)

Lynda Ellenshaw went onto a successful career in visual effects. She worked for Richard Edlund's BOSS Films (1984-1987) on features such as *Ghostbusters* (1984) and *Big Trouble in Little China* (1986). She was the visual effects producer on a number of projects for Buena Vista Visual Effects including *Dick Tracy* (1990), *Dave* (1993), and *James and the Giant Peach* (1996). Most recently, she was the visual effects producer on *The Zookeeper* (2011).

## JESSE SILVER

Jesse Silver continued his matte painting talents in *Total Recall* (1990), *The Tommyknockers* (1993), *Mars Attacks!* (1996) and *Astro Boy* (2009). He also supervised visual effects on *A Little Princess* (1995) and *Rosewood* (1997).

## JOHN VAN VLIET

John Van Vliet left Disney to open an independent VFX shop. Between 1984 and 2000, he contributed to more than fifty films including *Ghostbusters, Captain EO, Who Framed Roger Rabbit, Ghost, Honey I Blew up the Kid, My Favorite Martian* and *X-Men*. He freelanced as an independent visual effects supervisor and designer on such films as *Miss Congeniality* (2000), *Hart's War* (2002), and *Herbie: Fully Loaded* (2005).

## CHRIS CASADY

Chris Casady continued his effects animation in films including *The Adventures of Buckaroo Banzai Across the 8th Dimension* (1984), *My Science Project* (1985), *Short Circuit* (1986), *Back to Neverland* (1990), and is one of the premiere instructors in Flash animation on www.lynda.com.

## DARRELL ROONEY

Darrell Rooney went onto direct the critically acclaimed and successful direct-to-DVD sequels for Disney including *The Lion King 2: Simba's Pride* (1998), *Lady and the Tramp II: Scamp's Adventure* (2001), and *Mulan II* (2004).

In 2011, his first book, *Harlow in Hollywood: The Blonde Bombshell in the Glamour Capital; 1928 -1937*, was published by Angel City Press to commemorate Jean Harlow's hundredth birthday.

## PETER GULLERUD

by Greta Blackburn (edited for space)

"Ever since I could hold a pencil, I've drawn," Peter admits. As early as the 5th grade, Peter was winning art contests.

Self taught, Gullerud went straight from one year of theological college to the Disney Studios. There he worked his way up to the prestigious position of Visual Development Artist on their feature films. At Warner Bros. he continued work developing characters. After toiling four more years as a studio artist in animation features, for what most people would consider an irresistible salary, Peter chucked it all and followed the siren's call of his muse.

"I wanted to do my wildlife work but I wanted it to be authentic. I had a couple of choices. I could study exotic animals at zoos and circuses, I could move to Namibia, or I could hang out with the wildlife right here in southern California in a habitat that was natural to them. Luckily, I had worked with the Mountain Lion Foundation, helping to keep California's largest feline safe from the trophy hunters' sights."

Peter met the admirable [actress], Tippi Hedren. She saw how comfortable he was with a Siberian tiger and other exotic animals. She asked half-jokingly if he'd like to become a night watchman at her preserve, Shambala. "To her surprise and mine," Peter acknowledges, "I accepted."

For thirteen months, Peter ate, slept and breathed exotic animals.

Today, Peter brings to his work all of the talent, expertise and authenticity earned during his years as a paid artist and as a nocturnal observer. His work has been described as an unusual mix of Munch, Van Gogh, Peter Max and the old tiki artists of the '50s and early '60s. You can find his work at www.painterofpaint.com.

## ROB HUMMEL

Rob Hummel has had stints at Disney Post-Production, TV Animation, and Imagineering, DreamWorks, Technicolor, Warner Bros. Sony, and DALSA. He is now President of Group 47, LLC, formed to license hundred year digital storage media originally developed by Kodak. While at Warner Bros., he supervised the critically acclaimed digital restoration of *Blade Runner* (1982). While at Warner Bros. he found all the original visual effects negatives for *Blade Runner* that had been "lost" for twenty-five years.

"Everyone thought the negs had been destroyed, but I was the only one that remembered that we cut them into the 65mm blow up negative (from the 35mm Anamorphic) for making 70mm prints."

Hummel currently serves as the Chair of the Public Programs Committee of Academy of Motion Picture Arts & Sciences' Science and Technology Council. Hummel has hosted several programs at the Academy on film formats, film technology, and 3-D stereoscopic imaging. He is also an associate member of the American Society of Cinematographers and was the editor of the 8th edition of the *A.S.C. Manual*.

## ARNE WONG

Arne continued experimenting with special effects and 2-D traditional style animation. For the next two decades his company, Tigerfly Studios, produced and directed TV commercials, music videos, short films, and theme park rides.

Wong was invited to animate Tarna's fight scenes in the animated feature *Heavy Metal* (1981). He won an Emmy for "Bean Sprouts" in 1981, and a CLIO for "Sunkist Orange," best animated TV commercial in 1986.

The 1990s proved to be the transition period from 2-D to 3-D. Tigerfly Studios worked for James Cameron's production company, Digital Domain, by directing the 3-D animation sequences in *T2/3D* (1996) for Universal's theme-parks. Wong also animated the General Cinemas Logo. He continued to direct and storyboard Nickelodeon's *Dora the Explorer* and *Catdog*.

In 2000 he joined forces with Jean "Moebius" Giraud in co-creating a feature film *Thru the Moebius Strip*, the first 3D animated feature produced in China. Wong was then accepted at the Academy of Art University in San Francisco to teach art and animation, a position he still holds today. Most recently he directed his first full-dome digital animated film *The Tales of the Maya Skies*, which is now a permanent exhibit at the Chabot Space & Science Center in Oakland. In his spare time, he is an avid surfer and travels between Hawaii and Kelly's Cove in San Francisco and teaches Tai Chi & Qi Gong.

## RAULETTE WOODS

Raulette Woods continued to work in the visual effects industry. Her film and television credits include *Max Headroom* (1987), *Highlander II* (1991), and *Lifepod* (1993). From 1989-1997, she was co-owner of Stargate Films whose credits include *Unsolved Mysteries* (1987) and *The Outer Limits* (1995). She is currently a producer/designer for Studio 186.3 and is an active member of the Visual Effects Society.

## GLENN CAMPBELL

Glenn Campbell continued work in animation and visual effects in numerous television shows and films. Campbell worked his camera magic on *Spaceballs* (1987), *Dick Tracy* (1990), *Robot Chicken* (2005), and supervised visual effects on *The X-Files* television show (1996-1997), and *The Glass House* (2012).

## DOUGLAS EBY

Douglas Eby not only worked on many of the visual effects on *Tron*, but also helped create the iconic poster for the film. After the film, he decided to change the course of his career.

"*Tron* was a grueling project, and although I did some effects work after, I felt burnt out and decided not very long after *Tron* to take a break, and re-think my life, and pursue my interests in psychology getting a Masters degree (not PhD)."

Eby is affiliated with the American Psychological Association [APA] Division Ten - Psychology and the Arts; International Society for Gifted Adults and Advocates; Institute of Noetic Sciences.

## ART DURINSKI

Following *Tron*, Art Durinski continued working with the Walt Disney Company as art director of computer imagery for the stereoscopic Disneyland film entitled *Magic Journeys* (1982). Afterwards he worked as art director at Digital Productions, and won a Clio Award for the first Sony Walkman commercial. Later he became creative director at Omnibus Computer Graphics in Los Angeles, continuing to work in television graphics, commercials, and motion pictures. In 1986 Durinski moved to Tokyo, Japan (for a year and a half) as a consultant to the Japanese media company,

Imagica. In Japan, he directed various visual effects and computer graphics-oriented television commercials and motion graphics projects.

In the late 1980s, he established his own design and consulting company, The Durinski Design Group, and has been a designer/director/ and visual effects supervisor for numerous American and Japanese television graphics, commercials, motion pictures, and special venue projects.

After thirty-five years, Durinski continues to work in the industry as a director, consultant, and as a mentor to students at various Institutions.

## KENNY MIRMAN

As writer, designer, director, visual artist, and educator, Kenny Mirman continued to excel. As designer-director of CGI and live-action television commercials, Mirman has been the recipient of over thirty film-festival awards including five Clio Awards, the New York Film Festival Gold Medal, and the Best in Show Award from the National Computer Graphics Association, given to Mirman by the late Roy Disney, Jr.

At visual effects studio Digital Domain, Mirman served as Visual Effects Art Director and designer-director of the CGI simulation of the ill-fated *Titanic* (1997). At Rhythm & Hues Studios, he was the lead designer and creative director of IMAX's first 3-D CGI ride-film, the award-winning *Race for Atlantis* (1998).

Mirman was writer-director of hit videos for MTV, VH1 and BET for recording artists Toni Braxton, Al Green, Babyface, Jermaine Jackson, and Tracie Spencer. Mirman's music videos focused on exposing the beauty of our vulnerability as a path to self-empowerment. As a visual artist, Mirman has produced a wide range of installations: his most recent for the UCLA/DaVita Dialysis Center in Los Angeles, titled *Spirits Triumphant*, a 35ft-tall steel sculpture. While living in Bali, Indonesia, Mirman filmed traditional Balinese dancers to photo-illustrate his inspirational picture book, *The Princess of Bali: One Girl's Most Remarkable Relationship with Fear*.

Since 2006, Mirman has served as a volunteer teacher for InsideOUT Writers. He has been a popular guest speaker in universities, schools, feature-film production companies and museums.

## TIM MCGOVERN

Tim McGovern supervised visual effects on films including *The Last Action Hero* (1993), *Look Who's Talking Now* (1993), *Money Train* (1995), *Supernova* (2000) and *A Sound of Thunder* (2005). He won a Special Achievement Award from the Academy of Motion Picture Arts and Sciences for *Total Recall* (1990).

## JEFFREY KLEISER

Jeffrey Kleiser continued to break new ground in the world of digital visual effects. He worked with his brother, director Randal Kleiser, on *Flight of the Navigator* (1986) and *Honey, I Shrunk the Audience* (1994). Visitors to Universal's Islands of Adventure theme park in Orlando, Florida have been impressed by Kleiser's work on *The Amazing Adventures of Spider-Man* attraction (1999). Throughout the 2000s, Kleiser and his partner, Diana Walczak, have worked on films and commercials including *X-Men* (2000), and the Sun-Maid Raisin Growers television campaign.

## MICHAEL BONIFER

Mike Bonifer was one of the pioneers of Disney Channel after its debut in 1983. He produced and directed the episodes of *The Disney Family Album* from 1984-1985. Some of the people he focused on were Frank Thomas, Milt Kahl, Woolie Reitherman, and Marc Davis.

When *Toy Story* (1995) was about to be released, Bonifer directed *The Making of Toy Story*. He encouraged both the Walt Disney Company and Pixar to enter the world of the Internet by producing the *Toy Story* web site.

In 2007 he was the Chief Storyteller for the Live Earth concerts. In 2008, Bonifer wrote the book, *GameChangers—Improvisation for Business in the Networked World*, and launched a company called GameChangers that conducts leadership, communication and creativity programs for organizations and teams.

## ALVY RAY SMITH

"The group now known as 'Pixar' started on Long Island at the New York Institute of Technology in 1975, when I joined having just come from the fabled Xerox Palo Alto Research Center. We conceived then of being the first group to make a completely computer-generated movie. It was while the group was at Lucasfilm that I directed the Genesis Demo in *Star Trek: The Wrath of Khan* (1982), which just slightly preceded *Tron*, and hung out with Steven Lisberger and Bonnie MacBird at various parties while they were enthusiastically creating the latter. Everyone was curious at what Disney would do. I negotiated a major deal with Disney to create and build their CAPS, or Computer Animated Production System. Then George and Marcia Lucas divorced leaving George without enough money to fund us, so Ed Catmull and I cofounded Pixar as a spinout from Lucasfilm, with Steve Jobs as the venture capital. Luckily we had hired John Lasseter while at Lucasfilm, so we took him and thirty-seven others from Lucasfilm into the new company as the first employees. At Pixar we completed CAPS and cemented our relationship with Disney. Just after it looked like *Toy Story*, the movie we had waited almost twenty years to make, was a go with Disney, I spun out Altamira Software from Pixar, and subsequently sold it to Microsoft where I became Graphics Fellow. I left there in 1999 and have been writing books since then. I am currently writing a book on computer graphics, which I am sure will surprise nobody, while in Oxford on (my wife's) sabbatical."

## NOTES

Names are in order of how they appeared in the end credits of *Tron*.

Although Alvy Ray Smith did not work on *Tron*, his contribution to computer simulation was significant.

Some participants asked to rewrite their biographies. The author agreed to this and on occasion performed some editing for space. The author wrote the biographies for Jeff Bridges, Bruce Boxlietner, Wendy Carlos, Chris Casady, Douglas Eby, Jeffrey Kleiser, Bonnie MacBird, Tim McGovern, Syd Mead, Ron Miller, Cindy Morgan, Rosanna Norton, Frank Serafine, Dan Shor, Jesse Silver, Tom Wilhite, and Raulette Woods.

# IN MEMORIUM

Robert Abel (March 10, 1937-September 23, 2001)
Richard "Dr." Baily (February 16, 1953-April 20, 2006)
Richard Berger (died 2004)
Roy E. Disney (January 10, 1930-December 16, 2009)
Peter Ellenshaw (May 24, 1913-February 12, 2007)
Barnard Hughes (July 15, 1915-July 11, 2006)
Eloise Jensson (November 5, 1922-February 14, 2004)
Bill Kovacs (October 25, 1948-May 30, 2006)
Peter Lloyd (died 2009)
Dr. Phil Mittelman (died 2000)
E. Cardon Walker (January 9, 1916-November 28, 2005)

# KODALITHS EXPLAINED BY HARRISON ELLENSHAW

Originally published in *Cinefex*, April 1982
Article by Peter Sørenson
Entitled "Tronic Imagery"
Printed with permission from publisher Don Shay
Additional text by Harrison Ellenshaw (2011)

## 1982

Fifty-three minutes of the electronic world was shot first in 65mm on Double-X black-and-white film. The reason for the large format is to maintain quality. You take a piece of 65mm negative that has been developed and you put it into a photo-roto—which is nothing more than an enlarger—and you enlarge each frame onto a 12½by20-inch piece of kodalith transparency film. You process it with continuous tone chemistry and what you get out appears to be a black-and-white cel with a photograph on it. That is then taken and a contact print is made of it on the same kind of film—but it's processed this time with high-contrast chemistry, so what you get is a high-con reverse of the first. Now if there's a person in the scene, you have to produce a body matte to hold that person out from the background. When you make the negative enlargement, the black lines that were the circuit designs on the costumes become clear, so we could light them up, but the black behind the characters also became clear, so we had to make what we call a circuit reveal, and to do that you have to paint out all that clear area behind the characters. Then you have to make a matte for the face and the reversal of that—a face reveal—where everything is black but the face. And there we just add a little more exposure to the face, to make the face a little lighter than the body. When you put this on the animation stand, you combine photo elements with at least two cels. For example, when you do the backgrounds you always have to have a body matte over it. When you expose the circuit on the costume, you put down the hi-con and the circuit reveal. Then you run through the one element, shooting it, and you back up the film, run through another element, back up the film, et cetera—as much twenty-five passes on one piece of VistaVision film. We never went smaller than VistaVision. Since the release prints are 35mm Panavision and 70mm, we shot in VistaVision to maintain quality.

It's really beautifully simple. The complexity comes when you think about the *volume* of work. We have seventy-five thousand frames of live-action in the electronic world. That means we have seventy-five thousand continuous tones, seventy-five thousand hi-cons, seventy-five thousand body mattes, seventy-five thousand circuit reveals. Forty percent of the time we have face reveals and face mattes: fifteen percent of the time we have eye reveals. And we've got seven hundred backgrounds to worry about—some of which are set pieces that you may have to generate separate elements for, some of which are computer-generated, some of which are painted. If you look at all the elements—not counting backgrounds—that we used on the film, and stacked them five-feet high, that row would be fifty-eight feet long! I had to figure that out just to see how much room we would need to store it.

In essence, the live-action for the electronic world was shot in black-and-white so that it could be made into both positive and negative transparent enlargements which could then be used, in effect, as stencils for backlighting.

## 2011

To add for your understanding.

Kodaliths (or just non-cap'd "kodalith"), both the CT (Continuous Tone positives) AND the corresponding contact negative image HCs (High Contrast negatives without midtone gray - that's what made them Hi-Cons) were sent to Taiwan and and that's what the rotoscopers/inkers/ painters used as guides to paint the "mattes" on separate same size clear cels. After that was done the Kodaliths AND the corresponding cels had to be shipped back to the US for photography. The cels needed (drawn by hand) were, at the least, circuit reveals (CR) and body mattes (BM). But depending on the scene, there might also be needed (again drawn by hand): a face matte and/ or eye/teeth blob (to go over the circuit reveal so there's no glow on the eyes, for example); circuit separation (e.g. a bad guy in the same shot as a good guy); a face reveal (to go over the CT); an eye reveal (making the eyes brighter in close-ups); and even a teeth reveal in a small number of shots.

# STEVEN LISBERGER AND JOSEPH KOSINSKI: AN INTERVIEW

*On April 5, 2011, Disney released both* Tron *and* Tron: Legacy *on Blu-ray and DVD. As the author of this book, I thought it would be a treat for readers to get into the minds of directors Steven Lisberger (*Tron*) and Joseph Kosinski (*Tron: Legacy*), and the technological and generational differences between the directors and their films. This article and interview was originally posted on my website,* <u>www.fromscripttodvd. com</u>.

The image is surreal. Jeff Bridges reprises his classic role as computer hacker, Kevin Flynn. He is telling his young son, Sam (Owen Best), about the Grid. His son listens intently. The audience does not see Flynn's face too much, but he certainly looks youthful. However, Bridges is not really in his thirties anymore. He is in his sixties now. It is a new century. Has Bridges stepped into a time machine? In a way, he has. Along with him is the original writer/director of *Tron*, Steven Lisberger. Via modern digital visual effects, Bridges has been made to look young again.

*Tron: Legacy* brought back Kevin Flynn to the big screen. It also brought back the mythology created in the 1982 cult classic, *Tron*. The 2010 film won mixed reviews from critics, but went on to earn over $400 million in worldwide box office receipts. It has spawned an animated television series on Disney XD and a rumored sequel. The long-lasting appeal of *Tron* has certainly surprised many people, for the original film was thought to have been a financial disappointment. In reality, the film made a profit, spawned computerized visual effects and animation, jumpstarted a moribund Disney studio, and changed how we see films today.

Lisberger kept faith in the ideas of *Tron*. He envisioned cyberspace as a frontier of extraordinary possibilities. "Programs" took human ("Users") instructions and tried to make their own world a better place, even in the face of a corrupt Master Control Program. Unfortunately, the computer frontier became corrupt with viruses, slander, and naughty things. Not quite the world Lisberger envisioned. Nonetheless, Lisberger was persistent and *Tron: Legacy* was made with updated ideas.

I spoke with Steven Lisberger, who wrote and directed the original film, and Joseph Kosinski, who directed the second film. For Lisberger it was almost like going home for the first time in years. The landscape and technology ushered in by *Tron* was a lot different. Many of the people who worked on *Tron: Legacy* were either small children or had not been born when *Tron* was released. Lisberger was home again. For Kosinski, a high-profile commercial director, it was an opportunity to refresh the world of *Tron*.

I met Lisberger and Kosinski during the release of *Tron: Legacy* and *Tron* on Blu-ray and DVD. The public was able to meet both directors during an autograph signing event on April 5, 2011 at the Best Buy in West Hollywood, California.

**KALLAY:** What was it like for you to step back onto the Game Grid?

**STEVEN LISBERGER:** I had mixed feelings. One strange sensation is the opposite of what you would think—in that you're standing there with Jeff (Bridges) and you're on a *Tron* set and he's wearing a *Tron* costume. And suddenly it's like, "Wow! All the years in-between disappeared. Why do we both look as old as we look?" My son Carl wasn't born when *Tron* came out. Joe [Kosinski] was whatever he was, seven years old. You started hearing the ages of people working on the film in relationship to when the first film came out. Then you realize a whole generation has grown up in those years.

**KALLAY:** It was a reunion with Jeff Bridges and Bruce Boxleitner being on the set.

**LISBERGER:** It was sweet. It was under such happy terms to come back together for. This was a great way to do it. Jeff hasn't changed. Still as flamboyant as ever.

**KALLAY:** Do you recall what it was like for him to step back into the *Tron* world?

**LISBERGER:** I know that Jeff is freaked about the technology. He worries about his cyber alter-ego. The funny thing is that, although he plays this computer genius in the film, he's really a low-tech kind of guy in real life. He spends more time worried about technology than he does, I think, actually using it. But he likes the fact that *Tron* provides an arena for him to be so far out.

**KALLAY:** It's kind of like him playing a kid again.

**LISBERGER:** That's one of the strange things about the first *Tron* compared to the second. Even though we have way more technology this time, we built so much more in front of the camera. When we did the first film, it was just an empty stage and it really felt sort of Shakespearian. You're wearing your gladiatorial costume. You're standing under a spotlight on an all black empty stage, and you might as well be doing *Hamlet*. But on this one, Joe built everything. You really were in that nightclub or in Flynn's safe house. It was really like you were there. We didn't cheat about anything. Even the fabric was picked out perfectly on every couch and every pillow. You have to remember all the costumes were totally practical. They actually glowed.

**KALLAY:** The original film was shot in 65mm. That footage went through different stages to get the *Tron* look. VistaVision, Kodaliths and Technirama formats were used. The sequel was filmed in digital 3-D. What were some of the challenges that you recall with that new format?

**LISBERGER:** It's funny because there were so many times on *Tron: Legacy* where you think you could take the new technology that exists and it would make things a hundred times easier than on the first film. But damn if we didn't figure out a way to make it just as hard in every category. [On the original film] we had these enormous 70mm cameras. They were the size of dishwashers. The new cameras are this big (mimics small camera size). But nope. We shot it in 3-D with a beam-splitter and a rig that holds the two cameras. And we ended up with a giant, huge metal box that was about as big as our 70mm camera! So it went right back to let's make this as hard as we can. The same happened with the CGI computer capability. One frame of the Light Cycles in *Tron: Legacy* has more computer processing in it than all of the frames in *Tron*. You could do the whole movie probably in a week in terms of the computers. We rezzed up every centimeter of that "Electronic World" to the point where we barely got it done in eighteen months.

**KALLAY:** In a way it was the same as using Kodaliths. There were truckloads of Kodaliths on the Disney studio lot in 1981. They were needed just to handle the amount of Kodaliths coming back from the Cuckoo's Nest in Taiwan. On *Tron: Legacy*, the amount of computer data is just crazy.

**LISBERGER:** It's true. I didn't even think of that. There was all of this physical storage of the handmade film, and then there was all this cyber/digital storage of this one (*Tron: Legacy*).

**KALLAY:** Both you and Joseph come from extensive artistic and architectural backgrounds. Did you collaborate on storyboards or animation?

**LISBERGER:** Joe came in from a completely different place. I went to film school. Joe studied as an architect. In a way, I think, Joe approaches it a little more like he's a natural. He studied architecture and he had his style. He moved that whole style into film. He's more of an individual. I was more of a team kind of studio guy. I had my own little studio. I like that ensemble feeling. We were all involved from the beginning. That's not really the contemporary approach. Joe worked with Digital Domain, so they were a part of this team. He's more of a contemporary director.

[Joseph Kosinski arrives after being stuck in Los Angeles traffic. Greetings are exchanged and Kosinski joins the conversation.]

**KALLAY (to Kosinski):** I love the opening of *Tron: Legacy* in which the audience sees Sam Flynn's bedroom. There are posters on the wall for *The Black Hole* (1979) and *Tron*. When you were growing up, were you into Disney films?

**KOSINSKI:** We were trying to populate a 1988/1989 bedroom of a seven year-old kid, which is younger than I was at the time. I remember seeing *Tron*. I had the *Tron* yo-yo. I remember *The Black Hole*. I had *The Black Hole* record and the board games. All that stuff. So that was all selected on purpose. We're working on a script for *The Black Hole* [remake]. Why not throw it in there? [to Lisberger] I'm curious. Was there any relationship between Maximillan the robot and the Recognizers in *Tron*?

**LISBERGER:** No.

**KOSINSKI:** You based the Recognizer on something. Was it a computer part?

**LISBERGER:** Yeah. I don't remember if I showed you this, but we had the *Computer Dictionary*. It was a paperback book. I think it's fifteen pages with eight entries on each page. The word avatar isn't in there.

**KOSINSKI:** Bits and bytes are in there.

**LISBERGER:** Yeah, bit and byte are in there. I would go through and I would look for words and hope they were called something that was provocative because they were provocative that way.

**KOSINSKI:** I did the same thing. A rectifier is a piece of a computer. It's a transistor that rectifies a current and makes it pure.

**LISBERGER:** I looked it up. The Recognizer was some term, I forget what it was. That basic design really never changed. [John] Norton did that very early on and nobody wanted to take it on.

**KOSINSKI:** It's iconic.

**LISBERGER:** Syd Mead and Moebius looked at it and said, "I'm not doing it. It's fine! Leave it alone."

**KALLAY:** It's a very striking character in both films.

**LISBERGER:** For me it's sort of the front half of a gorilla.

**KOSINSKI:** Yeah, it's the face.

**LISBERGER:** That head and that mass. It was sort of a cyber King Kong.

**KALLAY:** Was it a challenge for you to remain faithful to Steven's original vision, as well as yours in bringing *Tron: Legacy* to the big screen?

**KOSINSKI:** I never thought of it as a challenge. I thought of it as this incredible soup of great ideas and designs that was an amazing starting point. Steven pointed out to me that the Light Cycles in the original *Tron* movie were not exactly how he really intended them to be. That kind of canopy that they ended up having to put on the top. The enclosed bike was not the initial sketch that Syd Mead did and Steven wanted to do. Because of the technology, they had to do it that way. When he told me that, I was like, "Oh great. Now we're going to get to do the open body Light Cycle where the rider really becomes part of the bike." It was fun to sit with him and talk about the things they weren't able to do. [We] used that as a seed for a whole new generation of designers. How do we evolve those initial ideas forward? What would that be like after 28 years of evolution?

**LISBERGER:** There was a lot we couldn't do. On the first film, many of the things we came up with, we made them look good, but they had to be really efficient and economical like the handlebars coming up and you grab them.

**KOSINSKI:** I just noticed for the first time, you can see the matte of the whatever the wooden thing that Bruce Boxleitner is crouching on. It's covering the bottom of his leg.

**LISBERGER:** The Blu-ray's too good! I talked to [John] Scheele who did the new DVD [Blu-ray] of *Blade Runner*. They couldn't find the negative of *Blade Runner*. They wanted to scan the negative. So they couldn't find it. Finally, it might have been Rob Hummel, but somebody found it in some basement after they'd given up, "Hey! I found the cans with the original negative of *Blade Runner!*" So they brought them out and they scanned them and resolution was way too good. You could see all the junk mattes. They spent a fortune and then they had to start all over.

**KOSINSKI:** I saw the 4K version of that in that final cut and it looked incredible.

**KALLAY:** What do you both make of the influence of *Tron* and *Tron: Legacy* to this point?

**LISBERGER:** I meet people who say, "I saw your film and I got into computers and video games and writing software." And I feel really good about that. But then I get really nervous. Does that mean when someone says, "Hey, I saw *Lethal Weapon* and I really got into blowing people away?" Either film influences people or it doesn't. I get that and it's pretty satisfying. It's cool when it comes full circle. You can picture—there's Joe, whatever he is, seven years old, seeing *Tron* and he gets a spark of something. Then it goes full circle, comes all the way around and now I'm seeing that spark play out and go, "Oh that's cool. I didn't think of that." But in terms of the larger media influence, I can't really track those. I find it really entertaining or funny.

**KOSINSKI:** My wife was watching *Dancing with the Stars* the other night and all of a sudden, one of the dance performances and everyone is wearing siren suits and he's dressed like Zeus.

**LISBERGER:** Halftime at the Super Bowl (2011) [The pop singing group, Black Eyed Peas, wore *Tron*-inspired costumes].

**KOSINSKI:** Black Eyed Peas. It's pretty cool. I can speak for all the people who worked on *Tron: Legacy*. It was the easiest movie to recruit people to work on. I mean it's the only movie I've ever done, but I think I was spoiled. So many of the artists that I hired on this movie said they got into this business because of the original *Tron*. It's clear to me that was all positive influence. I haven't heard of a negative *Tron* influence.

Special thanks to Click Communications, Dre Birskovich, Amelia McPartlon, Adam Becker, Steven Lisberger and Joseph Kosinski

# *TRON NOTES*

## MISSING INTERVIEWS

In the course of writing this book, I attempted to contact as many people from *Tron* as possible. Although modern digital technology has made the world smaller and made it seemingly easier to track down people, it was not always possible. In particular, I was not able to conduct an interview with cast member David Warner. Like many readers of this book, I value his tremendous talent and presence in *Tron*.

## 70MM SCREENINGS

In 1999, Roger Ebert featured *Tron* in his "Ebertfest" annual film festival in Champaign, IL. Steven Lisberger was the guest of honor. Disney had sent out a poor quality 35mm and that prompted Lisberger to demand that the studio strike a new 70mm print. They complied and the print made its way around the country for the next few years. El Capitan Theatre in Hollywood, CA held an engagement in 1999, and there was a repeat screening at El Capitan in 2004 with a panel discussion hosted by Harrison Ellenshaw.

Additional 70mm screenings include:
- Carpenter Center of the Performing Arts, Long Beach, California (1999)
- Oslo, Norway (2005)
- Samuel Goldwyn Theater, Beverly Hills, California (2006 with panel discussion between Bill Kroyer, Richard Taylor and Steven Lisberger)
- Castro Theatre, San Francisco, California (2006 and 2011)
- American Cinematheque's Aero Theatre, Santa Monica, California (2007 and 2011, both screenings with cast and crew panel discussions)
- Cinerama, Seattle, Washington (2008 and 2011)
- Widescreen Weekend Film Festival, Bradford, England (2011). Both a 70mm print of *Tron* and an Imax 3-D print of *Tron: Legacy* were shown.
- National Film Theatre/British Film Institute, London, England (2011)
- American Cinematheque's Egyptian Theatre, Hollywood, California (2011, double feature with *Terminator 2: Judgement Day*—the 70mm print for *Tron* was not available for the Amer-

ican Cinematheque, as that print was being shown at the AFI in Silver Spring, Maryland. The film was shown from a Blu-ray disc instead.)

- ⚲ American Film Institute (AFI) (Silver Spring, Maryland—July 2011)
- ⚲ Landmark Theatres screened the film (in 35mm) during midnight showings across the United States (2011)
- ⚲ There were at least two 35mm screenings in the Los Angeles and Orange County area—Edwards Cinemas (Santa Ana, California) in 2005, and at the Nuart Theatre (Los Angeles, California) in 2006.
- ⚲ A digital version of the film was shown at the Disney-sponsored fan convention, D23, in Anaheim, California in 2009.

But Richard Taylor believes that *Tron* should be presented in a movie theater the proper way—in 70mm.

"The 35mm print [of *Tron*] is beyond awful. Embarrassingly bad. There is no other print that can be shown as far as I'm concerned."

There may have been more screenings of *Tron*, but they could not be confirmed as of this writing.

## 35MM, 65MM/70MM, AND VISTAVISION

These are film formats. They vary in size. Generally, the larger the film gauge, the sharper and brighter the picture becomes when projected on a movie screen.

The standard film format is 35mm and is universally used around the world.

The 70mm format is twice the size of 35mm and generally has better picture quality, depending on the original film elements or how the film was lit and/or processed. The term 70mm is a bit of a misnomer. In reality, films like *Tron* or *Lawrence of Arabia* were filmed in 65mm. The extra five millimeters are reserved for multi-track stereophonic sound, hence 70mm prints for distribution to theaters.

VistaVision was a film format that Paramount Pictures developed in 1954 to counteract the widespread use of 20th Century Fox's CinemaScope. VistaVision was used on quite a few films and had superior picture quality to CinemaScope. But VistaVision fell out of favor by 1961. Walt Disney Productions continued to use the format for many of its visual effects for many years. Richard Edlund rediscovered the format and used it on *Star Wars*. Since then, numerous ILM visual effects productions used VistaVision for years.

The advent of digital technology essentially replaced VistaVision and other large gauge film formats for use in visual effects. However, a few recent visual effects films have used VistaVision and 65mm film.

## *THE BLACK HOLE* SOUNDTRACK

*Tron* was groundbreaking in its sound design and quality, but it is worth noting that Disney's previous big budget film, *The Black Hole*, also had an excellent soundtrack. Stephan Katz and William

J. Wylie helped create the film's distinctive sound palette by using state-of-the-art synthesizers and various electronic sound techniques. Most of Disney's films of the era utilized either its own sound library or sound effects by its sound personal. *The Black Hole* was also one of the rare films for Disney, and of the era, to utilize a 70mm Six-Track Dolby Stereo mix. As early as 1977, Disney employed the use of Dolby's noise reduction and Dolby Stereo on films such as *Pete's Dragon* (1977), *The Watcher in the Woods* (1980/1981), and *Night Crossing* (1982).

## GENESIS DEMO/GENESIS EFFECT/PROJECT GENESIS

In *Star Trek: The Wrath of Khan*, the film's CGI sequence of a dead moon coming alive has been referred to with different names. In this book, Alvy Ray Smith calls the sequence the "Genesis Demo." In some articles from 1982, including David Hutchison's *Starlog* article, "Behind the Genesis Effect," the sequence is referred to as the "Genesis Effect." In the actual film, the sequence is called "Project Genesis."

The team who brought the CGI sequence to life included Loren Carpenter, Ed Catmull, Pat Cole, Rob Cook, Tom Duff, Dr. Robert Langridge, Robert D. Poor, Tom Porter, Bill Reeves, Alvy Ray Smith, and Jim Veilleux.

## *STAR TREK: THE WRATH OF KHAN* TITLE

The film title had a colorful and confusing history. It went through a few title changes prior to its 1982 release, according to *Starlog* magazine (July 1982).

Titles included:

- *Star Trek: The Genesis Project*
- *Star Trek II*
- *Star Trek: The Vengeance of Khan* (George Lucas objected, as his upcoming *Revenge of the Jedi* sounded too similar. That film was retitled *Return of the Jedi*—1983.)
- *Star Trek: The Undiscovered Country*
- *Star Trek: The Wrath of Khan*

When the film was released in the summer of 1982, the on-screen title was *Star Trek: The Wrath of Khan*. In articles in both *Time* and *Starlog*, the film was refered to by that title. However, posters and newspaper ads of the era show the Roman numeral "II" in the title. Only when the film was released later that year on home video was the on-screen title renamed *Star Trek II: The Wrath of Khan*. The new title has remained ever since.

## SARK

There is a small country in the English Channel called Sark.

## JIM JIMIRRO

Not only did Jimirro found The Disney Channel, but he is credited for starting Walt Disney Home Video in 1979. Both The Disney Channel and Walt Disney Home Video were championed by Ron Miller.

## EPCOT

For clarity, the name EPCOT has been used in this book. Originally when the theme park opened, it was known as EPCOT Center. Disney later shortened the name. In various publications, including Disney's, the park has been referred to as EPCOT Center, Epcot Center, EPCOT and just plain Epcot.

## *TRON* INFLUENCES

Over the years since *Tron* was released, a number of films, television shows and fan videos have been influenced by the landmark film. This list is by no means complete, but it should give readers an idea of how many tributes have been given to *Tron*.

- Donald Kushner produced a television series on ABC called *Automan* (1983-1984). Actor Chuck Wagner portrayed a computer generated crime fighter and his sidekick was a computer character named Cursor animated by Bill Kroyer.
- The Ice Capades featured a segment called *Tron on Ice*.
- A number of music videos have based their looks and sequences on *Tron*.
- VH1's *I Love the '80s: 3D* used graphics to evoke Richard Taylor's war room map on Sark's Carrier.
- Television shows *The Simpsons, Robot Chicken, South Park, The Fairly Odd Parents*, and *Family Guy* spoofed *Tron*.
- "Tron Guy." A fan of *Tron*, Jay Maynard, created his own costume based on the film. He developed such a reputation that he appeared on the Internet, in short films, and on television programs such as *Jimmy Kimmel Live* and *TOSH 2.0*.
- Some television commercials borrowed heavily from the 1982 classic. Honda featured its Civics racing across the Game Grid, for example. Duck Brand had a clever commercial using its duct tape in a Light Cycle battle featuring the "Tron Guy."
- Professional skateboarder Tony Hawk also found himself on the Game Grid in a television commercial.

⅄ Feature films that were inspired by *Tron* include *The Lawnmower Man* (1992), *The Matrix* trilogy (1999-2003), *Atlantis: The Lost Empire* (2001), *Spy Kids 3-D* (2003) and *Speed Racer* (2008).

## LOS ANGELES TIMES

*Los Angeles Times* writer Kenneth Turan was so enamored with *Tron* that he listed it as one of the most influential films of the last 125 years of cinema. The newspaper ran a special commemorative supplement in its May 21, 2006 edition.

On his list were *The Great Train Robbery* (1903) *Pulp Fiction* (1994) and *Tron*.

He wrote, "Think of the movie business for a moment not as an entertainment enterprise but as an enormous cargo ship. Turning on a dime is not this vessel's specialty; even attempting to change direction is a herculean task that may take a while to show results. But there have been moments in Hollywood history when the opposite has happened, when lightening has struck and films have come around that so shattered existing paradigms that change was inevitable."

# BIBLIOGRAPHY

## BOOKS

Bach, Steven. *Final Cut—Dreams and Disaster in the Making of Heaven's Gate*. New York, NY: Plume, 1985.

Beard, Richard R. *Walt Disney's EPCOT Center—Creating the New World of Tomorrow*. New York, NY: Harry N. Abrams, Inc., 1982.

Canemaker, John. *Walt Disney's Nine Old Men & the Art of Animation*. New York, NY: Disney Editions, 2001.

Ellenshaw, Peter with Gordon, Bruce and Mumford, David. *Ellenshaw Under Glass "or Going to the Matte for Disney."* Camphor Tree Publishers, 2003.

Maltin, Leonard. *Of Mice and Magic—A History of American Animated Cartoons*. New York, NY: Plume, 1980.

Maltin, Leonard. *The Disney Films*. New York, NY: Disney Editions, 2000.

Meyer, Chris and Trish. Creating Motion Graphics with After Effects. San Francisco, CA: CMP Books, 2000.

Morton, Ray. *King Kong—The History of a Movie Icon: From Fay Wray to Peter Jackson*. New York, NY, 2005.

Rubin, Michael. *Droidmaker—George Lucas and the Digital Revolution*. Gainesville, Florida: Triad Publishing Company, 2006.

Smith, David R. *The Updated Official Encylopedia: Disney A to Z.*, New York, NY: Hyperion 1998.

Stewart, James B. *Disney War*. New York, NY: Simon & Shuster, 2005.

Thomas, Bob. *Walt Disney—An American Original*. New York, NY: Pocket Books, 1976.

Thomas, Bob. *Building a Company—Roy O. Disney and the Creation of an Entertainment Empire*. New York, NY: Hyperion, 1998.

Thomas, Frank and Johnston, Ollie. *The Illusion of Life—Disney Animation*. New York, NY: Hyperion, 1981.

Vaz, Mark Cotta and Duignan Rose, Patricia. *Industrial Light + Magic—Into the Digital Realm*. New York, NY: Del Rey/Ballentine Books, 1996.

Vaz, Mark Cotta & Barron, Craig. *The Invisible Art—The Legends of Movie Matte Painting*. San Francisco, CA: Chronicle Books, 2002.

## PERIODICALS

Associated Press. "Stock Decline After Screening of 'Tron' Irks Disney Studio." *The New York Times*, July 9, 1982.

Author Unknown. "Billboard Videocassette Top 40." *Billboard*, December 25, 1982.

Author Unknown. "Billboard Videocassette Top 40." *Billboard*, January 8, 1983.

Author Unknown. "Billboard Videocassette Top 40." *Billboard*, January 15, 1983.

Author Unknown. "Corporations: Running Disney Walt's Way." *Time*, August 16, 1976.

Author Unknown. "Khan's 'Vengeance' Turns to 'Wrath'." *Starlog*. July, 1982.

Author Unknown. "Let's Go to the Movies: 'Tron'." *Disney News*. Summer 1982.

Author Unknown. "Show Business: Disney After Walt Is a Family Affair." *Time*, July 30, 1973.

Author Unknown. "Tremors on Dopey Drive." *Time*, July 19, 1982.

Benson, Shiela. "High-Tech 'Tron': All the Lines." *Los Angeles Times*, July 9, 1982.

Broeske, Pat H. "'Tron' Sparkles as Computer Age Draws." *The Register*, July 9, 1982.

Coate, Michael and Kallay, William. "Presented in 70mm." *Widescreen Review*, 2001.

Corliss, Richard; Smilgis, Martha. "Cinema: Steve's Summer Magic." *Time*, May 31, 1982.

Corliss, Richard; Dutka, Elaine; Smilgis, Martha. "Cinema: Hollywood's Hottest Summer." *Time*, July 19, 1982.

Daniels, Bill. "Lucasfilm Ltd. Spins Off the Last Segment of its Computer Division." *Variety*. February 11, 1986.

Gentry, Ric. "Fraker Records Memoirs of An Invisible Man." *American Cinematographer*, December 1991.

Houston, David. "The Magical Techniques of Movie and TV Special Effects: Part IX—The Matte Artist: An Interview with P.S. Ellenshaw [Harrison Ellenshaw]. *Starlog*, June, 1978.

Houston, David. "A Black Hole at the Crossroads: Executive Vice President Ron Miller discusses the future of Walt Disney Productions." *Starlog*, February, 1980.

Hutchison, David. "Behind the Genesis Effect." *Starlog*, November, 1982.

Linck, David. "MAGI's Animation Magic." *Box Office*, February, 1983.

Loynd, Ray. "Wilhite Out As Prod'n V.P of Disny Pix." *Variety*, November 7, 1983.

Loynd, Ray. "Disney Unfurls a New Banner." *Variety*, February 24, 1984.

Maslin, Janet. "Disney 'Tron.'" *The New York Times*, July 9, 1982.

Naha, Ed. "The Re-Making of Star Trek." *Starlog*. July, 1982.

Pizzello, Stephen. "The Lawnmower Man: Mind-Expansion Run Amok." *American Cinematographer*, April 1992.

Reed, Rex. "Tron—Ouch!" *The New York Observer*, 1982

Sammon, Paul M. "Inside The Black Hole As Told by Disney's Special Effects Experts." *Cinefantastique*, Spring, 1980.

Sansweet, Stephan J. "Analysts Audition For a New Role As Movie Reviewers." *Wall Street Journal*, July 8, 1982.

Sorenson, Peter. "Tronic Imagery." *Cinefex*, April 1982.

Stone, Judy. "A High-tech 'Tron' Turns on Critic." *San Francisco Chronicle*, July 9, 1982.

## INTERNET

www.boxofficemojo.com

Carlson, Wayne. "A Critical History of Computer Graphics and Animation." Winter 2007. http://design.osu.edu/carlson/history/ID797.html

Coate, Michael. "70mm Cinemas and 70mm Films in San Diego, USA." November 1, 2003. http://www.in70mm.com/library/70mm_in/usa/san_diego/index.htm

Ebert, Roger. "Tron." January 1, 1982 [July 9, 1982] http://rogerebert.suntimes.com/apps/pbcs.dll/article?AID=/19820101/REVIEWS/201010350/1023

Ebert, Roger. "Interview with Tom Wilhite." July 18, 1982. http://rogerebert.suntimes.com/apps/pbcs.dll/article?AID=/19820718/PEOPLE/207180301

Kallay, Bill. "Interpreting the Sound and Theory: A Look Back at Motion Picture Sound." September 4, 2004. http://www.fromscripttodvd.com/sound_theory.htm

Kallay, Bill. "Steven Lisberger and Joseph Kosinski: An Interview." April 9, 2011. http://www.fromscripttodvd.com/steven_lisberger_joseph_kosinski.htm

www.tron-sector.com

United States Copyright Office. http://www.copyright.gov/

Variety Staff. "Tron." July 9, 1982. http://www.variety.com/review/VE1117795896/

## CORPORATE REPORTS, CATALOGS AND MEMOS

Ellenshaw, Harrison. "Lucasfilm." February 22, 1983.

Ellenshaw, Harrison. "Visual Effects." October 20, 1982.

Le Blanc, Doug. "Lucasfilm's Ltd.'s Computer Graphics. March 18, 1983.

Kinsey, Stan. "Lucas Computer Research Division." February 15, 1983.

Miller, Ron. "Touchstone Films." February 24, 1984.

Rees, Jerry. "Computer System." January 19, 1983

Ross, Daniel. "Visual Effects Consideration for: TRON." January 7, 1983. The Academy of Motion Picture Arts and Sciences.

"Walt Disney Home Video" catalog. 1982.

"Walt Disney Productions 1980 Annual Report." 1980.

"Walt Disney Productions Quarterly Report 1982." March 31, 1982.

"Walt Disney Productions Annual Report 1983." 1983.

## DVDS

"20,000 Leagues Under the Sea." Buena Vista Home Entertainment. 2003.
"Behind the Canvas with Disney Legend Peter Ellenshaw." Collector's Editions. 2002.
"The Black Hole." Buena Vista Entertainment. 2004.
"Ellenshaw Under Glass—A Documentary Feature of Disney's Finest Matte Artist." Disney. 2004.
"The Pixar Story." Leslie Iwerks Productions. 2007.
"The Simpsons—Season Seven." *Treehouse of Horror VI*. 20th Century Fox Film Corporation. 1995.

## BLU-RAYS

"The Last Starfighter." Universal Studios Home Entertainment. 2009.
"Tron." Walt Disney Studios Home Entertainment. 2011.

## SCREENPLAYS

MacBird, Bonnie. "Tron." March 14, 1980.
Lisberger, Steven. "Tron." September 1980.

# AUTHOR INTERVIEWS

Ioan Allen, 11/4/10
Jim Blinn, 6/13/08
Peter Blinn, 5/3/08
Michael Bonifer, 4/12/07
Bruce Boxleitner, 8/31/11
Jeff Bridges, 4/11/07
Glenn Campbell, 5/16/06
Wendy Carlos, 4/26/07
Chris Casady, 10/12/10
Art Durinski, 5/23/06
Douglas Eby, 3/26/07
Harrison Ellenshaw, 9/18/10
Lynda Ellenshaw (Thompson), 10/12/10
AnneMarie Franklin, 4/26/07
Michael Fremer, 4/10/07
Jeff Gourson, 4/10/09
Peter Gullerud, 10/29/10
Rob Hummel, 5/21/08
Jeff Kleiser, 10/18/07
Joseph Kosinski, 4/5/11
Bill Kroyer, 5/21/06
Donald Kushner, 11/14/06
Chris Lane, 1/28/08
Steven Lisberger, 6/28/06, 10/19/09
Bruce Logan A.S.C., 6/25/07
Bonnie MacBird, 6/7/06, 6/27/06
Tim McGovern, 11/13/06
Syd Mead, 9/2/06
Ron Miller, 4/3/08
Michael Minkler, 3/23/11
Kenny Mirman, 1/17/11

Cindy Morgan, 4/29/07
Rosanna Norton, 5/6/08
Jerry Rees, 11/28/06
Darrell Rooney, 4/5/07
Frank Serafine, 5/3/07
Dan Shor, 8/12/11
Jesse Silver, 4/14/07
Alvy Ray Smith, 3/21/07, 3/22/07, 7/17/09
Richard Taylor, 4/12/06, 10/18/10
Tom Wilhite, 4/15/08, 4/24/08, 10/21/10
Arne Wong, 6/28/06
Raulette Woods, 12/9/10
John Van Vliet, 5/16/06

In addition to email, audio and videotape interviews, there have been follow-up email questions to clarify information.

# ABOUT THE AUTHOR

William Kallay is an award-winning filmmaker and writer. His film, *Green Tea*, won the prestigious Outstanding Writing Commendation Award from the 48 Hour Film Festival in Los Angeles (2004). His follow-up, *Backyard Universe*, enchanted audiences in 2006.

Kallay's writing has taken him from studio lots to the red carpet. He has written extensively about filmmakers, film technology and has reviewed hundreds of DVDs and Blu-rays for his website, www.fromscripttodvd.com. He is a former contributing editor to *Widescreen Review* magazine and writer for *Go*, the official magazine for AirTran Airways.

Kallay lives in Southern California.

Printed in Great Britain
by Amazon.co.uk, Ltd.,
Marston Gate.